THE EUROPEAN UNION, MERCOSUL
AND THE NEW WORLD ORDER

THE EUROPEAN UNION, MERCOSUL AND THE NEW WORLD ORDER

Editors

HELIO JAGUARIBE
ÁLVARO DE VASCONCELOS

Routledge
Taylor & Francis Group

LONDON AND NEW YORK

First Published in 2003 in Great Britain by
Routledge
2 Park Square, Milton Park, Abingdon, Oxon, OX14 4RN
270 Madison Ave, New York NY 10016

Transferred to Digital Printing 2011

Website http://www.routledge.com

British Library Cataloguing in Publication Data:
The European Union, Mercosul and the new world order. 1. European Union.
2. MERCOSUR (Organisation). 3. European Union countries – Foreign relations –
Latin America. 4. Latin America – Foreign relations – European Union countries.
I. Jaguaribe, Helio. II. Vasconcelos, Álvaro.
327.4'08

A catalogue record for this book is available from the British Library

ISBN 0–7146–5405–1 (cloth)
ISBN 0–7146–8338–8 (paper)

Library of Congress Cataloging-in-Publication Data:
The European Union, MERCOSUL, and the new world order / editors,
Helio Jaguaribe, Álvaro de Vasconcelos.
p. cm.
Papers presented at seminars held Jan. 17–18 and Dec. 12–13, 2000, Lisbon, Portugal.
Includes bibliographical references and index.
ISBN 0–7146–5405–1 (cloth) – ISBN 0–7146–8338–8 (pbk.)
1. European Union–Congresses. 2. MERCOSUR (Organisation)–Congresses.
3. Globalization–Congresses. 4. International economic integration–Congresses.
I. Jaguaribe, Helio. II. Vasconcelos, Álvaro.
D887.E97 2003
327.1'7'090511–dc21   2003043550

A catalog record for this book is available
from the Library of Congress

Typeset in 11/13 pt Monotype Ehrhardt by Servis Filmsetting Ltd, Manchester

Publisher's Note
The publisher has gone to great lengths to ensure the quality of this reprint
but points out that some imperfections in the original may be apparent.

Contents

Notes on Contributors

Christoph Bertram studied law and political science at the Universities of Berlin, Bonn and Paris. In 1967 he joined the International Institute for Strategic Studies in London, serving as the Institute's director from 1974 to 1982. He left in 1982 to become a senior editor of *Die Zeit*, writing on international and strategic affairs. Since 1998 he has headed the Foundation of Science and Policy, a research centre on international affairs, which advises the German government and parliament. His publications include *Europe in Balance: Securing the Peace Won in the Cold War* (1995) and *Europa in der Schweber: der Frieden muss noch gweommen werden* (1997).

Aldo Ferrer gained his PhD in economics from the University of Buenos Aires in 1953. He has taught economics at the National University of la Plata and at the University of Buenos Aires. He worked in the United Nations Secretariat between 1950 and 1953, as economics consultant of the Argentinian government in the London embassy in 1956, and was Minister of Economics and Finance, District of Buenos Aires, from 1958 to 1960. His publications include *De Cristobál Colón a Internet: America Latina y la globalización* (December 2001); *Argentina y Brasil en la Globalización* (January 2001, in collaboration with Helio Jaguaribe); *Historia de la Globalización II: La revolución industrial y el segundo orden mundial* (January 2000); *El Capitalismo Argentino* (January 1998); *Hechos y Ficciones de la Globalización* (January 1997) and *Historia de la Globalización: Orígenes del Orden Económico Mundial* (January 1996).

Clodoaldo Hugueney Filho is currently Under-Secretary for Integration, Economic Affairs and Foreign Trade of the Ministry of Foreign Affairs of Brazil as well as Special Representative of the President for Mercosur. He graduated in law from the Catholic University of Rio de Janeiro and did postgraduate work in economics at the University of Chile. In 1966 he was admitted to the diplomatic academy and two years later he joined the Brazilian diplomatic corps. Ambassador Hugueney's official assignments include postings in, among others, Santiago, Washington and London. Between 1988 and 1991 he worked in the Ministry of Planning and Economy in the area of multilateral financing. In 1993 he was appointed Ambassador to Venezuela. Between 1999 and the beginning of 2002 he served as head of the Brazilian Mission to the European Community.

Charles Grant studied modern history at Cambridge University and took a diploma in French politics at Grenoble University. He wrote for *Euromoney* and in 1986 joined *The Economist*. He was posted to Brussels and in 1992 his writing on economic and monetary union won the Adelphi Foundation's Prix Stendhal. His biography of Jacques Delors, *Delors: Inside the House that Jacques Built*, was published in 1994. In 1996 he helped set up the Centre for European Reform, and in January 1988 he left *The Economist* to become its first director. He is the author of several CER publications. His latest publication is *Europe 2010: An Optimistic Vision of the Future*.

Samuel Pinheiro de Guimarães, Brazilian Ambassador and Secretary-General of External Relations, is former head of the Economic Department of the Brazilian Ministry of Foreign Affairs and a former director of the Instituto de Pesquisas em Relações Internacionais (IPRI).

Pierre Hassner is Research Director Emeritus at the Centre d'Etudes et de Recherches Internationale, Paris and Senior Professorial Lecturer, Johns Hopkins University European Centre, Bologna. In addition to teaching at the Political Science Foundation in Paris (1964–2002) he has taught at the University of Chicago (1998) and at Harvard (2000). His publications include *Violence and Peace: From the Nuclear Bomb to Ethnic Cleansing* (1995; English trans. 1997); *The Empire of Force or the Force of Empire?*, Chaillot Paper 54, September 2002, and he has written many works on political philosophy and international relations.

Helio Jaguaribe studied at the Law School of the Pontifical Catholic University of Rio de Janeiro and has PhDs from the Universities of Mainz, Buenos Aires and Paraiba. His books include *Political Development* (1973); *Brasil, Homem e Mundo* (2000) and *Un Estudio Critico de la Historia* (2002).

Carlos Pérez Llana is Professor of International Relations at the University of San Andres and Torcuato Di Tella University, Buenos Aires. From 2000 to 2002 he was Argentine Ambassador to France. He is the author of numerous books and articles about foreign affairs. His most recent book is *El regreso de la historia. La política internacional durante la posguerra fría, 1989–1998* (1999).

Ricardo Andrés Markwald has a BSc in economic sciences from Buenos Aires National University and an MSc in Public Sector Economics from the Pontifical Catholic University, Rio de Janeiro. He has worked as a research expert with the Institute of Applied Economic Research since 1980. In 1995 he was appointed Research Coordinator at the Foreign Trade Studies Centre Foundation (FUNCEX). From 1995 to the present he has been General Director of FUNCEX. An assistant lecturer at PUC-Rio de Janeiro, he has published several articles in *Perspectivas da Economia Brasileira, Pesquisa e Planejamento Econômico* and *Revista da ANPEC*, as well as discussion papers for the ILO and UNDP, with parallel contributions at the IPEA, CNI and FUNCEX.

Amaury de Souza was Professor of Political Science at IUPERJ and the Department of Economics of PUC-Rio de Janeiro. He has also been a visiting professor at many US universities. He was a fellow of the Woodrow Wilson International Center for Scholars and is currently a member of the planning committee of the Comparative Study of Electoral Systems of the University of Michigan. His publications include *The Politics of Population in Brazil* (co-author, 1981); 'Dilemmas of Industrial Relations Reform', in *Brazil and South Africa: Comparative Perspectives* (1996); 'Redressing Inequalities', in *Brazil Under Cardoso* (1997); 'Collor's Impeachment and Institutional Reform in Brazil', in *Corruption and Political Reform in Brazil* (1999); 'Cardoso and the Struggle for Reform in Brazil', *Journal of Democracy* (1999); and 'Brazil', in *Guidance for Governance: Comparing Alternative Sources of Public Policy Advice* (2001). Dr de Souza holds a PhD in political science from the Massachusetts Institute of Technology.

Álvaro de Vasconcelos has been Director of the Institute for Strategic and International Studies (IEEI), Lisbon, since 1980. He is editor of the IEEI's journals *Estratégia – Revista de Estudos Internacionais* and *O Mundo em Português*. He has written many works on International affairs and both regional and interregional integration, European and Portuguese foreign policy, and security and defence issues. He is co-author of *Portugal: A European Story*; editor of *Valores da Europa*; and co-editor of *Portugal: An Atlantic Paradox* and *La PESC – Ouvrir l'Europeau monde*; editor of *Européens et Maghrébins – une solidarité obligée* and *Portugal no Centro da Europa – Propostas para uma Reforma Democrática do Tratado da União*

Europeia. He is a member of the editorial board of *The Journal of North European Studies*, *The International Spectator* and *The Journal of European Integration*. He is a member of the EuroMeSCo Steering Committee and coordinator of its secretariat, co-organiser of the Euro-Latin-American Forum, and serves on the board of TEPSA, the TransEuropean Policy Studies Association.

Foreword

Written several months after the book it presents, this foreword has the advantages and benefits of hindsight. It is thus able to point at recent events that support or modify its main arguments. Three events have struck me in this sense: first, the unfolding of the Bush administration's attitudes and policies; already before 11 September and even more afterwards; second, Argentina's crises and bail-out after much hesitation by the IMF; and finally, the judgement of the WTO in favour of the European Union in its conflict with the United States over the Foreign Sales Corporation Act. Each of these trends bears on the themes of this remarkable book, which itself offers a framework for understanding them. In turn, they help us to search for a way out of the dilemmas raised by these debates.

The main theme of the Bush administration seemed to be, before 11 September, in terms of ends, the primacy of America's national interest, narrowly conceived, and in terms of means, the primacy of unilateralism. It is the first administration since that of Theodore Roosevelt to have, at least in part, an openly imperialist ideology. Simultaneously, it lacks an integrating imperial ideology, which would give a stake in its success to the rest of the world. It oscillates between an imperialist and an isolationist tendency, combined with elements of pragmatism and, when it directly serves the interests of the US, elements of multilateralism, such as the FTAA (Free Trade Agreement of the Americas) project. In spite of ideological proclamations to the contrary, it seems to follow in the footsteps of the Clinton administration. This is both for the better (the aid to Brazil and the provisional bail-out of Argentina), and for the worse (the possibility of a military intervention in the fight against drugs in Colombia). The lesson seems to be that American hegemony currently takes such an aggressive and unpredictable form that even the most moderate advocates of multilateralism, or even of empire, are drawn or tempted to become resistant states (in Professor Jaguaribe's terminology) and to dream of multipolarity. After 11 September, the United States has found its 'mission', to use President

Bush's expression: it is the war against terrorism. This legitimate cause has enabled it to gather a broad coalition for its intervention in Afghanistan, and to enter into a kind of loose concert with its past and potential enemies, Russia and China. But the imperialist ideology has been reinforced, the unilateralist method has reached new heights (with the coolness towards NATO's invocation of Article 5 after 11 September, or with the campaign against the International Penal Court) and the narrow conception of the national interest has been confirmed both in economic terms (with the farm tariffs and the help to the steel industry) and, even more strikingly, with the lack of legal guarantees for non-American prisoners.

The second element, from the point of view of Mercosul and the EU, shows how far this dream is from being attainable today. Neither Brazil, nor even less Argentina, is capable of dispensing with outside aid. This comes not from Mercosul or the EU, but rather from the IMF (a multilateral organisation controlled by the US). As Ricardo Lagos, the current Chilean president of the Rio Group, said at their meeting on 19 August: 'We are only the observers of what happens in our countries. But the effects of the system hit us in our most important spots.' Globalisation and interdependence certainly do not, by themselves, produce multipolarity.

Yet the third event seems to lean in the opposite direction: the judgement of the WTO Commission, which American sources compare to a bombshell or to a nuclear attack, shows that multilateralism is not necessarily a way to, or an instrument of, hegemony. Together with the EU's earlier opposition of a merger between two American giants, it shows that, on the contrary, multilateral institutions can lead to multipolarity, or at least to the limitation of hegemony.

As I see it, this dialectical relationship between multilateralism and multipolarity is precisely the most fascinating lesson of this book. Of course, it analyses with unprecedented precision and frankness the relations between Europe and South America, or, more precisely, between the EU and Mercosul. It therefore examines the needs and possibilities of regionalism, the resemblances and differences between the two enterprises of regional integration, and the modifications that their collaboration could bring about in the international system. However, precisely from the point of view of understanding the latter, in theoretical terms the real subject is the relation between multipolarity and multilateralism.

In reading the book, I was struck by the fact that most of the South American contributions greatly emphasised the goal of multipolarity, and the preferably collective (but if not, national) resistance to American hegemony. Interestingly, most of the European contributions emphasised multilateralism, and the goal of channelling and harnessing American hegemony into a system of rules and restraints, rather than attacking it frontally with the aim of replacing it with a multipolar balance.

There is a simple explanation for the difference: South America has a much more direct and brutal experience than Europe of North American hegemony. Furthermore, the experience is not mitigated, as in Europe, by the other even more brutal dominations (German and then Soviet) against which America has played the role of defender, liberator or protector, and of a much milder counter-hegemon. However, there is another explanation that emerges from the studies of this book, and from the events I have quoted at the beginning of this Foreword.

The South American writers show no complacency about the power relationships on their continent, or their economic strength or vulnerability. They also show no complacency about the political cohesion or division of their respective countries, the institutional advancement of Mercosul, or its current ability to protect its members from economic storms and political pressures.

By contrast, the European contributions – while quite lucid and even pessimistic about the EU's ability to act alone, or to become a genuine federation – demonstrate a quiet confidence in its achievements, and in the inevitability of multilateralism in the modern world. Paradoxically, this leads them to a much less antagonistic view towards the US and towards a more modest ambition concerning regional entities such as the EU and Mercosul. They would not be far from agreeing with another European – and a Frenchman to boot – Jean-Marie Guéhenno, when he declares:

> If power is only national power, if it becomes the *ultima ratio* of security which makes it possible for a country to go its own way, regardless of other countries' interests and concerns, then, indeed, there is little incentive in the rest of the world to welcome American power. But if legitimacy is recognised as the necessary complement of power in a democratic world, if multilateral institutions are understood to be not only a constraint on power, but also a foundation of power, because they make power more acceptable, the rest of the world has no problem with American power.[1]

Of course, Guehénno was speaking to an American audience, and I do not think he was representative of 'the rest of the world', or even of the rest of France. After all, France is the European country whose foreign minister has coined the expression: 'America as a hyper-power' and whose president has outlined the vision (curiously coinciding with some old formations by

Nixon and Kissinger) of a multipolar world based on a balance between four or five great powers, like the European concert of the nineteenth century.

Personally, without going as far as Guehénno, I tend to be on the side of the majority of Europeans and the minority of French who disagree with the notion of multipolarity as constituting, by itself, a valid description of a future international system and a valid objective for foreign policy. I am tempted (and reinforced in this by the reading of this book) by the idea expressed by two other Frenchmen, that the ideal of multipolarity is an expression of weakness.[2] This is the same weakness that induces Russia's need to be constantly confirmed in its superpower status, precisely because it knows it has lost it. I think that the notion of multipolarity, which has an obvious validity and relevance if one defines its context, can be very misleading, both theoretically and politically. It can lead one to forget the difference between poles, both in terms of power and in terms of ties. If one wants to avoid the so-called 'billiard ball model' of international politics, one must, on the one hand, recognise transnational ties, affinities and cleavages. On the other hand, one must acknowledge the fact that multipolarity means neither equality nor equidistance between the different units.

The international system is both unimultipolar and unimultilateral. All states maintain, to various degrees, a certain freedom to act unilaterally and a certain necessity, obligation or interest in respecting and using some multilateral framework. It is within these multilateral frameworks that multipolarity makes sense, just as, conversely, multilateralism by itself has no chance of moderating and channelling hegemony if it is not associated with an element of multipolarity, which enables the other members of the system to resist and retaliate against hegemonic unilateralism. In this respect, the threats implied by the policies of the Bush administration demonstrate the wisdom of Helio Jaguaribe's notion of resistant states. However, on the other hand, this resistance can be successful only if the policy of the states has a more positive content than just opposing the US. Furthermore, they cannot fall into the illusion that an abstract multipolarity (balancing the US with Russia, China and India, for instance) can erase the inequalities, the constraints and the solidarities of the Western capitalist and liberal democratic world.

Thomas Schelling, defining the mixture of cooperation and conflict that characterises international politics, proposed 'a theory of incomplete antagonism and imperfect partnership'. Similarly, we could suggest that all politics are a combination of *incomplete inequality* and *imperfect reciprocity*. Of course, to increase reciprocity, one needs to reduce inequality, but even in the most unequal relationship there is an element of reciprocity; and even in the most orderly and harmonious reciprocity there is a dimension of inequality.

It follows, too, that Professor Jaguaribe's trinity of ruling, resistant and conditioned states, while valid and illuminating, must be complemented by the recognition that even the ruling hegemon is somehow conditioned (if only by physical factors and by the nature of its own society). Furthermore, even the most conditioned state has some capacity for resistance. However, this applies above all to the intermediary category: that of states that may be resistant, but are at the same time part of the ruling system and conditioned by their relative weakness before both the hegemon and the global system. It is they who, as Professor Jaguaribe points out, have the capacity to increase their ruling dimension and the risk of being increasingly conditioned or dependent. The outcome of this dilemma, however, depends on their ability both to unite, or at least to coordinate, and to propose constructive social and political solutions as an alternative to economic determinism. In this respect, President Cardozo's statement at the 2001 FTAA meeting in Quebec, 'The FTAA is a choice, but Mercosul is a destiny', quoted by Amaury de Souza in Chapter 9, while valid geographically and culturally, could not be reversed. If not the FTAA, at least globalisation and capitalist interdependence, and the central role of the US are, in a sense, destiny – just as, on the other hand, are parochial reactions in the name of ethnicity or nationalism, or a renaissance of revolutionary romanticism. By contrast, the creation of intermediary levels capable of mediating between the two extremes on a regional and multilateral basis, such as the EU and Mercosul, is a deliberate choice, which requires both imagination and perseverance.

In my opinion, this book is both a very stimulating encouragement and a very compelling analysis in that direction.

Pierre Hassner
Centre d' Etudes et de Recherches Internationale, Paris

NOTES

1. Guehénno, Jean-Marie, 'Is the US too powerful?' paper for conference *France and the United States in New Century*, Centre on the United States and France, 24 May 2000, Brookings Institution, Foreign Policy Studies.
2. Melandri, Pierre and Justin Vaisse, 'L'empire du milieu', Paris, Odile Jacob, 2001.

Preface

This book is the result of a joint project promoted by the Instituto de Estudos Políticos e Sociais (IEPES), of Rio de Janerio, with the collaboration of the Instituto de Estudos Estratégicos e Internacionais (IEEI), of Lisbon. Two seminars were held in Lisbon on 17–18 January and 12–13 December 2000. English was adopted as the research language as it was common to all the contributors. The first seminar established the research methodology, the structure of work, and the tasks for each author. Jean-Marie Guéhenno, one of the intended authors, contributed to the project until taking up his current position with the United Nations as under-secretary-general for peacekeeping operations.

The project's central idea was to analyse the present international system after the implosion of the Soviet Union, and thus the end of the bipolar regime that regulated the second half of the twentieth century. Furthermore, the research and the seminars facilitated a discussion on the prospective development of a new world order in the first decades of the twenty-first century.

Considering such objectives, the research aimed at a triple and interrelated analysis: (i) of the current and the most probable future tendencies of the European Union and countries such as France, Great Britain and Germany, vis-à-vis the more likely alternatives of a future world order; (ii) of the position of Mercosul, as a regional market and as an international protagonist, vis-à-vis those alternatives; and (iii) of the positions of Argentina and Brazil, vis-à-vis those same alternatives.

In order to pursue this outline, it was agreed that each author would prepare a first draft for group discussion. Subsequently, during the second seminar, second drafts were evaluated and discussed. After consideration of the comments made at both meetings, final drafts were completed.

The developments in the international order that occurred after the final drafting of the papers, all of which were written before 11 September 2001 and the crisis over Iraq and most before President Bush was elected, were taken into consideration by the author of the Foreword or by the editors in their concluding chapter. However, in our judgement, those developments have in no way challenged the scenarios for the evolution of the international system discussed in this book, even if they have made the implementation of recommendations of most authors for empowering the multilateral order much more difficult. Indeed, it is too early to conclude whether a multipolar system will replace the old bipolar order. The analysis contained in this volume, however, does point to many serious obstacles standing in the way of an international order firmly based on universally accepted norms and rules, in which regional groupings would play a greater role.

The editors wish to express their gratitude to the Inter-American Development Bank, which generously provided the funds that made it possible to undertake this research.

Helio Jaguaribe
Álvaro de Vasconcelos

July 2002

Abbreviations and Acronyms

ABM	Anti-ballistic Missile
AIEA (IAEA)	International Atomic Energy Commission
ALADI	Associação Lationo-Americana de Integração
ALCA	American Free Trade Area
APEC	Asia-Pacific Economic Cooperation
ASEAN	Association of South East Asian Nations
CAP	Common Agricultural Policy
CEPAL (ECLAC)	Economic Commission for Latin America and the Caribbean
CET	Common External Tariff
CFSP	Common Foreign and Security Policy
CONAE	Comisión Nacional de Actividades Espaciales
CSDP	Common Security and Defence Policy
CSFP	Common Security and Foreign Policy
CTB	Comprehensive Test Ban Treaty
ECAP	European Common Agricultural Policy
ECLAC	Economic Commission for Latin America and the Caribbean
EFTA	European Free Trade Area
EMP	Euro-Mediterranean Partnership
EMU	Economic and Monetary Union
EU	European Union
FCO	Foreign and Commonwealth Office
FTAA	Free Trade Agreement of the Americas
GATT	General Agreement on Tariffs and Trade
GDP	Gross Domestic Product
GNP	Gross National Product
GWP	Gross World Product
ICC	International Criminal Court
IEEI	Instituto de Estudos Estratégicos e Internacionais

IEPES	Instituto de Estudos Politicos e Sociais
IMF	International Monetary Fund
LAIA	Latin American Integration Association
*Mercosul	Southern Cone Common Market
MPCC	Mechanism for Political Consultation and Co-ordination
MTCR	Missile Technology Control Regime
NAFTA	North American Free Trade Agreement
NATO	North Atlantic Treaty Organisation
NGO	Non-governmental organisation
NMD	National Missile Defence
NPT	Non-proliferation Treaty
OAS	Organisation of American States
ODA	Overseas Development Administration
OECD	Organisation for Economic Cooperation and Development
ONGs	Non-governmental organisations
PMBD	Partido do Movimento Democratico Brasileiro
PRC	Peoples Republic of China
SAFTA	South America Free Trade Area
SAD	South African Development Community
SELA	Latin American Economic System
SHAPE	Supreme Headquarters Allied Powers Europe
UK	United Kingdom
UN	United Nations
UNCTAD	United Nations Conference on Trade and Development
US	United States of America
WB	World Bank
WEU	Western European Union
WTO	World Trade Organisation

* The terms 'Mercosur' and 'Mercosul' are used interchangeably in this text as the former is the Spanish variant and the latter the Portuguese form.

ONE

————◄◦►————

General Introduction

HÉLIO JAGUARIBE

THE POST-COLD WAR WORLD

After the implosion of the Soviet Union and the de-communisation of its European satellites, the only superpower left in the international system was the United States. President George Bush (Senior) initially maintained that the result of the downfall of communism would be the creation of a new era, marked by universal peace and harmony. This suggestion expressed the American myth that communism was the cause of international problems and that, with its suppression, the 'free world' would realise its possibilities harmoniously and peacefully. It was also a way for the US, as a superpower, to manifest reassuringly its intention of intervening only consensually – and not unilaterally – in the international scene.

A few years after the fall of the Berlin Wall and the division of the Soviet Union (with Russia receiving the lion's share of the legacy), the international situation began to exhibit post-Cold War characteristics. Furthermore, various areas of turbulence in Africa, in the former Yugoslavia and in the ever-troubled Middle East have made it clear that the international system is not self-adjustable. In the preceding bipolar regime, each superpower exerted controls over its area of dominance or influence. However, the disappearance of these controls has exposed the world to continuous conflicts that the United Nations, not receiving the necessary aid from member states, lacks the resources to prevent or settle.

On the other hand, given the new conditions and the relative impotence of the UN, the US, in an increasingly unilateral way, has started to exercise a 'world monitoring' function practised in the name of the 'international community'. This is allegedly in defence of democracy and human rights, in addition to promoting America's own national interests. Despite being the only superpower and possessing unchallengeable economic technology and military supremacy compared to any other country, the US lacks the conditions to exercise effective unipolarity, although it frequently seeks to achieve it.

As Samuel Huntington has pointed out, the present world regime cannot be classified as unipolar, but, rather, has special aspects that one might call 'unimultipolarity'.[1] Unimultipolarity is characterised by the fact that the US enjoys a general power to veto important international proposals or anything that affects vital American interests. It is also characterised by the fact that US participation has become an indispensable factor in the success of any important international initiative. Finally, it is distinguished by the fact that the US has considerable scope for unilateral intervention in international affairs. However, this depends, in important areas, on the minimum support from countries such as France and Germany, and the almost automatic support from Great Britain.

The unimultipolarity regime currently in force has, of necessity, a transitory character. This stems from the fact that following the collapse of the Soviet Union, the US has had a high but not unrestricted capacity for unilateral intervention in the international scene. Therefore, in the coming decades this world order will be inclined either to consolidate itself into an unchallengeable American unipolarity, or to turn into an effectively multipolar system.

LIMITS TO UNIPOLARITY

Despite its status as the only superpower and the new unilateral assertiveness of President George Bush (Junior), there are currently two main circumstances (domestically and internationally) preventing the US from achieving the unipolarity level. Domestically, the fact remains that North American society and institutions are not geared towards running a world empire. The American people also refuse to assume the financial and personal sacrifices that would be required. Internationally, the fact remains that despite its unassailable economic-technological and military supremacy, the US, given its internal restrictions, faces sufficient resistance from various world powers.

The US is a mass democracy, although subject to a high degree of oligarchic control. The world empires from Mesopotamia, Ancient Egypt and Rome, to the Iberian empires of the Renaissance, and even to the recent British Empire, were constituted and directed by authoritarian regimes. (Although in the British case, it was under the guise – and with the resulting restrictions – of an aristocratic democracy.) In addition to the significant decline in relative power experienced by the UK after the First World War, it was a middle-class democracy under Gladstone, which increasingly became a mass democracy under Attlee, that made the continuance of the British Empire untenable.

In the case of the US, the important protestant ethic residue, which continues to manifest itself in the American people, makes violent or malevolent forms of coercion unacceptable for public consumption. In addition to the socio-economic restrictions stemming from the regime, this lack of coercion means, on occasion, that it is impossible to preserve an imperial system. It was the image on American television of a little, terrified, Vietnamese girl fleeing naked from a napalm bomb that led the American people to oppose the continuing military intervention in Vietnam.

Aside from the unassailable American economic-technological and military supremacy, such resistance (as mentioned above) has proved efficient. It has done this both in itself and by the fact that the domestic limitations that surround the US deprive it of the opportunity of a direct preventive confrontation with major opponents to its hegemony.

Without elaborating too much on the question of a limited unipolarity, it is worth highlighting three of its most restrictive aspects. Two of these points are closely connected to the domestic limitations facing the American power elite in any attempt to exercise uninhibited world hegemony.

The first relates to the need to transmit an image of legitimacy for US external interventions, to the American people. Interventions delegated by the UN (Kuwait) immediately confer this legitimacy. However, recent American interventions (before 11 September) have not counted on the support of the UN and escaped its condemnation only by virtue of the US power of veto. To make up for this, NATO-conferred legitimacy can be a useful second bet. In the absence of this, however, the express opposition of the Europeans, most notably from countries such as France and Germany, has an inhibitory effect.

The second restrictive aspect of an uninhibited American unipolarity is the fact that, in many circumstances, unilateral intervention would have to be exercised in a malevolent or violent way. This in turn would give rise to strong domestic opposition. The international practice of violence on the part of the US requires two things. First, there must be formal aspects of legitimacy (in the view of American institutions and the moral sensibilities of the public). Second, there is a demand for the prior 'demonisation' of the target country and/or leader – for example, Iraq and Saddam Hussein.

The third restrictive factor for the US exercising a full unipolarity is the strategic and tactical need to prevent the formation and consolidation of dangerous 'anti-hegemonic' coalitions. The US enjoys a clear unchallengeable economic-technological and military superiority over any other country, most notably China, India, Russia, Iran and Iraq. The formation of an anti-hegemonic coalition between such countries, whether all or some, would assume grave proportions. It would require incomparably greater effort and sacrifice than that demanded from the US by the Second World War, among other reasons, because of the potential for a major nuclear conflict.

Under present conditions, the above-mentioned countries are all against American hegemony and all aspire to see a reduction in the US area of predominance and influence. Nevertheless, one could not describe the relations among such countries as being co-operative; in fact competitive or even antagonistic would be nearer the mark. In this context, the US seeks to avoid any exacerbation of the anti-Americanism of these countries. This is in fear of them overcoming their reciprocal differences and banding together against America.

SCOPE FOR INTERVENTION

General aspect

Within the internal and external limitations mentioned above, the US still has considerable scope for intervention. To analyse this question, it is necessary to view it from two perspectives: first in terms of the main objective pursued by the US in its international policy, and second, the means at its disposal to achieve such an objective.

What is sometimes called the 'American Empire' is something quite different from the traditional empires, from the Roman to the British. These were marked not only by the effective submission of the areas under their control or predominance to metropolitan sovereignty, but also by their formal submission. Authorities appointed by the metropolis as pro-consuls, governors and viceroys exercised, with the required military support, effective power in the provinces or colonies of the empire. The inhabitants of those regions, in compensation, enjoyed certain benefits conferred by the empire. These ranged from, in the Roman case, the institution of a rational and equitable juridical system, regulated by the *jus gentium* and supervised by the *praetor peregrinus* – to the Caracalla edict, extending Roman citizenship to all the provinces – to the status of a British citizen, with the corresponding rights (different from those conferred by UK citizenship) to Commonwealth subjects.

The predominance of the US in the international system is not exerted through the formal imposition of American sovereignty on the territories and people subject to it. The American 'empire' is not an empire. It is a field, in the same sense as a magnetic field or field of gravity. It is a field in which multiple conditionings are exerted, conditionings of an economic, technological, cultural, psychological, political and military character. It comes from the US, without harming the continuing nominal sovereignty of the countries encompassed by this field. Wherever possible, the US seeks to influence the choice of local governments. However, it is not essential for American predominance that the leaders of the 'provinces', whose domestic institutions continue to exist, are people appointed by Washington or pointedly aligned to it. The system of conditionings operates independently of the will of the leaders of these areas, formally independent but subject to American predominance, generating constraints which would be extremely costly or simply unfeasible to ignore.

In stubborn cases or acts of blatant defiance, the US exerts strong direct pressure and according to the circumstances adopts a policy designed to make the country or leader in question, an international pariah (Khadafi, Hussein). Particularly in the cases of international terrorism, the US launches a campaign to 'demonise' such countries and leaders in the eyes of the American people and world public opinion.

The US pursues three main objectives in the international arena related respectively to: American power, the expansion of its economy, and the dissemination of its values and institutions.

Military power

The objective of preserving, strengthening and expanding American national power at the international level is understandably the most important of the three. Having managed to become, without resorting to war, the only superpower, the US gives top priority to preserving and consolidating this status. To this end, the US considers it essential to satisfy two requirements:

1. to maintain its control over Eurasia; and

2. to prevent the proliferation of nuclear weapons. (Particularly to make sure that no major power – besides the consummated fact of Russia – reaches a critical nuclear capacity and to make sure that no unreliable or rogue country shall have the means to inflict serious damage on American territory.)

As Zbigniew Brzezinski[2] has pointed out, the huge continental land mass that stretches from the Iberian Peninsula to the sea of Japan, together with the Japanese Islands, constitutes the key area of the world. Whoever controls this area is thus guaranteed world control. If unable to dominate completely and fully Eurasia, the US has endeavoured to achieve the following objectives in this region:

1. to maintain a close military alliance, under American command, with Europe and Japan;

2. to maintain an active co-operative economic relationship with Russia avoiding, on the one hand, any growth of anti-American feelings, and on the other, any decline in their prejudices against China. Thus, potentially allowing the formation of an anti-hegemonic coalition;

3. to maintain co-operative economic and technological relations with China, so as to link Chinese development to American co-operation, thus avoiding the formation of anti-hegemonic coalitions with Russia and Japan; and

4. to maintain co-operative relations with India and impede the latter from forming an anti-hegemonic coalition with China.

Europe is the key-figure for preserving the American system of supremacy, hence the decisive importance for the US to maintain the Atlantic Alliance and its military arm, NATO. The end of the Cold War and the implosion of the Soviet Union have made the preservation of NATO particularly difficult, as it was expressly formed as a defence against an enemy – the Soviet Union – which no longer exists.

It goes beyond the limits of this brief study to carry out a detailed analysis of the conditions and circumstances that have allowed NATO to continue. One might just mention, among the most important factors, the radical British opposition to any weakening or dissolution of NATO, the alliance with the US being more important to Britain than its links with Europe. One should also mention the lingering European fear towards Russia and a probable recovery, in the not too distant future, of her national power. A third factor is that France has not found, within an exclusively European orbit, compensatory mechanisms for the growing disequilibrium that has resulted from the inferiority of its economy and international status when compared to post-reunification Germany. Finally, one should mention the fact that the Europeans do not possess an updated defence system and are faced with multiple difficulties and inevitable delays in their proposals for adopting one. At the moment, as the crisis in the former Yugoslavia made so patently clear, they need to use NATO to tackle problems of this type.

As far as preserving its nuclear superiority is concerned, the US recognises the maintenance by Russia of the bulk of the Soviet Union's former arsenal (albeit in highly unsatisfactory conditions) as a factor to be reckoned with. They do not consider the fact that Britain and France have a modest nuclear system at their disposal particularly dangerous. However, they are making every effort to avoid the proliferation of atomic weapons, although they have been unable to block nuclear development in China. The spread of nuclear weapons, in some cases, already has a critical mass available (in Russia) or at least achievable within a few decades (in China), as well as the problem of the wild adventurism of certain leaders. Thus, the US is leaning, under very different conditions, to Reagan's old project of protecting America with a reliable missile-interception system. This project is strongly contested by Russia, which considers quite rightly, that the installation of such a system, besides violating already signed nuclear accords, would make the US militarily invulnerable, thus consolidating definitively American world hegemony.

In addition to the policies and measures mentioned above, American concern about the international preservation of its power supremacy has led the US to pay particular attention to the question of regional powers. To this end, the US seeks to identify both the respective local predominant power and the secondary power, most likely to dispute regional primacy in the main regions of the world. From the American point of view the regional powers and their respective contenders are:

1. in Europe; France and Germany, allies but competitors for supremacy, with Great Britain also as a contender;

2. in the west of Eurasia; Russia, with the Ukraine as a contender;

3. in the Far East; China, with Japan as a contender;

4. in South Asia; India, with Pakistan as a contender; and

5. in South America; Brazil, with Argentina as a contender.

In such a situation, American policy is studiously two-faced. On the one hand, it seeks to win the support of the predominant power and to act as a local link in the US network of influence, making use of material and honorary incentives to achieve this end. On the other hand, it nourishes the current or potential contentiousness of the secondary power, using the same resources, with a view to reducing the capacity for action and leadership of the predominant local power.

Economic power

American economic supremacy, besides its marked technological-economic superiority, stems from the fact that the country enjoys particularly favourable conditions generated by the globalisation process. The economic superiority of the US in comparison with any other country is striking. Boasting the largest GDP in the world and representing about one-quarter of world GDP, the US also enjoys considerable technological and managerial superiority. It controls the high-tech sectors of the economy and shows, on average, and in the most important sectors, significantly greater competitiveness than other countries. It should be added that this formidable productive and commercial system is operated by a network of multinationals that dominate the world market. In addition, the socio-cultural conditions of the US favour the existence and expansion, in the domestic market, of a large number of small companies with a high capacity for technological innovation. This supplies the market with a never-ending and increasing flow of new technologies and new products.

As previously mentioned, the marked technological-economic superiority of the US is particularly favoured by the globalisation process. This process – the origins of which go back to the mercantile revolution, followed by the industrial revolution – has not resulted from the initiative of any one country, including the US, or of any particular economic group. It has resulted from the aggregate effect of the technological revolution in the final decades of the twentieth century. This incorporated the entire world into a system of immediate intercommunication and close interdependence. It occurred both in terms of the supply of goods and services coming from, and destined to, every part of the world, and, even more significantly, in terms of the almost instantaneous financial movement of many billions of dollars. Within the conditions generated by the globalisation process, the marked economic-technological superiority of the US and its multinationals is making globalisation correspond increasingly to a general Americanisation of the world economy.

It is in such circumstances that the economic-technological conditionings regulated and manipulated by the US are particularly efficient, both directly and through international agencies. These agencies are conceived and structured in a consistent way with these conditionings, such as the World Trade Organisation (WTO), the World Bank, the

International Monetary Fund (IMF), and others. These condition-ings obey neoliberalistic logic, which leads to international super-competitiveness and the creation of new rules. Combined, they strongly favour the American economy and its multinationals, particularly to the detriment of countries with less developed and less competitive econo-mies. Therefore, these economies are faced with two alternatives. The first option is to open their internal market to an invasion of goods and services offered by the multinationals. This would mean the elimination of autochthonous productive capacity and a growing loss of operational control over their own economy, thus becoming a mere segment of the world market. The second option would be to insist on the practice of traditional protectionism, and thus bring about an increasing technology lag that would subject them (in the name of free trade and liberal and democratic principles) to intolerable sanctions on the part of the interna-tional agencies and the US itself.

Cultural power
The cultural power of the US is frequently underestimated and considered only in terms of its scientific-technological aspects. Certainly, science pro-duction shifted during the course of the twentieth century from Europe to the US at an ever-increasing rate. Perhaps even more significant here is the concentration in the US of the technological and innovation capacity in this area. Notwithstanding this predominance, the dominant cultural influence of the US at the 'pop-culture' and 'American way of life' level is no less apparent. The American cinema exerts an immeasurable multiplying effect in this respect. It is an effect that is also self-multiplying in the sense that the screens of the world (with few exceptions) show mostly American films. The odd non-American movie sometimes manages a screening as well, but predominantly by American distributors..

The immense and powerful dissemination of American values and cul-tural styles has a corresponding effect on the configuration of values and styles of life in the other world cultures. Without getting into too much detail on such a consequential question, one might highlight just three of its most important effects. The first concerns the fact that modernity and modernisation, particularly from a youth point of view in almost every country in the world, are seen as being equivalent to a process of Americanisation and as something resulting from it. Furthermore, American institutions and procedures, such as democracy, neoliberal eco-nomics, super-competitive individualism and high and unrestricted consu-merism, are seen as universally desirable. Finally, and which tends to lead to disastrous consequences, the conviction is spreading among every nation and social class, that the American way of life and its high and unrestricted consumerism are universally accessible whenever American institutions and procedures are adopted.

INTERNATIONAL CONSEQUENCES

The enormous scale and intensity of the American impact on the world is producing very profound and varied effects. Among the countless consequences of this impact, three aspects should be highlighted as being particularly important. The first relates to the image the US has of itself and its international actions, the second concerns stratification, and the third concerns its real economic-social effects.

America's image of itself

The Americans do not view their country as an imperial power and do not aspire to such. They are fully aware and proud of being the only superpower and intend to preserve and consolidate this position. For many, including significant numbers in Congress and the Executive, this position confers unipolarity on the US. Unipolarity carries the obligation of performing a regulatory role in international affairs, which can, and in principle should, replace the work of the UN in a more efficient and internationally beneficial way.

The Americans see their country as a benign power – which tendentiously it actually is – that seeks to contribute to the institution of world peace, to democracy and the defence of human rights and free trade. The super competitiveness of the American economy giving it advantageous access to all the markets not subject to a protectionist regime, prompts the country to actively defend free trade. From the American point of view, it is fair that the most competitive should prevail and the effects of this competitiveness are beneficial for consumers in every country in the world.

The view the Americans have of themselves and their role in the world is genuinely positive. It is true in the short run, both for the ordinary man in the street involved in his daily life, and for political leaders, conditioned by the short duration of elective mandates. The great scholars, such as Brzezinski and Huntington (among others), have a historical view of their country. It leads them, on the one hand, to an awareness of the transient nature of all hegemonies, from the Roman to the British and, by necessity, the current American hegemony. However, they share the favourable self-image that Americans have of their country and its international actions.

From this conjugation between historical awareness and self-complacency arises the interesting idea that the US will be historically the last superpower. American hegemony, even though non-unipolar, will contribute towards the universalisation of democracy, respect for human rights and a progressive modernisation of the world. It will generalise higher living standards for all nations and thus establish an era of universal peace and prosperity.[3]

World power stratification

American supremacy and the unipolarity regime, viewed in terms of world power stratification, leads to a world differentiated at three levels.

1. the level of the ruling countries;

2. the level of the resistant countries; and

3. the level of the conditioned or dependent countries.

Strictly speaking, the US has become the only fully sovereign country. It enjoys the power of veto, not only in the Security Council ritual, but also at the practical level, in any international deliberation of great importance or conflicting with vital American interests. Furthermore, the US is an indispensable partner in any important international initiative that hopes to succeed. It is militarily invulnerable, having at the same time the capacity to intervene effectively in any part of the world. Nevertheless, as mentioned before, the US, by virtue of domestic inhibitions and efficient international resistance, does not enjoy effective unipolar power. The international actions of the US are subject to legitimacy requirements dependent on the approval of the UN Security Council and, in the final instance of the European countries (particularly France and Germany, besides the habitual, almost automatic alignment of Great Britain).

This circumstance, plus the very weight of the EU itself, grants co-participation status to the European countries, although to a lesser degree than the US at the ruling power level. At this level, also to a lesser degree, Japan co-participates by virtue of its position as the second economic-technological power in the world. In addition, the fact remains that the US depends on the Japanese alignment to maintain its influence in the Far East.

Countries that are in a position to resist American supremacy but not contest it head-on occupy the second level of world power stratification. This position is typically that of China. To a lesser degree, countries such as Russia, India and Iran take part at this level. Iraq, if it manages to overcome its traditional rivalry with Iran, which led to a bitter war between the two countries, might have access to this level, as a supporting player of its former enemy. If Brazil manages to consolidate the Mercosul and overcome its current policy of international financial dependence, it might also have access to the level of resistant countries.

The third level of international power stratification is that of the conditioned or dependent countries, which comprises the rest of the world. This level is predominately occupied by countries subject to the technological-economic logic of the Euro-Nippon–American system and without options of their own. At this level there are also a number of Asiatic countries dependent in different ways on China, the most typical case being that of North Korea. Switzerland occupies a singular position in this level and is a small highly developed country which prefers not to join the EU. Such a union would give it greater international participation but deprive it of its assumed neutrality.

Social-economic effects

The globalisation process, which is rapidly spreading throughout the world within the international power stratification regime mentioned above, produces extremely varied social-economic effects. These effects are conditioned, on the one hand, by the international power level at which a country is situated. On the other hand, for countries situated at the dependent level, these effects vary. This is according to whether the country manages to achieve a satisfactory position in the international market as an exporter of primary products, or remains an under-competitive industrialised country.

Countries situated at the ruling level have managed to achieve a high level of general development, enjoy satisfactory living standards (although in the case of Europe, there are excessive unemployment rates) and maintain internationally balanced economic, cultural and political relations. These characteristics are presented in full in the US. The continual international trade deficits, tolerated for the benefit of domestic consumers and the logic of its own multinationals, are amply compensated by the huge inflow of profits and interest and also (in the extreme) by the self-constituting capacity of its own financial reserves. In the case of the European countries, the EU provides them with international and domestic protection, highly compensatory for the restrictions to national sovereignty arising from this same Union.

The position of countries situated at the resistance level is more complex and varied. Fundamentally, this level provides them with a wider range of options than the dependent countries. This fact provides a margin of national autonomy, which the dependent countries are deprived of. This margin of autonomy in turn enables them to promote their own development with a significant degree of independence from the ruling countries. The opportunities provided by this level, however, require a considerable and consistent national development effort, which also needs to be implemented rapidly. The resistance level has a comparatively short horizon. Countries that fail to achieve a satisfactory level of development within the next few decades are unlikely to be able to do so in the course of the second half of the twenty-first century, and will find themselves in the position of a dependent country. This is clearly the case of China, but also for Russia, in terms of its need to rapidly overcome the chaotic conditions of the post-communist aftermath. In the case of Iran, it is in terms of the need to overcome Islamic dogmatism and become a modern society.

Countries situated at the dependency level, which covers the great majority of countries in the world, present a huge variety of situations, according to their relative level of development and their demographic statistics. As already mentioned, a small highly developed country such as Switzerland can enjoy advantageous conditions without belonging formally to the ruling level. Underdeveloped countries with a small population which manage, however, to place their primary products in the international market on a satisfactory basis (such as Costa Rica) also enjoy relatively favourable conditions. This level, however, is extremely unfavourable to underdeveloped countries with a large population (like Indonesia and Nigeria) or for countries also with a large population, predominantly industrial, but whose productive system is not sufficiently competitive (like Brazil). Brazil, as will be briefly discussed next, finds itself in an intermediary situation between the resistance and the dependency level. Its final status will depend, domestically, on the extent to which it is able to overcome its current reliance on the international financial system, and internationally, on how far Mercosul can consolidate itself and expand to the rest of South America, resisting its absorption by the FTAA (Free Trade Agreement of the Americas).

EVOLUTIONARY TRENDS

General aspect

The current international system and its three-power strata offer little stability. There is inherent instability in the unimultipolarity status of the US, tending in the course of the coming decades to turn into an effective unipolarity or become a new multipolarity. There is instability in the status of countries situated at the resistance level, as is clearly the case with China. The latter will either achieve equipollence with the US by mid-century, or it

will slip into a dependency relationship, amidst considerable crisis and turbulence. Furthermore, numerous countries now situated at the dependency
level are exhibiting, both domestically and internationally, signs of extreme
instability. This is clearly apparent in the cases of Africa and Indonesia, but
also, within its own conditions in the case of Brazil. The huge populations of
these countries are not compatible with recalcitrant underdevelopment and
a continued situation of international dependency. Such countries, if they do
not develop and acquire satisfactory conditions of domestic equilibrium in
the coming decades, will become explosive centres of international upheaval.

The instability currently found in the international system will bring
about great modifications in the decades to come, which will evolve at three
main historical-social levels. We can describe these levels as:

1. the economic-social;

2. the international; and

3. the civilisation level.

These levels correspond to processes of different duration and velocity.
The economic-social level corresponds to phenomena already being felt,
resulting from the domestic and international non-viability of the majority
of the countries situated at the dependency level. Such phenomena occur,
at great speed, in a relatively short space of time. The international level
concerns the configuration of the new world order, which will result from
changes in the current unimultipolar situation. The corresponding processes develop in the medium term, their effects tending to materialise from
the mid-twenty-first century onwards. The civilisational level corresponds
to long-term processes. It consists of the gradual formation of a planetary
civilisation, through the fusion of elements coming from the currently
existing civilisations into planetary universal, which will exhibit distinct
characteristics in each of the original bases.

Economic-social level

As has been pointed out by Aldo Ferrer,[4] the current globalisation process
constitutes the third wave of a phenomenon whose origin lies in the maritime discoveries of the fifteenth century and the resulting mercantile revolution. A second globalisation wave occurred with the industrial revolution.
The third and present globalisation wave has resulted from the technological revolution of our own time.

The globalisation process has acquired steadily growing proportions, both in terms of geographic extension and in terms of its intensity as it has passed from one stage to the next. In all three stages, this process has been marked by the asymmetry – growing geometrically – of its effects. The Asian world in the fifteenth century exhibited a civilisational level equal or superior to that of the West. With the mercantile revolution, the Western world began to enjoy an economic advantage of around two to one in its relationship with the Asian world. With the industrial revolution, this advantage became ten to one. With the current technological revolution it has become 60 to one.[5]

The effects of this extraordinary asymmetry are extremely destabilising for underdeveloped countries. They exhibit great differences, among other things, according to whether the countries come from major ancient civilisations, such as India or China, from the Iberian cultures, such as Latin America, or whether they are still in a pre-national stage, as in the case of Africa. Despite the profound differences that exist between these countries, the underdevelopment from which they are suffering expresses the effects of the deep asymmetry generated by the globalisation processes.[6] Besides having exponentially raised the difference in levels between underdeveloped and developed countries (the GDP per capita in the case of Africa is around US$500, against US$30,000 in the most developed countries) the third and present globalisation wave has brought the masses of the underdeveloped world, through television and other media, into immediate contact with the affluent world. This includes the islands of influence existing in the poor countries themselves, generating acutely destabilising effects, particularly in countries with a large population.

The entry of underdeveloped countries into the Euro–Nippon–American economic-technological system imposes inhibiting constraints on their development, particularly on social development. It also arouses completely unrealistic expectations, generating frustrations that are expressed in all kinds of violence and rising crime rates. These countries are heading rapidly towards a state of ungovernability, as one can already see in Africa, in Indonesia and in the Andes region of South America. In Brazil itself, the destabilising effects generated (particularly by the Landless Peasant Movement and large and extended urban criminality) are extremely disconcerting. This is despite the stability of its democratic regime, the relatively high average level of the country (US$5,000 per capita) and the important high-tech sectors that it has.

Any attempt at a more detailed analysis of the conditions of countries at the dependency level falls outside the scope of this brief study, but one should just point out, in relation to the asymmetry process, that overcoming underdevelopment requires, among other conditions, balance of trade and balance of payments equilibrium in these countries. This is in order to allow economic growth, as it is up to institutions like the World Bank and the IMF to facilitate this process.

Civilisation level

From the end of the nineteenth century and in a process that gained pace after the First World War and even more so after the Second World War, Western Civilisation[7] began to exhibit characteristics that required differentiation from its preceding tradition. One might use the term Late Western Civilisation to denominate it, in the same way that Classical Civilisation, after Constantine, became known as Late Classical Civilisation. The Christianisation of the classical world, with the resulting loss by Rome of its previous religious beliefs, led to profound changes in the ancient world. Transformations in the long term and in the course of great vicissitudes, gave rise, after the disintegration of the Carolingian Empire, to the emergence of Western Civilisation.

In the same way the growing laicisation of Western Civilisation, the crisis of transcendent values (with Nietzsche and after him) and the non-open *de facto* replacement of the belief in God, as the basis of the Western cosmovision, by the belief in science and technology, have made the Western Civilisation of today something very different from the preceding tradition. Thus, it is a late expression of that civilisation.

Concomitant with this process and more markedly after the Second World War, another process has been taking place at a much slower rate. This is the gradual fusion of the civilisations to the present day into a general, single civilisation, which can be entitled a Planetary Civilisation.

This second process began at the end of the eighteenth century, through the growing influence of the important elements of Western Civilisation on the other remaining civilisations: Islamic, Indian, Buddhist and Sino-Japanese. The initial penetration of Western Civilisation was in the technological and military areas. Confronted with Western technology and its military applications, the other civilisations realised that if they were to survive, they needed to incorporate these crucial elements of Western superiority. They tried to do this, preserving in the other cultural domains (particularly in the religious and institutional domains) their traditional characteristics. However, in the course of time, this intent proved to be impossible. Western technology brought with it the parallel need to adopt Western science with all its ramifications, in the conception of the world and organisation of society. Fundamental conceptions for Islam, such as that of structural unity in the community of the ummah of political, civil and religious dimensions, were not compatible with the modernisation of Islamic society. Turkey took the recognition of this incompatibility to its ultimate consequences, converting Islam into a subjective religion and imposing completely Western Turkish characteristics on society and the state. Japan moved towards complete Westernisation, except in respect of its ethical values. For the Indo and Buddhist civilisations, the conception of samsara, related to the transmigration of souls and central to their religious-philosophical convictions, has proved to be incompatible with modern biology and psychology.

The gradual and growing Westernisation of non-Western civilisations has not occurred in a linear and continuous way. Thus, it has given rise in different regions to occasionally violent reactions, such as Islamic Fundamentalism. Nevertheless, the process in the long term follows an inexorable logic. The modernisation of the non-Western world is synonymous with Westernisation. It so happens, however, that the Westernisation of the non-western world corresponds, albeit to a lesser extent, to an ample penetration in Western Civilisation of elements from other civilisations, as well as African culture. Buddhist practices and concepts have considerable influence on sectors of Western society. Afro-Americans, to affirm their differences from the Anglo-Saxon world, have adhered on a large scale to Islam. Neo-Confucian ideas are dispersed throughout the world. Black influence is predominant in Western pop music. The illustrations are countless. What results from this process of reciprocal influences is the gradual formation of a Planetary Civilisation: a civilisation whose scientific-technological bases come from Late Western Civilisation, but which tend to present marked differences according to the original pillars of this civilisation. These differences came from the non-Western civilisations that survived until the twentieth century.

This hypothesis for the gradual formation of the Planetary Civilisation differs fundamentally from the ideas put forward by Huntington in his book, *The Clash of Civilizations*, mentioned previously. However, what Huntington does visualise is the strong tendency for the major conflicts of the twenty-first century to pit the US,[8] and its possible allies, head-on against China, and in terms of terrorism and guerrilla conflicts, against the Islamic countries. It happens, however, that Huntington's predictions, although concerning antagonisms that might well come about, will not represent a civilisational clash. Rather, they will represent a dispute for world power within the context of a Planetary Civilisation in the process of formation.

As previously pointed out, the world order in force after the implosion of the Soviet Union, characterised by the unimultipolarity of the US, does not look set for long duration. The unimultipolar regime will tend, by the mid-twenty-first century, to change into either an effective American unipolarity or, more likely, head towards a new multipolarity. Furthermore, the three-way stratification of world power, split into a ruling country level, a resistant country level and a conditioned or dependent country level, is also unlikely to last. The resistant countries will tend, by the mid-twenty-first century, to divide into those that achieve ruling country status (as will probably occur with China) and those that slip back into a dependency relationship. Among the dependent countries, however, the underdeveloped countries with large populations that do not manage to move towards sustainable development in the relative short term will tend to experience profound destructive crises. They will lose internal conditions of governability and constitute explosive centres of upheaval in the world.

It is difficult to forecast the ways in which these different probable processes will manifest themselves and interrelate during the first half of the twenty-first century. There will be a tendency for the ruling countries to use constraining solutions in their respective local areas. These solutions, for the upheavals caused by the disruption of non-viable societies, will employ suitable coercive means. However, the globalisation process, which will continue to spread and intensify, contains inevitable channels of inter-communication – everyone with everyone and everything with everything – in an operationally unified world. Under such conditions, islands of affluence, no matter how powerful they may be militarily and technologically, will be unable to survive surrounded by a sea of rebellious, wretched populations.[9] The massive extermination of the impoverished masses could be adopted, if it were feasible. However, what makes it impossible is the inevitable contamination of the planet as a whole, which would result from using mass extermination methods such as nuclear or chemical–biological weapons. This is in addition to the fact that the higher cultures cannot preserve their own values if they violate them on a large scale in the process of exterminating the outcasts of the world as a whole.

In the long term, the world is faced with a single alternative. Collective suicide or the institution, within the emerging Planetary Civilisation, of a rational and equitable world order. In the form of a modern *Pax Universalis*, the *Pax Perpetua* would be established, which Kant, in the conditions of the eighteenth century, understood as being the only possible way of regulating the world.

ARGENTINA, BRAZIL, MERCOSUL

Mercosul

What is the situation of the member countries of Mercosul and of the latter, as an integrating system in southern South America, *vis-à-vis* the situation and the international conditions previously mentioned?

Mercosul is both a common market project for its members as well as an initiative for co-ordinating efforts designed to provide its members with greater external weight and better international negotiating conditions.

Mercosul has represented a market of growing importance for its members. In the period between 1991 and 1998[10] aggregate intra-regional trade was 36.9 per cent, 16.5 per cent, 79.6 per cent and 80.5 per cent for Argentina, Brazil, Paraguay and Uruguay, respectively, with the rest of the world. In this situation, if the relative trade importance of Mercosul is less for Brazil than for the other countries, one should take into account that Brazilian exports to Mercosul are products of high aggregate value, in which manufactured goods represent 90 per cent of the total. To get a comparative idea, Brazilian exports of manufactured goods to the EU represent only 38.5 per cent of the total. In addition, besides the current importance of Mercosul, intra-regional trade has grown at significantly higher rates than the trade of member countries with the rest of the world. From 1991 to 1997 intra-regional trade grew by 771 per cent, against an increase in trade of 142 per cent[11] for the rest of the world.

From 1999 to the writing of this study in mid-2001, a serious crisis confronted Mercosul. The Argentinean stagnation was ascribed, by some sectors, to the negative effects of Mercosul. The new Uruguayan government, under President Jorge Battle Ibañez, is unsupportive of Mercosul. Therefore, Mercosul is faced with the alternative of either reaching new institutional arrangements and becoming stronger and consolidated, or converting itself into a less ambitious free trade area, with the probability of being later absorbed by the ALCA (American Free Trade Area).

When considering Mercosul independently of its 1999–2001 crisis, one must consider two main aspects. First, Mercosul as a regional market and second, Mercosul as an international protagonist.

As a regional market in the relative short term, Mercosul faces the option of expanding throughout the rest of the South American continent. This would incorporate, if not all the other countries, at least countries such as Chile, Bolivia, Peru and Venezuela. Brazil strongly supports this alternative. Opposed to this, there is another option that the US intensely supports. It consists of instituting an American Free Trade Area (ALCA), extending from the present North America Free Trade Area (which currently incorporates the US, Canada and Mexico) to the whole of Central and South America.[12]

As the 1990s came to a close, the position of Mercosul, and also of Brazil, remained extremely ambiguous in relation to these two alternatives. On the one hand, the Latin American countries have signed declarations of intent with Washington, in respect of ALCA, to finalise the accord by 2005.

On the other hand, there is a prevailing view in Brazil that a free trade treaty for the whole of the Americas will eliminate Mercosul's common external tariff, which in practice means ending the union. The Latin American country's competitiveness, particularly in sectors of high aggregate value, is well below that of the US. This disequilibrium, with the implementation of ALCA, is recognised in the region as possibly reducing the members of Mercosul and the other countries of the region, to what they were until the 1930s (mere exporters of primary products, with an enormous decline in their per capita GDPs and employment levels). On the other hand, in many South American countries, including the ideas of Minister Cavallo in Argentina, there is a prevailing view that ALCA is preferable to Mercosul.

One possible outcome would be a restructuring of Mercosul in conditions favouring Argentinean demands, in which case Mercosul would not be absorbed by ALCA. Another possibility is the acceptance of ALCA by all South American countries, with the exception of Brazil. If the US would not suppress all non-tariff barriers, Brazil would refuse to join. An important variable in the game is the behaviour of the EU. An opening of the EU to Mercosul would change the present picture in favour of the Brazilian position significantly.

The other important aspect of Mercosul, supposing its consolidation, is the extent to which it functions as an international protagonist, representing the interest of its members. The political importance of Mercosul is in fact considerably greater than its commercial importance. Certainly, for Paraguay and Uruguay, Mercosul represents a market that absorbs 80 per cent or more of their exports. In the case of Argentina, although on a lesser scale, Mercosul receives about 40 per cent of that country's exports. For Brazil itself, as already pointed out, Mercosul has an important role as a market for Brazilian manufactured goods. Nevertheless, the political importance of Mercosul is even more significant, as only under its auspices do the member countries enjoy any international bargaining power. In the short term, this bargaining power gives them access to the resistance level in the international power stratification, opening up a space in the longer term for access to the higher level. In isolation, not even Brazil would manage to rise in the short and medium term to the resistance level. Potentially, in the long term, assuming that the country achieves a satisfactory level of national development by 2020, Brazil would be in a position to maintain itself at the resistance level, even without Mercosul, with the possibility of making subsequent progress. In the absence of Mercosul, the ALCA will absorb the other South American countries by 2005, thus perpetuating their dependency status. More than just a regional common market, Mercosul is a passport to history for its members.

Argentina

Besides external obstacles to its consolidation and expansion, such as those arising from the ALCA project, Mercosul is facing serious internal difficulties. These relate in general, to the considerable hesitations on the part of Argentina in its relationship with Mercosul, and in particular, to Brazil. Predominantly, this is due to three main factors of a political, economic and psychic-cultural nature.

On the political plane, there are those in Argentina who assume that Brazil, due to its large geographic, demographic and economic size, will inevitably be the leader of Mercosul. This will reduce Argentina to a secondary position. For others, this question has little relevance, as any attempt at exercising arbitrary power or even excessive influence by a member country of Mercosul (in this case Brazil) can be avoided through appropriate institutions. In addition, many people consider it much more advantageous for Argentina to belong to Mercosul, rather than to remain isolated and totally dependent on the major powers. In this situation, there would be resulting benefits for Argentina, even if Brazil exercised a controllable leadership over it. There are those, however, for whom the prospects of Brazilian leadership, seen as an exercise in sub-imperialism, is quite unacceptable. In such a case, it seems preferable to be subject to US leadership.

On the economic plane, the problems facing Argentina are more objective and relevant, although compatible with satisfactory solutions. Such problems stem from the fact that Argentina, having opted in the previous military regime for a de-industrialisation policy, is currently faced with insufficient capacity and industrial competitiveness compared with that of Brazil. Therefore, trade with Brazil tends to be characterised by the low aggregate value of Argentinean exports and the high aggregate value of Brazilian exports to Argentina. This problem is real, and certainly not desirable. Nevertheless, both in the short and medium term, various corrective measures can be taken, and in the long term, the problem can be completely rectified. Among the corrective measures particular importance should be given to setting up large bi-national corporations and to a high rate of Brazilian investment in Argentina. This can be in addition to measures that will ensure a balance of trade between the two countries, which in recent years has been showing an Argentinean surplus. In the short term, Argentina's new Economic Minister, Domingo Cavallo, decided, with a reluctant Brazilian agreement, to suppress external tariffs for capital goods for a certain time. This was in order to stimulate a new developmental effort. It is already visible that a future agreement concerning Mercosul will have to reconsider, in a broad way, the question of the common external tariff.

The third factor underlying Argentinean hesitations is of a psychic-cultural nature. This relates to the Argentinean discontent with Brazilian economic and political pre-eminence in Mercosul.

It goes beyond the scope of this study to get into a more detailed discussion of the possible factors underlying Argentinean hesitations in its relationship with Brazil and Mercosul. Let it suffice to highlight just three important points. The first concerns the fact that any fears Brazil might exercise within Mercosul and/or in its bi-lateral relationship with Argentina, any form of sub-imperialism as proponents of the Brazilian sub-imperialism thesis claim, are completely unfounded. This is due to the obvious fact that in a confrontation with American hegemony, any form of arbitrary power on the part of Brazil, within Mercosul or South America, would allow the country which was the target of such arbitrary action to withdraw from the system and join ALCA. Brazilian sub-imperialism would only be possible if Brazil, instead of aspiring to an autonomy level, became a regional agent of American imperialism.

There is a thesis, according to some, that the supposedly inevitable secondary position of Argentina (behind Brazil) in Mercosul would render preferable the adhesion of Argentina to a system under the immediate leadership of the US. However, this does not take into account the terms on which the participation of a country like Argentina are made, in one case or the other. In fact, within Mercosul, the position of Argentina, far from being secondary and despite the size of Brazil, is crucial, because the very existence of Mercosul as a level of international negotiation depends on it. Without Argentina, the Brazilian position would blur Mercosul, and make the union irrelevant. In Mercosul, Argentina is a fundamental participant, whose relationship with Brazil, despite its greater size, is on the same level. A link between Argentina and the US, without Mercosul, would make it one of the countless dependent countries, less important than the Ukraine, which has nuclear arms, and Egypt, which is a key country in the Arab world.

A third point to consider concerns the economic advantages that Argentina reaps from its participation in Mercosul, in contrast with the disadvantages that would follow upon its withdrawal. Primarily, as previously mentioned, Mercosul absorbs about 40 per cent of Argentinean exports, which in itself is extremely important. Furthermore, precisely because Argentina is a crucial participant in Mercosul, it enjoys enormous bargaining power and therefore is in a position to ensure balanced trade relations. It also enjoys particularly favourable conditions for expanding its industrial capacity and increasing its competitiveness. In contrast with this situation, withdrawal from Mercosul would not bring about any expansion in Argentina's industrial capacity or any increase in its competitiveness. In fact, it would lead quite to the contrary. Defenceless and exposed to the tough vicissitudes of the international market, Argentina would be forced to resort to an expansion of its traditional agricultural sector, missing the opportunity, which Mercosul offers, to re-industrialise.

Brazil

On account of its continental size, Brazil is inevitably the central player in Mercosul. However, this does not mean, as mentioned before, that it is in a position to exert predominantly unilateral leadership. On the contrary, the fact that Mercosul lies in the region that is subject to the most uninhibited American hegemony, and is currently, in the course of the early years of the twenty-first century, facing the serious challenge of ALCA, means that Brazilian leadership can only be exercised with the consensus of the other member countries. This signifies leadership that stems not from coercive means, but from the capacity to put forward measures of general interest and contribute towards a rational and equitable administration of the system.

It is important to stress the fact that currently, the position of member countries within Mercosul is of a different nature according to whether one is looking at Brazil or the other member countries. This situation will tend to prevail in the hypothesis of other South American countries being incorporated into the system. For Brazil, which constitutes the major market to which the other countries of the region are seeking access (while the other national markets are relatively small for Brazil) the main importance of Mercosul is political in character. Mercosul is a predominantly economic arrangement for the other members, without detracting from its political importance. For Brazil, without detracting from its economic importance, Mercosul is predominantly a political system. More than being just a market for its exports – notwithstanding the importance of this – Brazil is seeking through Mercosul conditions that will enable it to preserve its national autonomy. This is within the international power stratification participating at the resistant country level.

Brazil's position means an obligation to satisfy various requirements in order to consolidate and expand Mercosul. These requirements are of two distinct types. On the one hand, the consistency of Mercosul depends, particularly in view of the current crisis of the system, on the internal conditions. On the other hand, in order to take advantage of the benefits that Mercosul can provide, there are conditions which Brazil itself depends on.

The internal consistency of Mercosul, in relation to Brazil, depends whether the other participants find satisfactory stimuli to remain coherently within the system, as well as the significant disadvantages of withdrawing from it. Coercive leadership, as a hegemonic power might exercise, depends on the penalties it can inflict on those that do not follow it. The leadership that a non-hegemonic power like Brazil can exercise, lacking any coercive means, depends on the advantages it can offer to those that follow it and the disadvantages that result from not doing so.

Within these conditions, Brazil has to be clear about what is primarily involved in the task, together with the corresponding costs. Brazil must reassure the other participants that their membership to Mercosul is advantageous and any withdrawal consequently disadvantageous. This task, with its respective costs, generally involves the adoption by Brazil of compensatory measures for the greater average competitiveness of its industry, *vis-à-vis* that of the other members. For instance, one of the new arrangements could be a revision of the common external tariff, reducing significantly its incidence on capital goods. What matters most of all, is to facilitate access to the large Brazilian market for the other participants, and give them the conditions to achieve a balance of trade equilibrium.

Brazil is subject to the responsibility of reassuring the other members that their membership of Mercosul is an advantageous one and this may prove to be an excessively onerous task. There is an impression that Brazil will be the major beneficiary of Mercosul. However, the burden of sustaining the general optimisation of the system may subject Brazil to excessive demands. To correct this situation, Brazil needs to set up an alternative system for protecting its international interests, so that in the extreme hypothesis that Mercosul splits, the country has other means for preserving its autonomy on the international scene.

Once again, the scope of this study does not allow a further elaboration of how a country like Brazil can set up an alternative system for its international protection. Two of the most important requirements to this end are:

1. a system of close economic-technological co-operation with the other continental countries in the world – China, India and Russia; and

2. the negotiation of a wide-ranging co-operation accord with the EU. It should be added that such initiatives can and should be adopted concomitantly with the consolidation and expansion of Mercosul.

Besides working towards the consolidation of Mercosul and, in fact, as a condition for doing so efficiently, Brazil needs to carry out a profound institutional reform. The reform must significantly raise its level of governability, which currently is extremely low, and enable it to rapidly carry out a major comprehensive national development programme.

Mercosul, if it succeeds in consolidating itself, provides its members with the internal conditions to conclude their respective development programmes and raise their competitiveness. In terms of the international market and system, it provides them with protection for sufficient time to acquire international competitiveness. Furthermore, in respect of the international power stratification regime, it provides them with access to the resistance level, creating a satisfactory margin of national autonomy. For both these effects to occur, the members of Mercosul should adopt (at the national level) the corresponding measures and proceed actively to incorporate other South American countries into the system.

CONCLUSIONS

Events in the world are developing through three main processes, at different levels of historical-social depth and speed:

1. the economic-social process, within the ambit of the various countries and their reciprocal inter-relations;

2. the process of forming a new world order, with its different power tiers; and

3. the civilisation process, moving towards the gradual formation of planetary civilisation.

These processes are taking place, from the first to the last, at levels of growing historical-social depth and declining speed. The events related to the economic-social configuration of societies affect their daily existence and are being processed rapidly. The twenty-first century inherited societies marked by abyssal differences between each other, in terms of income, education and qualifications, from the century before. A small number of affluent countries in Europe, North America and Japan have a per-capita income of around US$25,000. This is in comparison with the rest of the world population, which has an average per capita income level of less than US$3,000 – with a large number of poverty-stricken countries with per-capita incomes below US$500. However, even greater gaps separate a

minority with living standards approaching those of the European countries, from a huge mass of excluded subjects within the underdeveloped
countries themselves.

Various circumstances and factors in an increasingly globalised world
have made this situation untenable, both on the international plane and
within the countries themselves. There are excessive differences in income
and education levels. The social situation of the world, internationally and
at the domestic level of extremely heterogeneous countries (particularly
those with large populations), is becoming explosive and will reach intolerable levels in the comparative short term.

The affluent countries, and within the underdeveloped ones, their affluent minorities, are inclined to consider the use of coercive means to contain
the excluded masses. However, as previously mentioned, it is not viable,
both ethically and operationally, to go ahead with what in the final analysis
would mean the extermination of the excluded masses. The world, therefore, at both the international and the national levels, must head towards a
much less inequitable economic-social regime. This means a whole set of
policies and costs. However, it also means, given the high degree of social
exacerbation already reached, there is a need for short-term compensatory
measures, which will inevitably require a great effort.

In the international system, events are heading two ways. On the one
side, they are heading towards the formation by the mid-twenty-first
century of a more stable world order, which will replace the present unstable unimultipolarity regime. On the other side, at a faster rate, the relative
positions of countries are changing in the three tiers of world power stratification previously mentioned. For the member countries of Mercosul, the
fundamental question concerns the extent to which they are able to overcome the current crisis, to reach resistance level, and stabilise themselves in
it. Then they can possibly raise themselves to the higher level in the future.

As has been previously discussed, the destiny of the countries in question depends on consolidating and expanding Mercosul and at the same
time securing their own respective national development. Positive results
will enable these countries to stabilise themselves at the resistance level,
which in turn favours their subsequent development.

In the short-term horizon up to 2005, the significance of Mercosul,
besides its international consolidation and expansion to other South
American countries, will depend on whether it can defend itself from
absorption into ALCA. Overcoming this important challenge, the significance of Mercosul in the longer term will depend on the type of world order
that has developed by the mid-twenty-first century. If a multipolar regime
prevails, a greater space for national development will open up for member

countries of Mercosul. Depending on how significant this development is, Mercosul may gain access to the ruling country level. A multipolar world will tend to be administered for a long time by a formal or informal management committee, comprising, although with unequal weight, the major world systems. Countries such as the US, China, possibly India and Russia, the EU, an equivalent grouping of Islamic countries and possibly Mercosul, are the likely candidates to sit on this management committee.

In the present stage of humanity's cultural and technological development and in a growing world rapidly being unified by the globalisation process, countries are faced, both individually and collectively, with the non-viability of maintaining intolerable economic and social differences (whether between each other, or within each country itself). Equally, the world is faced with the need to establish a stable world order, which will, through necessity, have to be rational and reasonably equitable. The alternative to a rational, reasonably equitable and egalitarian ordering of the international system and the countries that integrate it, for a large number of countries, is the explosion of uncontrollable social conflicts. For humanity in general, the alternative is collective suicide, which will result from a holocaust of global proportions.

Mercosul, faced with the broad historical-social process outlined above, is a collective union of very small proportions and modest weight. Mercosul, however, is not irrelevant for its members and the South American countries that might join. This is because the possibility of having any historical destiny and escaping the alternative of becoming mere segments of the international market depends absolutely on Mercosul.

Even in international terms, however, Mercosul is not irrelevant. A new world order is in the process of formation. The international posture of a representative system of the main countries in Latin America (except Mexico) constitute an important lineage of Western culture. As a union, they can exert an important catalysing effect in favouring the emergence of a multipolar world within a rational and reasonably equitable world order. Furthermore, they can contribute so that the entry of the US and the EU into this new system occurs consensually and without jeopardising their legitimate interests.

Moreover, it should be added that in the alternate hypothesis of the US consolidating its world hegemony, constituting a stable unipolar regime, Mercosul would continue to be a precious instrument. It would aid in securing a more favourable positioning for its member countries in this new world order. A dominant *Pax Americana*, in the conditions of the twenty-first century, as in its time did *Pax Romana*, will have to manage the world in a rational and reasonably equitable way. This is in order to maximise the self-sustainability of this world, minimising the need and the cost of corrective interventions on the part of the hegemonic power. A more efficiently consolidated and expanded Mercosul will provide the best economic-social conditions within the system for its members and the best economic-political conditions for its relationship with the hegemonic power.

NOTES

1. See Samuel Huntington, *The Clash of Civilizations, and the Remaking of World Order*, Ch. 1, Touchstone Books, London (1996), 1998, and 'A Superpotência Solitária', in *Política Externa*, Vol. 8, No. 4, March–May, 2000, pp. 12–25.
2. See Zbigniew Brzezinski, *The Great Chessboard*, New York, Basic Books, 1997.
3. See Huntington, *The Clash of Civilizations*, Ch. 5, *and Brzezinki, The Great Chessboard, Conclusion.*
4. See Aldo Ferrer, *História de la Globalización*, México, Fondo de Cultura Económica, 1996.
5. See Osvaldo Sunkel and Pedro Paz, *El Subdesarrollo Latinoamericano y la Teoria del Desarrollo*, México, Siglo XXI, 1970, and Jadish Bhagwati, *The Economics of Underdevelopment*, New York, McGraw-Hill, 1966.
6. The underdevelopment of Third World countries is not only due – often not even mainly – to the effects of the asymmetry. This was responsible, generally speaking, for the historical origin of underdevelopment, particularly in the case of Asia. During the twentieth century, especially in the second half, countries such as Brazil up to the 1970s, and more recently South Korea, managed to overcome the effects of asymmetry. An important factor in perpetuating underdevelopment has been the excessive cost of local elites, in relation to the surplus generated by their societies, as notoriously occurs in the case of Africa.
7. Western Civilisation began to take shape in Europe in the tenth century AD. The bases of Christian Society, which legitimised the Carolingian Empire and which was administrated by it, developed from the Classical-Christian culture of the Late Ancient World, with a powerful Germanic aggregate. In the course of time, from the Middle Ages to the Baroque era, Western Culture developed its main lineages: Germanic, Italian, French, Iberian and Anglo-Saxon.
8. It is important to note in relation to Huntington, that he identifies at the present time the West with the US, considering as anti-Western any resistance to American hegemony. Such an identification obviously has no basis to it. The US is only a transplanted segment of one of the branches, of Anglo-Saxon lineage, of Western Civilisation, which also includes the Germanic, French, Italian and Iberian branches.
9. The same rule applies in the context of extremely heterogeneous countries, such as Brazil, India, Indonesia and others in the relationship between their affluent elites and their wretched masses.
10. Data from the *Boletim de Integração Latino-Americano*, No. 23, Ministry of Foreign Affairs, p. 189, the data from 1998 corresponding, in the cases of Argentina and Uruguay, only to the January–June period.
11. See Note 10.
12. As a matter of fact, the ALCA project presents a strong appeal to most Latin American countries, including many Argentinean sectors and Chile, which has proclaimed its intention to join. Brazil is the most resistant country.

TWO

◄◦►

The European Union and the New Multilateralism

ÁLVARO DE VASCONCELOS

This chapter focuses on Europe's role in shaping a post-hegemonic world order. Europe's vision of world order and its role within it are both influenced by its own integration. Knowing whether the European Union (EU) will assert itself as a centre of power comparable to the United States (US), or if it will become a qualitatively different actor, is a key issue when attempting to outline the future of the international system. The question, therefore, is whether the EU is capable of presenting the international community with a common project for a new multilateralism, or if it will merely remain, from a political and a hard security point of view, a regional actor. At the same time, one must also ascertain what role regional groups, such as Mercosul, can play according to a European vision of the world system. Of course the feasibility of a world system regulated by principles and rules will depend to a large extent on the evolution of US foreign policy in the post-Clinton era.

THE OPEN EUROPE MODEL

The fundamental aim of European integration remains the same: to weaken nationalism and power politics in intra-European relations and to prevent war, particularly between France and Germany. Although most Europeans believe it is only through the Union's continued existence that the 'European Model' can resist the external forces of globalisation, it is also true that internal considerations drive the primary goals of the EU, and shape Europe's foreign policy. It was very apparent in the way the EU reacted to the fall of the Berlin Wall. The Union took steps aimed at accelerating the process of European integration and reinforcing cohesion among member states. Policies on the internal front have met with successes that have not been matched on the external front. Even as it has proceeded with economic union and the creation of a single currency, the EU demonstrated its political impotence to intervene in Bosnia. Successes on the path to political union continue to be meagre.

The Union as a whole has an inherent difficulty to act as a world power because it weakens power politics in relations between member states. The Union maintains internal peace by reshaping relations between neighbours and acting as a powerful motor for democratic consolidation and social cohesion. This was true for the founding members in the post-war period, it was also the case for the southern European countries that returned to democratic rule in the 1970s. The same can be said for the new democracies of Central and Eastern Europe. In order to achieve security, peace and democracy, the Union's key instrument is inclusion. In this context, it is important to note that the states most committed to the building of European integration are precisely those that have benefited most from the policy of inclusion. By contrast, those that adhered to the EU principally for economic reasons – to meet the challenges of an increasingly globalised economy that cannot be dealt with nationally, and to take advantage of the European market – have remained on the margins of some of the phases of deepening integration. This is the case with the UK, Sweden and Denmark, who have all failed to join the single currency and strongly resisted all initiatives leaning towards the creation of supranational institutions.

The debate that counterpoises 'European power' and 'European space' fails to reflect this dichotomy if the terms are not clarified. The aim of the promoters of a European 'power' project is not to build a European super state in the image of the US. Even France, the main supporter of the notion of 'European power' does not accept the possibility of a central European government to which it would cede national defence and social policy prerogatives. The tendency reinforced since Maastricht,[1] with the deepening of political union, has been to strengthen the European Council, an intragovernmental organ, to the detriment of the supranational European Commission.

In the context of Europe's extraordinary diversity, the main innovative contribution of the European model has been its capacity to make compatible a sense of national belonging with membership to a supranational community. Joschka Fischer and others like him understood this, hence Fischer's proposal for the creation of a federation of democratic states, rather than a federal state, based on the dual legitimacy of the Union: its states and its citizens.[2] To date, the main political forces in Germany and significant sectors in France and the countries of Southern Europe, share this vision, but it has failed to meet with support in the UK and the Nordic countries. Much more controversial is the idea propounded by Fischer in his Humboldt speech, of creating a 'hard core' or a vanguard of states to speed up the creation of a federation of states. (It is unclear whether such a core would consist of founding members or participants in the single currency.) This idea is rejected instinctively by the smaller member states that see it as a thinly disguised proposal for the creation of a *'directoire'*.[3] This is particularly so when the notion of 'vanguard' is mentioned in the context of international relations. The 'European power' versus 'European space' debate is relevant insofar as it outlines the basis of the international role to be played by the EU. If the EU were to be a 'federation of nation states' as proposed by Jacques Delors,[4] this would affect its action and role in the international system in two important ways: the definition of its identity and, concomitantly, of its frontiers.

The EU cannot establish a cultural or civilisational identity without reneging on the concept of citizenship and weakening the communities of citizens within each of its member states. Such an identity would militate against a cultural, linguistic and even religious pluralism, which is increasing daily within the Union and its member states. For instance, there are nearly ten million European citizens who are Muslims. The German decision to give citizenship to immigrants, including over two million Turks, and to begin to distance itself from an ethnically based nationality, is a fundamental step towards ensuring compatibility between national political systems and the European model. The tendency is for a Europe that is increasingly defined as an area of multicultural co-existence in which supranationalism is compatible with the preservation of historical peculiarities, as well as cultural and religious affinities within and beyond the European continent. Hence, the creation by France, Portugal and the UK of 'circles' of co-operation based on a common language. The internal affirmation of multiculturalism is a trump card in the formulation of international policy when it is felt in many regions that globalisation and the dominance of American popular culture is a threat to cultural pluralism. This feeling helps to boost identity-based nationalism, particularly of a religious nature, which presently constitutes the gravest and most threatening alternative to democracy.

Politics defines the identity of the Union. Membership is available to all European democracies that accept the *'acquis'* of the EU and are economically prepared for convergence with, and competition in, the single market. The European Council's decision to accept Turkey as a candidate for membership at Helsinki in 1999 explicitly stated that Turkey must fulfil these conditions. Predominantly, the conditions were political – the preservation of democracy, the rule of law, of human rights and the assurance of the protection of minorities. There were no cultural or religious conditions. Defined in this way, the EU provides no clear limits on its enlargement. Even its geographical limits, its frontiers, are unclear. A 30-strong EU is envisaged. Currently, the ongoing process of European reform is seeking to establish how to accommodate 27 states.[5] The future is unclear. Could the Ukraine become a member, or will it be the extreme eastern frontier of the Union? How can the Union deny the democratic and Europeanist sectors in Russia a place in the process of European integration? Herein lies the pertinence of the debate about variable geometry and 'circles' of European construction.

Could a European 'hard core', the 'vanguard' proposed by the Germans, (and less enthusiastically by the French), realistically become a centralised federal state within the union of states that is the EU? It seems unlikely. Such a nucleus would have to be open and it would tend towards full inclusion. At the same time, the most coherent, if not equivalent proposals by Fischer and Delors, advocate a model that creates a community of democratic states according to the precept of unity within diversity.[6] Clearly, there will be a group of states that will take integration further, faster. There will be reinforced co-operation between them in various areas under Union competency, including foreign policy and home affairs. Their ability to act in the international arena will also be concomitantly reinforced. Yet where security and defence policy is concerned, this more markedly federal nucleus faces a basic difficulty: the resistance of the UK. One of the pillars of the whole process is the consolidation of a European defence policy. This requires committed participation from the UK, which is unwilling to take part in any form of federal vanguard but is predisposed to contribute to European defence. In sum, there will be no single 'hard core' but rather various nuclei corresponding to uneven developments on the road towards supranationalism. It is possible that there will be an ever-growing group that participates in all the 'circles'. This will become the true core of cohesion, independently of the size of the states involved.

The European institutional system and decision-making process will remain enormously complex for the foreseeable future. This is because it must continue to guarantee the system of checks and balances that has ensured its success to date. A central entity for Common Foreign and Security Policy (CFSP), such as a High Representative with vaster and more precise powers than the current one, which would permit him or her to co-ordinate foreign policy rather than act as a mere spokesperson, can be defined. However, there will always be a multiplicity of interlocutors: the

Council, the Commission, the Parliament and the member states. The Union's foreign partners will thus probably continue to feel the difficulties of not knowing who their interlocutor is.

The consolidation of an open Europe, in the Popperian sense of a democratic, pluralist and culturally diverse society, means the affirmation of a universally appealing European model. The EU will continue to focus essentially on the consolidation of democracy on the continent through enlargement, and on the project of expanding an area of stability and development to the south, in the Mediterranean. Europe thus emerges as a regional actor upholding a model with universal repercussions. Indeed, the greater the 'internal' success with the consolidation of continental democracy, the greater the 'external' impact and prestige of the model.

The values upheld by the EU are projected onto its foreign policy. Hence the importance of democracy, human rights and humanitarian law in European declaratory politics and the application of political conditionality in EU agreements with Third World countries. The universal appeal of the European model and its adjustment to the era of globalisation, as well as the global ambitions of some of its member states, provide a window of opportunity for positive and effective action in the international arena. Thus, this reinforces its position as an open pole of power within a more balanced, multilateral and universal system.

There is an alternative path that would work against this scenario. With enlargement to the East and South, and in the absence of deeper integration, the Union could lose its power to decide and act. It could become diluted and eventually disintegrate, transforming into an economic giant with no political weight. It would have to abandon any hope of acquiring an international status. This would be left to a few member states. Yet, without the Union, these states would be relegated to secondary roles in the international arena. The main victim of such a scenario would be the multilateral project.

THE EUROPEAN VISION OF THE INTERNATIONAL ORDER

The EU is not just a powerful regional actor, it also has a substantial international role as a civil power. With 370 million inhabitants, the 'Europe of the Fifteen' is the main economic zone in the world, representing 28.6 per cent of gross world product (GWP), in contrast with 27.4 per cent for the US, 14.9 per cent for Japan and Mercosul's 3.8 per cent. The EU is also the world's main trading power as well as its main source of official development aid. It represents more than half of the world Overseas Development

Administration (ODA) total, in contrast with 4 per cent for the US and 18 per cent for Japan. In terms of military expenditure, both absolutely and as a percentage of Gross National Product (GDP), it is known that the US is far ahead of Europe; it spends US$265 billion on defence, whereas the EU spends US$169 billion. European Union expenditure represents 60 per cent of that of the United States but generates only around 30 per cent of its military capability.

However, more so regionally than internationally, the EU already exercises significant soft power. Its economic weight, the attraction of its model and its development and co-operation policy, means the EU can use economic power for political ends, relying on non-coercive means to help solve long-term regional problems. Nonetheless, despite the ambitious scope of the Euro-Mediterranean Partnership (EMP), the results of policy towards the countries of North Africa or the Middle East (which are the first extra-European priority of the Union), will be felt only in the long run. The weight of the Union in crisis situations is still modest, as demonstrated by its timid, divided and ineffective response to the Israeli–Palestinian conflict. Aid and trade agreements with Sub-Saharan Africa, a region for which the Union has been the main economic, political and even military partner, have often been a failure. However, in fairness, it must be noted that no other actor has succeeded in that region either. Africa is still buried in inter- and intra-state conflict, and without a resolution of the security problem there can be no development. In Asia, Europe's role is not very significant in terms of soft power politics, and it is negligible in terms of hard power politics. Furthermore, as discussed below, in Latin America it has failed to show the political will to match the ambitions of the project it has advocated.

These are the current limitations of the EU as a civil power in the global arena. Even at a regional level, its capacity for 'inclusion' and its attributes as a civil power have been insufficient in times of severe crisis. This was the conclusion reached by European governments concerning the crisis in the former Yugoslavia, namely in Bosnia and Kosovo, as they regretfully observed their impotence to respond to the crisis. This impotence is the result of the limitations of the EU as an exclusively civil power. Dependence on the US, on its military strategy and willingness to intervene or not to ensure security on the continent, was also demonstrated. The current European defence project launched in St Malo, in 1998, by France and the UK, was born out of that observation.[7]

The development of European defence capabilities over the next decade will consolidate the Union as a truly powerful regional actor, able to deal with most of the challenges confronting the European continent. Security relations with Russia, however, may prove more difficult, particularly if the latter insists on maintaining the status of a superpower, albeit without the means to be one. The situation might be different if Russia opts for a European power status that is more compatible with its economic situation.

Although timid and rather incoherent, the consolidation of a common foreign and security policy with the creation of a 'Mr CFSP' will contribute to greater coherence in the Union's external action. However, it would be a mistake to think that in the coming decade the Union could become a military power comparable to the US. If the EU develops a capacity to act in the realm of security, it can develop a significant role in the construction of a post-hegemonic international order during the first quarter of the twenty-first century. A consequence of this would be the achievement of greater equality in transatlantic relations.

The countries of the Union have shown increasing unease with unipolarity and have affirmed the need to evolve towards a more balanced world. There is a consensus of frequent criticism across the whole European political spectrum, of the unilateralism of the US, particularly of its attempts to impose the extraterritorial application of US law (the D'Amato and Helms-Burton Acts). It is a preoccupation, which not only exists in most of the 'Countries of the Euro', but also in the UK. The constant tensions have been confined to the realm of trade, and a threatening political overflow has been avoided thus far. However, European unease with US unilateralism is not only restricted to trade matters. European leaders have demonstrated deep concern over non-ratification by the US Congress of the Comprehensive Test Ban Treaty (CTBT), the American refusal to sign the founding treaty of the International Criminal Court, and its decision to proceed with the creation of an anti-missile shield, the National Missile Defence (NMD*)*.

Although there is strong Euro-American convergence regarding security in the European continent (which has permitted the post-Cold War survival and even the expansion of NATO), the same cannot be said for extra-continental affairs. As far as the Middle East and the Gulf are concerned, the nuances and differences are plain to see. Only the UK supports the sanctions against Iraq; the majority of member states opposing them either for their political and social effects, or because of their unilateral nature.

However, at the same time, the member states of the Union (France included) cannot conceive a viable alternative for the role that, for better or worse, the US now plays during this transitional period in the international system. Nonetheless, it is widely believed in Europe, that a system based on the hegemony of the US, even if benign, cannot be sustained in the long run.

This is due to the pluralism that characterises the world and the unwillingness of American society to pay the price of guaranteeing international
security. Further, the majority of the current member states of the Union
hold a different view of the international order to that advocated by the US.

France supports the creation of a multipolar order that could balance
the 'hyper-power' of the US (an expression coined by Hubert Védrine).[8]
The Chirac view is that other centres of power could be the EU, Russia,
Japan, India, and possibly Brazil and Mexico. There would be a system of
clearly defined poles, inspired by the European balance of power system
before the Second World War. Within this system, the EU could seek to
affirm its sovereignty and autonomy, although the negative impact on world
security would partly reduce thanks to the existence of multilateral institutions. In speeches in China, Brazil and India (all countries with international power ambitions), both Jacques Chirac and Hubert Védrine have
explicitly referred to the need to build a multipolar world as an alternative
to unipolarism. A case in point is the April 1997 Russian–Chinese declaration on the promotion of a multipolar world.

This French view is apparently not shared by any other state of the EU,
even though the expression 'multipolarity' is frequently heard in the
speeches of most European leaders. Despite Blair's surprising Warsaw declaration on the need for a superpower Europe, the UK in fact resists such a
vision. Its public opinion and political elite are overwhelmingly opposed to
the concept of 'European power', as it implies a high degree of federalisa-
tion. The statement was rendered meaningless days later in the UN, when
the UK voted with the US on the Middle East. Although the German vision
of the Union is an exceedingly political one, it is still predominantly seen as
a civil power, focused primarily on the widening and deepening of European
integration itself. Germany also places a great deal of emphasis on a balanced
relationship with the US. However, this does not mean a less intense relationship; Germany sees the US as a crucial international partner for the EU.

Spain and Italy favour the international affirmation of the Union, not
just in the Mediterranean, but also, particularly for Spain, in Latin America.
Portugal has the same position and emphasises the need for the European
Union to honour its responsibilities towards Sub-Saharan Africa.
Nonetheless, Aznar's Spain has gradually come closer to the US perspective, and Italy's international position is far from corresponding to its economic and cultural weight. Furthermore, these countries are, together with
the Netherlands, those closest to the UK vision of Transatlantic relations.

As traditionally non-aligned countries, the Nordic countries distance
themselves from the French view, instead emphasising the central role of
the UN as a regulator of conflicts in a multilateral system. Europe should

become a large Scandinavia of sorts, an example in terms of peaceful co-operation and social justice.[9] Belgium is the country closest to France, but its capacity to influence EU foreign policy is not great. Finally, despite recent positive developments in foreign policy, Greek foreign policy still focuses essentially on the Turkish question. In contrast with the Nordic countries, most of the candidates for accession – Poland, Hungary and the Czech Republic – as 'Atlanticist' countries, are at ease with a pro-security and defence posture, which is also a product of their political desire to join the EU. Moreover, they share a desire with most of the European Union states that NATO remain essentially a collective defence organisation

Thus, it is unlikely that the EU will become a traditional power centre exercising a power politics-based foreign policy. In all probability, what we are witnessing is the emergence of an influential global actor, which will fall short of replicating the full attributes of a traditional superpower. It will, nevertheless, have the ability to influence decisively the future shape of the international system.

There is no consensus in Europe as to the benefits of a multipolar system. Indeed, it remains unclear what impact the emergence of new power centres and the relations between them would have on international security. There are serious reservations in most European capitals about the impact that the emergence of totalitarian China, as a super or great power, will have on international stability. Similar doubts are voiced about the impact of the Sino-Indian rivalry on Asian stability. The Indian nuclear test could be a sign of the 'regional bad times' to come, because of the emergence of new power centres.[10]

Whatever the debate on the advantages and disadvantages of a multipolar world, there is consensus among European states (and increasingly so in London) that the current predominance of US unipolarity and unilateralism will be challenged by newly emerging powers. Thus, it is transitional and unstable.[11]

Whether the EU acts in a multipolar world or not (most probably it will), it is not in the nature of the Union to seek hegemony, pursue American-style power politics, or even cultivate a global balance of power system. The European model does not envision the transformation of the Union into a super state. Rather, it envisages an entity able to shape the formulation of international rules within a network of interdependent multilateral institutions, such as the WTO and the recently created ICC (the ICC bearing witness to the growing importance of international law). The EU's active support for international regulation will have great credibility. Not only is it backed by its own experience, but the creation of such rules corresponds with the need, felt by states in different regions, to manage and take

advantage of the process of globalisation. The Union envisions a truly efficient global multilateral system, and the creation of institutions able to regulate political and economic interdependence. The aim is to construct a
system, accepted by a majority of states, governed by international norms for
international trade, security, the protection of human rights and the environment. It is a 'third' model, which, stated by Jean-Marie Guéhenno, is:

> . . . based neither on the indefinite supremacy of the United
> States, nor on the pursuit of independence and sovereignty as
> the ultimate goal of a political entity.[12]

It would constitute the institutionalised organisation of interdependence, of
a 'structured multilateralism'.[13] The success of the World Trade Organisation
(WTO) in managing the conflicts between the EU and the US, testifies to the
importance of multilateralism in the new international context.

The promotion of regionalism is one of the essential components of the
Union's foreign policy and its vision of the world. Whether the European
experience is adopted elsewhere as a model or not, the Union considers that
multilateralism can only be effective if it is based on regional groups, which
are seen as the building blocks of the new multilateralism. Not only do regional
groups constitute a form of administering economic interdependence, but
they are also a way to establish reliable security relations between neighbours and to support UN crisis prevention and resolution. Indeed, in many
circumstances, regionalism is the only possible multilateralism. Hence the
importance of so-called group-to-group dialogue in the external action of
the Union. Whether with ASEAN, Mercosul, the Andean Community or
the SADC, the Union seeks interlocutors with which to share its vision of
the international order. Indeed, the Union seeks to establish inter-regional
agreements with such groups, developing multi-regionalism as the basis of
multilateralism. Seen from this perspective, relations between the EU and
the Mediterranean, or with Mercosul, are an essential part of the experiment in the new multilateralism.[14]

One of the components of the Union's multilateralism is its posture *vis-
à-vis* the relationship between sovereignty and citizenship. It is not mere
chance that the concept of humanitarian intervention was born in France,
and that it was a Spanish judge who requested the extradition of Pinochet.
Europe is built upon supranational foundations that have de-legitimised
the concept and sanctity of absolute sovereignty. Thus, the intervention in
Kosovo was supported by a majority of European states, particularly
France and the UK, but also Germany. France and the UK participated
actively in the Rambouillet agreement and in the military intervention.

When Kofi Annan stated at the last General Assembly of the UN that 'the sovereignty of a State cannot be a protecting "wall" for the violation of the rights of man', his posture did not shock, but rather it pleased the majority of Europeans. Does this signal a *rapprochement* with the position of the US? It seems not. For Europeans, a reformed UN must develop the capabilities to practise the new multilateralism announced by Kofi Annan. It must be the UN that legitimises interventions when grave human rights violations occur within any given state. This is not to be seen by European states as an unacceptable limitation on their sovereignty.

However, this vision is not shared by various southern states, which opposed intervention in Kosovo in the name of the defence of sovereign powers and in opposition to unilateralism. This was the position of the Latin American countries, many of which have suffered a long experience of illegal interventions from the North. At a time when the Union creates an intervention force, it is essential for its foreign and security policy to be able to get the greatest number of states possible to agree to the definition of conditions for intervention.

The success of the multilateral project largely depends on the multilateralisation of the US. The majority of European states perceive that the possibility of a more just international order depends on close co-operation between the Union and the US. Those who think that the management of the bipolar enmity of the Cold War could become the form of administering a Euro-American rivalry are mistaken. The Union's member states still see the US as their main partner. The Union seeks a re-balancing of relations with the US, so that they become equals, able to contribute to the creation of global rules.

For the EU, the ability to face crises within its strategic zone, to make its co-operation policy effective and to acquire clear international weight, depends on every state's observance of multilateral rules. It is obvious that when the world becomes more Grotian, the influence of the EU will increase.[15] However, as Grotius has yet to prevail over Hobbes, the Union must be able not only to sanction prevaricators with the application of political conditionality, but also to opt for military intervention when all other avenues have been exhausted.

EU–MERCOSUL RELATIONS AND THE 'US FACTOR'

The EU needs partners to make its vision of a world based on regionalism viable. There has been a clear tendency in a variety of regions to establish different integration and co-operation schemes. However, the majority of

such projects have not gone beyond a basic inter-governmental co-operation that is fragile in the absence of true political convergence. Mercosul is
an exception to this rule and therefore the EU identifies it as a strategic
partner. For the Union, various factors affect the credibility of Mercosul.
The first is that it is an integration project among democratic countries,
which introduced a democratic clause in its treaty providing for sanctions,
including expulsion if a member returns to authoritarian rule. The firm and
effective reaction of the countries of Mercosul to the *coup d'état* in Paraguay
in April 1996, was an important test that increased the credibility of the
regional group. The international legitimacy of Mercosul, which is based
on this democratic commitment, is underlined by the EU.

The second factor is the alteration of traditional relations of enmity and
rivalry between Brazil and Argentina. This change implied the mutual
abandonment of national military-oriented nuclear programmes. This is a
major achievement at a time when proliferation is a dominant security
concern.

Third, apart from the EU, Mercosul is the only regional group that goes
beyond free trade and aims to create a common market. Like the EU,
Mercosul is a deep integration process. It participates as a bloc in trade
negotiations. Both the EU and Mercosul have a different vision of regionalism to the US. The EU and Mercosul view regionalism as a way to affirm
autonomous regional groups and the importance of relations among them.
America, during the Clinton administration, view regionalism as a way of
shaping world order with itself at the core of each regional initiative – be it
APEC, the FTAA or the 'transatlantic marketplace'. This is not likely to
change dramatically under a new Republican administration. Robert
Zoellick, the George W. Bush man for international trade, wrote: 'The
United States needs a strategic economic-negotiating agenda that combines regional agreements with the development of global rules for an open
economy . . . If America links its economy to those of key regions, it can
also promote its political agenda.'[16] It remains to be seen how and if a more
unilateralist administration will be able to combine opposition to global
political rules with a multilateral and regional approach to trade and how
this will affect the FTAA.

Finally, the EU and Mercosul share a similar attitude towards globalisation. The triumph of the neo-liberal vision that has accompanied the
unfolding process of globalisation is viewed as a potential threat for deep
integration projects. This is because it can dissolve them into vast free trade
areas. For the Union, the aim is to seek compatibility between the demands
of a new economic order and the defence of the social cohesion at the basis
of its integration model. For Mercosul, a post-globalisation integration

model,[17] the aim is to create conditions favourable for the pragmatic implementation of liberalisation policies.[18] In sum, it seeks a process of controlled opening to compete globally. The EU and Mercosul share the aim of formulating rules to administer the process of globalisation in order to give a 'human face' to global interdependency.[19] As noted by the Euro-Latin American Forum:

> The European Union and the Mercosul have a common interest in the promotion of a world governed by multilaterally determined and universally applicable global 'game rules'. They have a mutual interest in that all actors, both powerful and weak, work towards a 'pact of mutual trust', based on the participatory creation of a new global agenda and regulations. In sum, they have a shared interest in replacing a *Pax Americana* with a *Pax Interdemocratica*.[20]

For all of the above, the EU identifies Mercosul as a potential partner for the establishment of a more balanced international system based on the essential pillar of regionalism. This is the fundamental difference between the EU and the US. For the US, Mercosul constitutes a form of 'trade deviation', a project that seeks to establish the international autonomy of Brazil (the France of the American continent). The US perceives it as an obstacle to the American project of the regionalisation of the Americas. According to the US, Mercosul should be simply absorbed into the FTAA. US negotiators are not keen on the fact that Mercosul participates as a bloc in hemispheric negotiations.

By contrast, for the EU, the greater the affirmation of the identity of Mercosul within the Americas, the better. Indeed, for the EU, the problem with Mercosul is its institutional deficit, the absence of a system of checks and balances that can help to balance power equitably among the participating states. The great asymmetry between member countries makes it both indispensable and hard to achieve. Widening to Chile and Bolivia will make clearer the institutional deficit and the limits of consensus rule. The 1998 financial crisis, which hit Brazil and, later, the crises in Argentina both affected relations between Brazil and Argentina and were seen by Europe as further proof of the need for greater macroeconomic convergence between the countries of Mercosul, and for the creation of a tribunal to manage trade disputes.

Given the crisis experienced by most Andean countries, with the trend towards democratic involution and the collapse of the state in Colombia, it is important for Mercosul, and Brazil in particular, to take an active political and security interest and not merely an economic interest, in the problems on its periphery. The South American Summit of August 2000 is a sign of this concern. It remains to be seen whether this 'South American dynamic' can become a strategy for Mercosul in its relations with its neighbours in the Andean Community, in particular, with Colombia.

The EU fears that Mercosul will dissolve into the FTAA if it does not institutionalise itself. The failure of President Clinton to have 'fast track' approved by Congress to negotiate a free trade agreement in the Americas, created a window of opportunity for the consolidation of Mercosul. Mercosul, however, had real difficulty in exploiting this because of the financial crises and because its member states remained strongly attached to sovereignty. Furthermore, domestic difficulties in the US over negotiating a trade agreement with Latin-Americans will not evaporate under the new republican administration. However, it would be a mistake to think that the FTAA will not become a reality, and that the dynamics of its working groups are not already having an impact on the countries of Mercosul.

Some sectors in the region, particularly Brazil, feel that the European vision of a Mercosul with institutions similar to its own is an attempt to export the European model. This is incompatible with the great asymmetries between the countries of the Mercosul. Nonetheless, the 'mirror effect'[21] in Mercosul–EU relations is a reality. The debate on the single currency in Mercosul, an option that Argentina believes increasingly to be necessary for the success of the common market, demonstrated the 'mirror effect'. There are also signs of this conviction in Brazil.

Is the EU willing to take on Mercosul as a strategic partner and give it a high priority in its foreign relations? Given the typical discrepancy between the best interests of the Union and the practice of its member states, it is not easy to give a positive answer to this question.

As noted above the EU is, first and foremost, a regional actor. However, as it develops a global vision and a common foreign policy, there will be increasing privileges for Mercosul as a partner. Some countries in the Union have supported the reinforcement of relations with Latin America and have been at the centre of various initiatives launched in the 1990s. This is, for historical reasons, the case for Spain, which has considerable weight in the external relations of the Commission with Latin America. It is also the case for Portugal, and to a certain extent for Italy, also for historical reasons. Germany is also supportive of relations with Latin America, given the scope of its economic interests in Brazil. For France, Mercosul and Brazil are part of its multipolar vision of the world, which explains France's promotion of Euro-Latin American Summits (the first took place in Rio de

Janeiro in 1999). However, these summits are dominated by rhetoric and demonstrate the difficulty that the EU has in giving substance to its relations with Latin America, despite all the progress made over the last few years. There are two important reasons for this. First, the framework of Euro-Latin American relations is asymmetric, with the EU on one side, and a collection of states belonging to disparate regional groups on the other. Second, given the essentially economic dimension of EU–Mercosul relations, a successful bi-regional trade agreement is the essential basis of substantial relations between the two blocs. This does not mean that relations cannot go beyond trade, with a deepening of bi-regional co-operation in the defence of democracy and human rights, and to combat the drug trade.

France is a promoter of Mercosul as a centre of power for a more balanced world system. Paradoxically, France is also the country that faces the most difficulties in overcoming the constraints to agricultural trade liberalisation, due to its powerful agricultural lobby. The scepticism of Mercosul, *vis-à-vis* current trade liberalisation negotiations with the EU, testifies to this reality. A free trade agreement that does not include agriculture is unacceptable to Mercosul.

The interest of the Union in pushing that agreement forward (its conclusion is planned for 2005) has declined due to the opposition of the US Congress to 'fast track' and the concomitant slow-down in hemispheric negotiations. There is an undeniable competition between the US and the EU, which pushes forward relations with Mercosul. Mercosul countries try to take advantage of this rivalry.

Relations between the EU, Mercosul and the US are the 'sides' of a triangle that is still not clearly drawn. The US–EU 'side' of the triangle is very strong. Relations between the US and Latin America are also intense, despite mutual suspicions, as all are members of the Organisation of American States (OAS). Closing the Atlantic triangle means reinforcing the EU–Mercosul 'side'. However, this does not mean internationalising a three-way alliance, or constituting a 'bloc' of Western democracies.[22] The non-Western world would regard such a bloc as directed against it, and it would therefore become a cause of instability.

In short, the EU does not aim to replace the unstable world of unipolarity and unilateralism with an even more unstable world based on a traditional multipolar balance of power system shaped by the frequent dissolution and reversal of alliances. Rather, it wants to build a new multilateralism based on regional integration groups, whose experience with the supranational regulation of relations between states can be put to good use. In other words, it seeks the transformation of the international system into a community that is based on the success of its own experience and on the reinforcement of international institutions, particularly of the UN. This system is also the most appropriate for the administration of a world that seems to be heading towards multipolarity, with the emergence of great powers that have adopted a power politics perspective of foreign relations.

The US is key to a successful multilateral project, which not only enables the international community to guarantee security by preventing crises, but also to intervene militarily when other alternatives have been exhausted. The success of the system also depends on the ability of the EU to combine coherently its economic power and the powerful attraction of its model with an effective foreign and security policy, and credible military capabilities. There is a fair chance that this could happen, but unfortunately, it is far from certain. The more that Europe becomes a political actor, the more it will seek to consolidate relations with other partners that have a similar vision of inter-state relations, and Mercosul, despite all its difficulties, is just such a partner.

NOTES

1. The treaty of Maastricht reflected the intention of the EU to broaden the scale of monetary and economic union, and to begin serious consideration of joint policies in regard to external affairs and security, citizenship, and the protection of the environment.
2. See Joschka Fischer, Humbold speech on www.german-embassy.org.uk/speeches_and_statements.html
3. The executive branch of the Republican Government of France, established in 1795 in accordance with the constitution promulgated by the National Convention. It consisted of five members. Each director held the presidency for a three-month term, and one director was replaced annually.
4. For a full account of Jacques Delors' vision of the European Union, see 'Jacques Delors, *L'Unité d'un Homme*', entretien avec Dominique Wolton, Editions Odile Jacob, Paris, November 1994.
5. The present candidates are Bulgaria, Cyprus, Czech Republic, Estonia, Hungary, Latvia, Lithuania, Malta, Poland, Romania, Slovak Republic and Slovenia. Negotiations with Turkey are pending depending on its adoption of appropriate democratic criteria.
6. The proposal of a vanguard, based in the six founder members of the EEC as suggested by Jacques Delors, or the 'Countries of the Euro' as suggested by Joschka Fischer, is strongly opposed by most European Union states.
7. For a good analysis of European Union Defence Policy, see Chaillot papers 'European Defence: Making it Work', Institute for Security Studies, Paris, September 2000. For the basic papers on CSDP see Chaillot papers 'De Saint-Malo à Nice: Les textes fondateurs de la défense européenne', Institute for Security Studies, Paris, May 2001.
8. Dominique Moïsi, 'Hubert Védrine dialogue avec Dominique Moïsi', *Les cartes de la France à l'heure de la mondialisation*, Fayard, Paris, 2000.
9. See Mario Telò, 'O Novo Multilateralismo, Perspectiva da União Europeia e do Mercosul', Euro-Latin-Américan Forum, Lisbon, 2001.
10. Thérèse Delpech, in Álvaro Vasconcelos (co-ord), *A European Strategic Concept for the Mediterranean*, Lumiar Papers, IEEI, Lisbon.

The EU and the New Multilateralism 45

11. See Charles Grant, Chapter 3, and Christoph Bertram, Chapter 4, this volume.
12. Guehénno, Jean-Marie, 'The Impact of Globalisation on Strategy, *Survival*, Winter 1998–99.
13. See Christoph Bertram, Chapter 4, this volume.
14. For a discussion of the new multilateralism, see 'Forging a New Multilateralism – A view from the European Union and the Mercosul', report, Euro-Latin-American Forum, October 2001.
15. Celso, Lafer and Gelson Fonseca Jr, 'A problemática da integração num mundo aberto de polaridades indefinidas', in A Integração Aberta – um Projecto da União Europeia e do Mercosul, Euro-Latin-Américan Forum, Lisbon, 1995, pp. 28–65.
16. Robert Zoellick, 'A Republican Foreign Policy', in *Foreign Affairs*, Vol. 79, No. 1, January/February 2000, pp. 71–2.
17. Celso Lafer and Gelson Fonseca Jr, in A Integração Aberta – um Projecto da União Europeia e do Mercosul, Lisbon, 1995.
18. Helio Jaguaribe, 'A Emergente Civilização Planetária e a Possível Contribuição Lusófona', Comunication in Lisbon International Conference, IEEI, 1994.
19. 'Discurso do Senhor Presidente da República, Fernando Henrique Cardoso, na abertura da III Reunião de Cúpula das Américas', Quebec, Canada, April 2001.
20. Euro-Latin American Forum 'Setting Global Rules – A Report', IEEI, October 1998.
21. Mónica Hirst, 'O Novo Multilateralismo, Perspectiva da União Europeia e do Mercosul', Euro-Latin American Forum, Lisbon, 2001.
22. A narrow vision of the civilisational bloc proposed by S. Huntington, which excludes Latin America.

THREE

Europe, Mercosul and Transatlantic Relations: A British Perspective

CHARLES GRANT

Discussions of transatlantic relations have, until now, always concerned the links between one large and powerful country, the United States (US), and one group of middle and small-sized less powerful countries, those of the European Union (EU). The transatlantic game has had two players. However, it is not inconceivable that, in the very long run, the focus of transatlantic relations could be the ties between three geostrategic entities, the third one being built upon the countries of Mercosul.

Many of the Europeans who think about foreign policy – admittedly, not a large number – would be happy to see a more coherent regional grouping emerge in Latin America. One reason for this is that they would be flattered to see that continent imitate aspects of Europe's own political development. The relations among the states of Latin America today may resemble those among the West European states circa 1955.

The other, and more important reason, is that some Europeans – and even some Britons – are, like some Latin Americans, concerned by America's hegemonistic tendencies. These Europeans would welcome a more solid Mercosul that could, alongside the EU, constrain the exercise of American power and steer the US towards working within multinational institutions. If Mercosul can build strong institutions, take in more countries, and develop common foreign policies, then, a few decades hence, transatlantic relations could be a game with three players.

This chapter examines the current difficult state of transatlantic relations. Then it looks at the evolution in British attitudes towards the EU's role in foreign policy. Next, it considers British views on Mercosul, and concludes by discussing how the evolution of Mercosul could help to promote a more multipolar world.

THE TROUBLED STATE OF TRANSATLANTIC RELATIONS

The view in London, as in many other European capitals, is that the two sides of the North Atlantic seem to be growing further apart. The arguments on defence are one indication of the current strains in transatlantic relations. The Europeans are developing their own defence capability, which few Americans understand or see the point of. Meanwhile, the Americans plan to develop a missile defence system, which few Europeans understand or see the point of. Each side fears that the new development on the other side of the Atlantic will create rifts in the alliance.

Of course, security issues are not the only ones that matter in transatlantic relations. Arguments over bananas, genetically modified organisms, hormone-treated beef, and agricultural subsidies, have dragged on for years.

The root of the problem, as far as many Europeans are concerned, is that the US has become the world's sole superpower. The result is that the US has started to see the rest of the globe as less threatening and therefore as less important. The evaporation of the Soviet menace probably made it inevitable that the US would begin a slow disengagement from Europe. America cut the number of its troops in Europe from 300,000 to 100,000 during the 1990s.

The US has become increasingly reluctant to commit itself to international treaties, conventions and organisations. The saga of money owed by the US to the United Nations (UN) continues. The US has failed to sign up to the International Criminal Court, to the convention limiting the use of land mines and to the recent agreement on genetically modified organisms. Congress has ratified neither the Comprehensive Test Ban Treaty nor the Kyoto Treaty on climate change.

The one international organisation that remains generally popular with American politicians is NATO. But US support for NATO is not necessarily eternal. During the Kosovo conflict, when it appeared that an air campaign would not suffice to expel the Serbs from Kosovo, the British government argued that America had to be ready to commit ground troops to Kosovo. If Milosevic defeated NATO, said the British, that would more or less be the end of the Atlantic alliance. This argument appeared to make little impact in Washington, where there was minimal support for committing troops to a ground war.

The countries of the EU, being much smaller than the US, have a natural interest in subjecting states to the norms and rules of international law. Furthermore, because of their own experience of working within the multilateral framework of the EU, they find it much easier to accept the authority of international organisations (though it should not be forgotten that it is the EU, rather than the US, which has most often flouted the rulings of WTO panels). The different stance taken by the US is a natural consequence of its size: a superpower stands a better chance of getting its way without resorting to the help of international bodies.

Americans pointed to the fact that their four principal presidential contenders – Bill Bradley, George Bush, Al Gore and John McCain – were solid internationalists. And that is true, to the extent that all of them want America to engage in world affairs. Both Bush and Gore believe that America needs to work with its allies. However, none of them argues that America should allow international organisations or treaties to constrain its ability to pursue its own self-interest. The view in European capitals, London included, is that little by little, America is becoming more unilateralist. One manifestation of this trend is the enthusiasm of America's political classes for a system of National Missile Defence (NMD). Republicans and Democrats alike have been unmoved by the objections of European allies and Russia, or by the prospect of the system breaching the Anti-Ballistic Missile treaty. The subject of missile defence has the potential to create huge rifts in the Atlantic alliance.

There is no longer much doubt that the US will proceed with plans for a ground-based missile defence system, designed to deal with the threat of ballistic missiles from rogue states. Reports from American intelligence agencies have convinced policy-makers in Washington that, within a few years, North Korea and Iran may develop the capacity to strike at North America.

The Europeans worry that NMD could lead to a 'decoupling' of US and European security interests: if a rogue state threatened the NATO allies, and if the US knew that NMD made its homeland secure, US policy might diverge from that of the Europeans. The Europeans also tend to be more relaxed about the potential threat of ballistic missiles. They also have many doubts about the efficacy of US anti-missile technology. Britain and France have a special concern of their own: America's NMD system may provoke the Russians to build a similar system, and that could then neutralise the British and French nuclear deterrents.

The likely decision of the US to proceed with NMD will create awkward choices for EU countries. Should they ignore the missile threat of ballistic missiles, or try to develop their own missile defence systems, together with the Americans? Many Americans believe that, once the Europeans understand the nature of the threat, they will want their own missile defence systems.

However, even if the Europeans were to share the Americans' analysis of the risk, it is not clear that they would wish to develop their own missile defence systems. They are trying to find the money to develop their own power projection capabilities (see below) and would be hard-pressed to come up with extra billions of dollars for missile defence. They also worry about the reactions of the Russians and the Chinese to NATO countries developing missile defence. Furthermore, many senior French policy-makers would have political objections to participating in a missile defence system that would, inevitably, be dominated by the US.

THE GLOBAL REACH OF THE EURO

Meanwhile, Europe is becoming more unified, and in ways that may disturb some Americans. The movement towards European integration is slow, faltering and often confused – but the direction is clear. Until a year or so before the launch of the euro, many American commentators believed that the Europeans would never create a single currency. Now that it is a fact, many commentators assume that the euro will not challenge the global role of the dollar, and that it therefore will not require the US to re-examine its own policies. They are probably wrong. Once the euro has established a track record as a solid currency, institutional investors and central banks will want to balance their dollar holdings with euro investments. Fred Bergsten, of the International Institute for Economics, is probably right to argue that in the long term between $500 billion and $1 trillion of assets will switch from dollars into euro. The establishment of a bipolar global financial system, with most of the Americas tied to the dollar, and most of Europe and parts of Africa tied to the euro, may well prove awkward for the US. It will no longer be so easy for the US to disregard the international ramifications of its economic policy. In the past, US administrations have often been relaxed to see the dollar sink and the current account deficit balloon. There have always been enough foreign institutions to buy dollar securities, even when the dollar was weak, for it was the only international currency of note. When the euro presents a viable alternative, however, America may not be able to finance its current account deficit so easily. It may have to run an interest rate policy and an exchange rate policy that appeals to foreign investors.

The dollar–euro exchange rate may well prove volatile, and that could in itself create transatlantic tensions. A persistently weak euro could provoke American complaints of Europe's 'unfair' competitive advantage, and protectionist sentiment in the US. A prolonged period of dollar weakness could have the reverse effect. In the long run, the US and the EU may have to agree on some system of target zones, in order to stabilise the link between their currencies.

At the moment, the US dominates international financial diplomacy. When the South East Asian economies suffered severe crises in 1997, the US led the international efforts to restore financial stability – although the Europeans, collectively, had lent more money to the region. The Americans tend to dominate meetings of the International Monetary Fund (IMF), the World Bank and the G-7 finance ministers, for they have just a few representatives, while the Europeans have many and are divided. Over time, this may change. There is some debate in European capitals over the merits of creating a 'Mr Euroland', who would represent the euro-zone countries to the rest of the world. He or she would take instructions from the euro-zone finance ministers and negotiate with third parties on, for example, financial crises, exchange rate targets or reform of the international financial institutions.[1] France and Germany have already discussed the possibility of merging their quotas at the IMF. Thus, on questions of currency and financial diplomacy, the US may be obliged to listen more carefully to European views.

THE CHALLENGE OF EUROPEAN DEFENCE

Europe is integrating not only economically, but also in the field of defence. Since the British and French governments unveiled their plan for a European defence capability at St Malo in December 1998, the Europeans have moved a long way. The principal motivation of the EU governments is their belief that they need a more coherent and effective Common Foreign and Security Policy (CFSP), and in order to achieve it they will need to be able to back up their diplomatic pronouncements with the threat of force.

The EU's 15 governments have agreed that the Western European Union (WEU), a little-used defence organisation, be merged with the EU. If, for whatever reason, the Americans do not want to take part, the EU itself will be able to organise military missions. Such missions would normally involve the Europeans borrowing command structures and equipment from NATO or the US, but in theory, the EU would be able to run 'autonomous' missions that did not involve NATO.

The Europeans have also agreed, at the insistence of the British, to focus on improving their military capabilities. The EU governments between them spend about two-thirds of what the US spends on defence. However, their ability to deploy force outside the NATO area is probably only 10 per cent of that in the US. The British believe that the best way of getting the US to support European defence is to show that it is about Europe being capable of doing more. The war in Kosovo exposed the Europeans' weakness in command, control, communication and intelligence systems, and in their ability to move equipment by sea or air. The EU governments have now committed themselves to be able to put into the field, by 2003, a Reaction Force of 50,000 to 60,000 men.

The EU's military ambitions have caused much anxiety in the US. Few Americans see the point of a European defence entity, given that NATO works well. Many Americans worry that the French, always ambivalent over NATO, have persuaded the other Europeans to join them in a scheme that will undermine it. Will the EU try to duplicate what NATO does by establishing a planning staff of the sort that NATO has at SHAPE? What if the Europeans assume that they would normally act through the EU, resorting to NATO only if a major war came along? Might the Europeans exclude non-EU NATO members (notably Turkey) from the new arrangements?

Most of these fears about the new institutional arrangements are probably misplaced. The ambition of most EU governments (and even of some figures in the French government) is to strengthen NATO, by enabling the Europeans to contribute more to it. The Europeans are working hard to find a way of associating Turkey and other non-EU countries in their new club, though the Turks will have to accept that they cannot be full members until they are in the EU. The Europeans do not want to duplicate much of what NATO does because that would cost money (the EU's new military staff is unlikely to contain many more than 100 people).

The Americans should humour the EU by allowing it the theoretical possibility of running purely autonomous missions. For in many European countries, such as Germany, the best way of getting politicians to spend money on defence is to say that it is in the cause of 'Europe'. The truth is that Europe's weak military capabilities mean that it would not normally want to embark on military missions without the assistance of NATO and the US. For example, Europe has none of the aircraft that are required to jam hostile radar systems and take out missile defences.

American commentators are right to be sceptical about Europe's ability to boost its military capabilities, so long as many countries (including Germany) continue to cut defence budgets. But while there is not much prospect of greater European spending on defence, there is a real chance that existing budgets could be spent more wisely. European governments are now coming under considerable peer-group pressure to follow the British and the French in developing professional and more mobile forces. Thus, Italy and Spain have already decided to abolish conscription.

Strobe Talbott, America's deputy secretary of state, is not the only American to have admitted that many of his compatriots are inclined to be schizophrenic about the CFSP. On the one hand, they have long urged the Europeans to get their act together on defence and foreign policy. On the other, when the Europeans seem likely to do so, Americans worry that the CFSP may act against their interest.

Americans such as Strobe Talbott and Robert Zoellick, an adviser to President George Bush, welcome the European defence initiative, at least in principle. They believe that a more capable Europe will be a more useful ally to the US. To be sure, there will be occasions when the EU opposes US policy. But, because Europeans and Americans share many values and interests, they will usually agree on the big questions.

However, many Americans do not regard European defence as benignly as do Mr Talbott and Mr Zoellick. Many of them do not like the idea of a more united Europe, because it could pose a threat to American power. Whether in NATO, the WTO, the UN or the IMF, a more solid European presence, they fear, would make it harder for the US to get its way.

Europe's single currency is still in its infancy, while its military organisation remains embryonic. When both have developed further, the predominant US reaction may be negative. Given that most Europeans scarcely understand how the EU is changing, it is hardly surprising that many Americans are concerned about its evolution. Nor is it surprising that Europeans are dismayed by America's growing reluctance to work with international organisations.

So, it is hard to be optimistic about the immediate outlook for transatlantic relations. In the very long run, however, the emergence of a more powerful and successful EU could encourage the US to accept a world order that is less unipolar and more rule-based than that of today. The transatlantic relationship may ultimately reach a new and more balanced equilibrium, but the transition is likely to be fraught.

BRITISH ATTITUDES TO THE GLOBAL ROLE OF THE EU: A SIGNIFICANT SHIFT

Napoleon famously said that the British are a nation of shopkeepers, and his epithet still carries much truth. The British joined the EU because they thought – rightly – that it would help to revive their declining, post-imperial economy. Unlike the six founding members of the EU, the British have never seen Europe as a 'project' to inspire emotion or devotion. They have never felt comfortable about the political side of the EU. Many of them still wish it was merely a Common Market.

The British essentially take a pragmatic approach to Europe. They will support it when it can deliver concrete benefits that the nation state cannot deliver on its own. Thus, they will vote to join the euro – if they ever do – not because it will advance the cause of 'Europe', but because it will enhance their economic well-being.

The Economist (where this author used to work) reflects these very particular British attitudes. In the late 1980s and early 1990s, *The Economist* supported the cause of economic and monetary union. Its leader-writers considered that EMU would promote economic efficiency. They pointed out that, in terms of economic theory, there was no reason why a single currency should lead to much tighter co-ordination of economic policy, or indeed to central political institutions. However, in the mid-1990s, when it became clear that many continental European leaders *did* want EMU to be matched by, and to engender, greater political union, *The Economist* turned against EMU on the grounds that political union was a bad thing.

Most Britons do not want the EU to become a political federation. They regard the EU as an inherently bureaucratic, undemocratic organisation. They do not understand what the word 'political union' means. They worry that the French and the Germans are driving the EU towards a centralising, taxing, regulating 'super-state'. Some Britons are also quite happy to have a 'special relationship' with the US. They value their links with the Commonwealth. They fear that, the closer the UK gets to the EU, the weaker its ties will be to the US, Australia, New Zealand and Canada.

In almost every respect, the traditional British view has been different from the traditional French view. The French have been reticent about the EU as a market, in which national protection is no longer permitted. But they have striven to create the idea of *Europe puissance*, Europe as a power. They have cared more about the political union than the Common Market. As Jacques Delors, the former Commission president, once said: '*On ne tombe pas amoureux d'un marché unique*' (Nobody falls in love with a single market).

A REVOLUTION IN BRITISH THINKING

As far as most of the British people are concerned, the attitudes described above remain true. However, Tony Blair's government, elected in May 1997, has adopted a very different position. Its support for an EU role in defence (as mentioned in the preceding section) is one indication of this change. In fact, the viewpoint of British officials evolved through much of the 1990s. They began to see the value of the EU becoming more than a single market, and that British interests would be served – at least some of the time – by a more coherent and effective common European foreign policy. At least four factors explain this shift during the 1990s:

- In the safer, post-Cold War world, it is less urgent for the Europeans to keep the Americans engaged in Europe. The British, like most Europeans, want the Americans to remain committed, but it is not catastrophic if they wind down their presence. Thus Europeans, the British included, are freer to challenge and question what the Americans say and demand. A more independent European foreign policy no longer risks exposing the British people to real danger.

- The British have become disillusioned with the quality of American decision-making. The increasing power of the US legislature over American foreign policy has caused dismay in Britain (and in other European capitals). Even if the administration can be convinced of the right course of action, Congress can prevent it from moving in that direction. The situation in Bosnia from 1992 to 1995 caused great stress in Whitehall. The British, the French and other Europeans had troops on the ground in Bosnia, as part of a UN force. The Americans did not, but they wished to bomb the Serbs, which would have put at risk the lives of European troops. And, as previously mentioned, the war in Kosovo, in the spring of 1999, also caused anguish in London. President Clinton refused to countenance the commitment of ground troops to Kosovo, even though NATO's air campaign failed (for several months) to dislodge Serbian forces from Kosovo. Tony Blair wanted the NATO allies to commit ground troops in order to save the alliance from possible defeat, but the Clinton administration seemed – at least some of the time – to be more concerned about how the war would affect Al Gore's chance of winning the presidential election.

- There has been a growing awareness in London, as in other European capitals, that the EU's machinery for co-ordinating foreign policy has been inadequate. The rotating presidency, with a different country taking on the leadership of the EU every six months; the lack of central institutions, on a par with the Commission's role in economic policy-making; the requirement that all decisions be taken by unanimity; and the disconnect between the EU and its military club (the obscure Western European Union), all helped to ensure that EU foreign policy was slow-moving and ineffectual.

- British officials have also begun to appreciate a real convergence of interests among the principal countries of the EU. The experience of working with the French on the ground in Bosnia, and with the French and the Germans on the ground in Kosovo, has done a lot to promote ties between these countries' defence establishments. At a more political level, too, there has been convergence. France has moved closer to NATO, and put its forces under US command in Kosovo. Germany has become a more 'normal' nation, committing thousands of troops to peacekeeping in Kosovo (the first time in its post-war history that it has sent troops on such a role). And Britain, as will be discussed below, has abandoned its opposition to an EU role in defence.

These factors created a climate that was favourable to a shift in British policy on the EU's role in foreign policy. Less than two months after winning power, Tony Blair agreed to the Treaty of Amsterdam. This introduced new foreign-policy machinery: majority voting on decisions on implementing policy; a new policy planning unit in the EU's Council of Ministers secretariat; and, crucially, the creation of the post of High Representative for foreign policy. This post, effectively that of the EU's foreign policy spokesman, has now been filled by Javier Solana. Britain supported all these changes.

However, the real revolution in British thinking came in defence. In the spring of 1998 Tony Blair was struck by the absence of the EU from the diplomacy surrounding the crisis in Kosovo. The Americans dominated the field, despite the Europeans having strong interests in Kosovo. A more political consideration also influenced Blair. He wanted Britain to lead in Europe, but it was outside the euro. Therefore he needed a policy area in which Britain enjoyed natural advantages. He thought, rightly, that defence was the ideal domain in which Britain could exert leadership. Hence the reversal of Britain's longstanding opposition to an EU role in defence and the St Malo initiative of December 1998.

The British government, therefore, is quite happy for the EU to become a more effective and decisive player in foreign policy. But this policy change has been confined to the policy elite. Most British people have little understanding of, or sympathy with, the idea that the EU should become a power. The government, well aware of the innate Euroscepticism of the British people, has made no effort to sell the idea of EU foreign policy to them. It prefers to let sleeping dogs lie. It remains to be seen whether the Conservative opposition, now thoroughly Eurosceptical, can succeed in waking this dog.

BRITISH VIEWS OF MERCOSUL

Most British people do not think about Latin America a great deal. This is true even among those who take an interest in foreign policy. The British media take more interest in the EU, the US, Russia, the Balkans, the Middle East, South Asia the Far East and even in Africa, rather than in the countries of South America.

In the Foreign and Commonwealth Office (FCO), ambitious young men and women choose to specialise in the EU rather than in Latin America. Among those who are interested in the region, there is concern that Britain – and indeed the whole EU – is losing out by failing to focus sufficiently on Mercosul. In the words of one FCO man, 'Mercosul looks to the UK and the EU, but we are not ready to respond.' The Department of Trade and Industry seems to take Latin America more seriously. It has, for example, made the Brazilian market a top priority for export promotion.

Among Britain's Latin American specialists, Mercosul is seen as the most dynamic and successful regional trade organisation other than the EU. Its common external tariff is thought to have boosted trade between its members, rather than merely to have diverted trade. The Andean Pact has more structured institutions, with a Parliament and Court, but is nevertheless seen as less successful, because its governments have been less committed to free trade and to free markets.

Nevertheless, the British view Mercosul's political institutions in Montevideo as dangerously weak. When Mercosul hits a problem, it is over-reliant on the governments getting together to sort things out. Thus in 1999, when Brazil devalued the real by 40 per cent and Argentina retaliated by introducing trade restrictions, there were no institutions to take the strain or to constrain the behaviour of governments. The crisis required a top-level presidential summit to resolve the arguments – and such summits are not always the best means of solving disputes. The FCO hopes that Mercosul develops new dispute-settlement mechanisms.

MERCOSUL, A TRADING ARRANGEMENT

The British, like most other EU governments, see Mercosul primarily as a trade organisation rather than as a political body. The British government is happy that the EU has (since February 2000) reached a trade agreement with Mexico. Following the start of negotiations in 2000 between the EU and both Chile (an associate member of Mercosul) and Mercosul, there are strong hopes in London that a similar, but wider-reaching free trade agreement can be reached with them during 2002. However, there are worries in London that no EU country is really pushing these negotiations hard. It seems that Argentina and Brazil are more enthusiastic than most of the governments on the EU side. The perception in London is that the deal with Chile will be easier to conclude than the deal with Mercosul: Chile seems to be more geared up for the negotiations, and more committed to the principle of free trade.

Farming may prove the biggest difficulty in these negotiations. The British, of course, as the perennial foes of the Common Agricultural Policy (CAP), are well aware that the European desire to maintain agricultural protection will create difficulties for the Mercosul countries. These countries are big exporters of farm produce, and their principal reason for wanting a deal with the EU is to gain new markets for food exports. On the EU side, the chief benefits would be new markets for capital goods and services, as well as more open public procurement.

MERCOSUL, AN EMBRYONIC POLITICAL ORGANISATION?

Although the EU's negotiations with Mercosul are currently focused on trade, they will, increasingly, take on a political element. Indeed, the free trade agreement under discussion is expected to include clauses on human rights, culture and political contacts.

European governments are well aware that a trading club can have political implications and ultimately develop supranational organs; they have watched their own Common Market evolving into the EU. Europeans also know that some Latin Americans see Mercosul as a counterweight to the US. Brazilians, in particular, sometimes see Mercosul as a way of enhancing their sovereignty, because it helps them to stand up to the Americans. Some Brazilians seem more interested in linking Mercosul to the Andean Pact, than in moving ahead with the idea of a Free Trade Agreement of the Americas (FTAA).

Many Europeans – if not many Britons – view the EU as a means of standing up to the US, so that same trait in Latin Americans does not bother them. Nor are they bothered by the increasingly political nature of Mercosul: Europeans regard imitation of their own historical evolution as a sort of flattery. Just as the EU has helped to overcome historic rivalry between France and Germany, so Mercosul has reduced tensions – over border disputes and armaments build-ups – between Argentina and Brazil, and also between Argentina and Chile. During Paraguay's political crises of 1999 and early in 2000, the British, like the other Europeans, were delighted that the 'Mercosul factor' helped the cause of democracy: Brazil's political intervention appeared to aid the democratic forces within Paraguay.

MERCOSUL AND THE CAUSE OF MULTIPOLARITY

The US appears to have little in the way of a policy towards Mercosul. Thus, there is a real opportunity for the EU to develop a close political and economic alliance with the cone of Latin America. Both blocs may, on occasion, wish to ally against the US, although more often they will be allied with the Americans. Mercosul's fundamental economic and political interests are, in most respects, similar to those of the EU and the US. To take one example: Latin American countries, like those of Europe and the US, generally believe, in certain circumstances, that intervention in another country's affairs, for humanitarian reasons, is justified. Russia, China and India, by contrast, think that such 'Kosovo-style' intervention is never justified.

The EU and its governments, as was discussed earlier, worry that America is becoming increasingly unilateralist. Many Europeans, including Britons, are worried that, in a unipolar world, the US is decreasingly willing to follow the rules and procedures of international organisations and conventions. One reason for welcoming the EU's slow emergence as a power in its own right – albeit a soft and slow-moving one – is that in a less unipolar world, the US will have more incentives to work within a multinational framework. It will not be so easy for the US to achieve its ends through putting bilateral pressure on individual states, if those states are bound together in regional bodies such as the EU or Mercosul.

The US should not fear the increasing coherence of the EU or, perhaps in the future, of Mercosul. For, as has been stated, most Europeans and Latin Americans have similar values to most Americans. A stronger EU and a more political Mercosul will be useful allies to the US. They will help it to shoulder the burden of sorting out the world's problems. However, the emergence of these regional entities will also create strong incentives for the US to deal with its allies in such groups, rather than individually, and to respect the principles of rule-based global governance. In any event, transatlantic relations promise to become a more complex game, with three, rather than two, principal players.

NOTE

1. Everts, S. 'The impact of the euro on transatlantic relations'. Centre for European Reform, London, 2000.

FOUR

Multilateralism, Regionalism, and the Prospect for International Order: A View from Germany and Europe

CHRISTOPH BERTRAM

For evident reasons, post-Second World War Germany has been and remains a champion of the multilateral approach to international problems. It was only by joining with others that the country could re-establish international acceptance and respectability. This recognition, first born from the weakness following defeat and partition, applied no less once the country obtained power and influence and even, in 1990, unification. Being part of a wider grouping protected the weak Germany and, for the first time in modern European history, made a stronger Germany acceptable for Europe and stronger Europe acceptable for Germany. Thus, multilateralism, in the case of Germany, has been dictated by national self-interest.

Structured multilateralism can be defined as an institution-backed process agreed among states for working out joint decisions and practising joint responsibility. It is based on common rules that restrict the sovereignty of each of them, for the sake of enhancing common sovereignty. This chapter will argue that structured multilateralism is not just in the German national interest, but indeed the best way to develop international order in the globalised world. The first section will analyse that a unipolar world cannot provide such order since it is inherently unstable. The second section will examine the experience and evolution of the European Union (EU) and its emerging relationship with the United States (US), with special reference to the experience and attitude of Germany. The third section will discuss the link between global and regional structures of order, and the final section will look at a special case of multilateralism – the relations between the EU and other emerging regional structures such as Mercosul.

WHY A UNIPOLAR WORLD IS AN UNSTABLE WORLD – AND EVEN
AMERICA NEEDS PARTNERS

Max Kohnstamm, the long-serving friend and disciple of Jean Monnet,
tells the story of how, in one of the many moments of despair (that the
architects of European integration have lived through), the great man
cheered them up. It was in early 1963, and French President de Gaulle had
just blocked the entry of Britain into the European Community, something
that continental Europeans had long worked for (and have since regretted).
Monnet, on the way out of a meeting with his dejected followers, suddenly
chuckled. When they asked him why, he replied, 'I just thought of how
tough it will be for the United States of America to accept that they, too,
will have to share sovereignty'.

In this new century, two features stand out: the proliferation of participants in the international system, and the pre-eminence of the US. This
contradiction will have to be mitigated by a conscious US policy of multilateral engagement, particularly with the EU.

The main reason why a unipolar world is an unstable world lies in the
fact that it cannot last, and that everybody knows it cannot. Of course, as
Helio Jaguaribe rightly points out in Chapter 1, it is possible for international order to be upheld by a single dominant power for some time, and
this can often be highly beneficial for the other participants in the system.
Thus, the US, by its very presence, assures a precarious peace in the world's
most volatile region: Asia. It provides the security framework within which
the industrial world can rely on energy supplies from the Gulf. It encourages the spread of international rules and deters those who seek to break
them. It has promoted European integration from the very beginning – the
Schuman Plan (Jean Monnet's brainchild to start the process) was a
response to the US urging for a cohesive policy towards Germany. The
passage from the Cold War to today's globalised world would not have been
as peaceful without American involvement and leadership. In other words,
the US has been willing to carry the burden of leadership for a long time
already.

However, while it is one thing to point to the considerable advantages
that US pre-eminence has produced, it is quite another to assume that this
role will last. The change will be brought about more by burden-fatigue
among the American public and by American self-interest, than by the
emergence of rival powers.

Burden-fatigue is not unfamiliar for the great democracy of the US. In
the Cold War years the dependence of US policy overseas on the priorities
of its citizens at home was symbolised by the title of an influential journal

article of the time: 'Will the Balance Balance at Home?' Even when the Soviet Union was regarded as a present danger by most Americans, the willingness of the voters to carry the costs of maintaining and underpinning the heavy defence effort and the commitment to the Atlantic Alliance, could not be taken for granted. Today, the costs for upholding international order *à l'américaine* are significantly less, yet the need to do so is also less evident to the man and woman in the street. It is only natural that widespread uneasiness with shouldering these remaining costs is rising.

The most obvious, if perhaps the most superficial manifestations of such uneasiness, lie in the combination of declining popular interest in international affairs with unilateralist tendencies, which are so visible in the US Congress. Hence the reflex of imposing economic sanctions on those who do not comply with US wishes, and thus, the determination to go forward with National Missile Defence. This is regardless of the concerns raised around the world, or the partisan bloody-mindedness with which the Comprehensive Test Ban Treaty was rejected by the Senate. In the field of trade and international finance, the tendency is no less pronounced. Congressional willingness to increase the defence budget, while persistently reducing funds for non-military international activities, conveys a general impatience with coalition crisis management, as opposed to unilateral military action, that is with the tough task of getting others on your side and keeping them there.

Yet such tendencies, while explainable and even understandable from the position of unchallenged and unchallengeable power, not only demand more sacrifices than the citizenry will want to bear, but also run counter to the requirements of the globalised world. Only in the military manifestation of power does the US enjoy a unilateral option, and a largely theoretical one at that. Both the US public and US leaders prefer the political and military risks of interventions to be shared with allies, from Kosovo to Haiti. In all other fields, even America needs partners to sustain her interests. Globalisation increases the reach of US trade and culture while simultaneously making America more dependent on the concurrence of others.

It is true that as Americans turn inward, they may be less prepared to rely on partners that are both weaker and more demanding. Jean Monnet was right when he warned that it would be difficult for America to accept the need for power-sharing. There are indications, however, that this may be more difficult for the politicians than for the people who, according to extensive polling, support a foreign policy of broad international engagement.

In the end, refusal of such engagement would imply a loss of American pre-eminence. Thanks to her weight and influence, the US can be confident that it will continue to play the major part in any multilateral organisation it engages in, thus assuring what unilateralism denies her. American self-interest will move the US in the direction of multilateralism, which trades dominance over others for more influence in conjunction with others.

Bill Clinton, the first post-Cold War president, clearly understood that since dominance cannot last, structured multilateralism – he called it 'robust multilateralism' – offers the only alternative. Even if domestic opposition made him drop the term, the practice of Clinton's foreign policy continued to reflect it, whether in the World Trade Organisation (WTO), the UN, or over the Balkan conflicts. If these steps were often more tentative than determined, they could at least count on majority support, if not from Congress, at least from the wider public. Furthermore, since they reflect a clear national interest of the US, the direction is likely to reassert itself once the ideologism of the newly elected president vanishes.

For both the creation and the efficiency of multilateral institutions, countries will need partners with whom coalitions can be formed and maintained. While this need applies to states everywhere, America too, is in a favoured position. This is not only because of her own weight, but also because she can be confident of an enduring special relationship to the EU. America has nursed and protected the EU from infancy and it has emerged, in all the traditional aggregates of power, as second only to the US. No less than in the Cold War, Europe and the US have become indispensable partners for each other in the globalised world as well.

THE EUROPEAN UNION AND HOW GERMANY WOULD LIKE TO
SEE IT DEVELOP

Initiated in 1950, launched in 1958 and evolving from a European Economic Community of six members to a European Union of soon to be 30, the EU has experienced an extraordinary rise in size, depth and weight. It has proven to be the best device not only to reconcile Europe with Germany and Germany with Europe, but also to extend the stability enjoyed by its members to the new and struggling democracies on its rim, which are keen to join. Through the membership of Finland, the EU now has a common border of some 1,300 kilometres with Russia; should Cyprus join, it will be part of the Middle East; should Turkey join, the EU will border on Iraq and the Caucasus region.

Had any European nation state expanded like this, it would have caused a major strategic upheaval, not only in the Old World. Counter-alliances would have formed to stop its advance, and major rivals would have seen the need to intervene in Europe. Political turbulence, even war, could have accompanied this rise to continental dominance. The EU has had an entirely different impact: it has proven a magnet for other countries, and the US has fostered its growth and continues to advocate its further enlargement. Even notoriously suspicious Russia, which likes to present the extension of NATO to Eastern Europe as a threat to its security, does not seem to mind the EU's extension here.

This is an extraordinary achievement. The movement towards greater integration, although never smooth and at times stagnating, has persisted throughout. Despite the resistance of national bureaucracies, the over-loading of EU institutions, the indifference of politicians, the reservations of public opinion and the continuous and demanding enlargement process, the transfer of powers from the national to the Union level has continued. Today, there is not only a common internal market with a common com-mercial policy toward the outside world, but a common system of law with the European Court of Justice at the top, a common currency for the major-ity of members, a common approach to immigration and visas, a blending of foreign policies and an emerging common defence policy with its own embryonic organisation.

Sometimes these advances have been the result of institutional initia-tives; sometimes they were brought about by the sheer habit of working together, as in the field of foreign affairs where EU governments are increasingly acting together despite the absence of strong institutions. One can even get the impression, at times, that the process of policy co-ordination has become second nature to most bureaucrats and their politi-cal masters.

This has been achieved in the absence of clarity over two aspects that should be vital for any international power: both the geographical borders of the Union, as well as its final constitutional nature, remain undefined. Some would argue that it has precisely been this lack of clarity that allowed integration to move forward – since there is no defined goal, each step does not commit those taking it to a specific outcome. Yet, the disadvantages of a largely open process are also becoming clear, particularly with new countries joining the club. As long as extending membership is the Union's chief foreign policy instrument, it will not be able to develop any other. As long as it does not know where it ends – with Turkey a candidate for membership the Union is no longer restricted to European countries – it does not know what it is: and as long as member states are allowed to avoid commitment to the final structure of their common edifice, there is no firm commitment to making it an integrated union either. To replace uncertainty with clarity in these two domains will be the major challenge for the Union in the coming decade. It is by no means certain that the challenge will be met.

Yet the contribution the Union has made and continues to make to European stability and prosperity is not in doubt. It is the most successful regional organisation ever. Although originally devised to put an end to European wars, it is even more relevant in the age of globalisation, by providing its members with an international weight which none of them, not even the major ones, could muster on their own. Today the Union is the major international actor next to, at times even on a par with, the US in all organisations of international economic and financial relations. It is the major donor of assistance to the developing world and the primary source of support for the UN. It has shown that regionalism works not only for its respective region, but also for the wider order. The very existence of the Union strengthens international multilateralism.

The Federal Republic of Germany has been, from the start, a staunch supporter of European integration, and it remains so to this day. Yet, it would be wrong to assume that Germany's motives for supporting the European experiment have remained the same since the days of the Schuman Plan, the first launch of a supranational European Community 50 years ago. Nevertheless, the policy has remained largely similar, spanning the period from post-war weakness to post-unification strength, from being the defeated challenger of the old European system to becoming the respected pillar of the new one. This underlines the depth of German support for European integration, as well as a firmly held conviction that it suits German interests best, in weakness and in strength.

The motives change of course. When Robert Schuman and Jean Monnet proposed the Coal and Steel Community in 1950, and well into the 1970s, Germany saw in European integration a chance for gaining equality in Europe, and acceptance in the global scene. In contrast to practically all the other countries, which joined in this unprecedented adventure, integration for Germany did not mean to give up sovereignty (she did not have full sovereignty under the Four Power Statute). Instead, it meant to gain stature and influence. For the weak Germany, it was the obvious choice.

Perhaps surprisingly, it became the same for the strong Germany that emerged from unification in the early 1990s. Now the chief motive, apart from the economic interest in a large internal market, is no longer more stature, but protection against resentments by others of the stature Germany enjoys. Successive German governments have realised the advantage of working through the Union rather than on their own. The Union has been a force multiplier for both the bigger and the smaller member states, and has also provided the structure for Europe to be reconciled with a strong Germany. This is an extraordinary achievement against the background of European history. An additional motive may increasingly be added: namely that the Union (should the US distance themselves from the old continent) could offer a secondary security network. Thus, all the quantum jumps in European integration taken after German unification – from the introduction of the common currency to EU enlargement and, more recently, the commitment to develop a European military component – have enjoyed solid German support.

It is true that enthusiasm for moving beyond the present level of integration to a federal EU has waned, in Germany no less than elsewhere in the Union. Concern that the process of a creeping transfer of powers from the nation state to the Brussels institutions has grown. Germany is now leading the initiative for a much clearer demarcation of respective responsibilities. This is partly prompted by the country's federal structure in which the individual states see their authority as being progressively drained by the transfer of powers to Brussels. Some clearly hope that such demarcation will tilt the balance back to member governments at the expense of the 'supranational' institutions – the Commission, the European Parliament, and the Court of Justice. No doubt, there is a real risk that under the guise of improving the functioning of the Union, member states will weaken what has, after all, been associated with its extraordinary success; namely its supranational, as opposed to a purely intergovernmental, structure.

The next few years will show whether this temptation can be resisted. Yet it seems likely that whatever German government will then be in power, it will not deviate significantly from the policies pursued by every administration since 1950. This is not the result of altruism, but of egotism: Germany remains committed to European integration because it is here that her national interests can be best pursued. Increasingly, this applies not only to the advantages outlined earlier, but also to those the Union conveys to its members in terms of international influence. To a remarkable degree, what differences existed between the foreign policies of member states even in the Cold War period, are rapidly disappearing in the age of globalisation. European multilateralism, in the form it has found through the Union, has become an essential condition for the successful pursuit of the common interest in global multilateralism.

REGIONALISM AND GLOBALISM

The EU is the most successful regional organisation in the world today. Despite this, it has not become an export article. Elsewhere, efforts for regional co-operation have occurred, but they have all stopped short of the transfer of sovereign powers to a common structure. This is the EU's hallmark, as well as one (if not the primary) condition for its achievements. It is also an achievement that followed after centuries of war and destruction. If that were the precondition for its establishment elsewhere, one would rather advise against it.

Yet, the globalised world has added its own weight to the arguments in favour of regional groupings. On the one hand, it has brought forth an impressive array of new global regulations: the WTO, the International Penal Court, the reaffirmation of the Non-Proliferation regime through the indefinite prolongation of the Non-Proliferation, as well as the Comprehensive Test Ban Treaty – to mention but a few. The process of expanding global rules is clearly under way.

Simultaneously, regionalism too, has steadily grown in importance, no less with the consequence of the ending of the Cold War. Then, every part of the world was a pawn on the chessboard of East–West rivalry. What happened in Cuba led to the most dangerous superpower crisis of the Cold War. Events in Korea, in Vietnam, in Angola or Nicaragua, were elevated to challenges of the system as a whole. Today, the protracted war in the Balkans, the interminable conflicts in Africa, and the strife in the Caucasus, are all separate issues, never seen as threats to the system, but as isolated events. It is not even a foregone conclusion that a nuclear exchange between, for example, India and Pakistan, would be regarded as a global disaster. Regions are on their own, no longer the inseparable part of an overarching strategic structure.

What is more, states now think of their region before they think of the world beyond. If Iran and Iraq seem intent on acquiring nuclear weapons, it is not because they see themselves in a global strategic relationship with other nuclear powers, but it is in order to balance, and possibly counter, nuclear rivals in the region. Despite globalisation, most national economies, even highly developed ones, do most of their trade with their immediate neighbours. Notwithstanding the global reach and acceleration of communication, the region still provides the most active network.

Therefore, global rules alone will not produce global order. They require, for their authority, the underpinning of functioning regional regimes. Furthermore, those places on the map where they do not exist are the most likely theatres of future conflict. The significance of regional conditions for the relevance of global rules is obvious when one looks at the fields of arms control or trade arrangements. The causes for nuclear proliferation, as pointed out, are regional – as present developments in South Asia and the Middle East, and past efforts in South America testify. Hence, the barriers to proliferation, too, must be erected at the regional level for global rules to work.

In trade and commercial relations, the contribution made by successful regional arrangements to the recognition of global rules cannot be over-rated. In most cases, whatever international rules are being agreed upon by the signatory states, the test for their sustainability lies in the regions. This should be an encouragement to regional actors to group together for greater regional stability and global impact, since global rules result not from the command of a superpower but from the groups of states agreeing first among themselves and then with other groups of states. The development and management of international agreements invariably requires regional initiative and involvement.

Just as global rules need regional support, regional co-operation, in turn, is the best response to globalisation. If regional security relations are stable, instabilities elsewhere are less likely to become a problem. If com-merce between the participating countries is intense, dependence on the existence of global rules declines. Globalisation thus requires regionalisa-tion, and regionalisation is the best way for reaping the rewards while reducing the risks of globalisation.

Thus, there is no alternative to regional integration in today's world. However, the step from recognition to implementation is not easy. While the model of the EU may not be transplantable to other parts of the world where traditions, cultural affinity and economic standards are different, it nevertheless makes clear that the mere decision of states in a region to do things together is not enough. If the commitment to regional co-operation is not underpinned by common and binding institutions, it will not be sus-tained.

European integration suggests that, like a positive cancer, once coun-tries seriously start down the road of integration with the help of such insti-tutions, the areas and issues affected multiply. At the beginning of Europe's experience, it was sufficient to subject the resources of coal and steel to common guidelines; now, as the recent (and misguided) sanctions against Austria have shown, the ideology of political parties in the government of another country is also regarded as a legitimate concern of the other members. Integration breeds more integration.

The decision to engage in effective regionalism is, therefore, a momen-tous one. When first contemplated, it usually gives rise to a massive coali-tion of opposing interests. It is no surprise, therefore, that governments in regions outside Europe have generally found it too demanding. However, it is difficult to imagine resilient structures for the globalised world of the twenty-first century unless supported by regional structures beyond

Europe. Moreover, it is difficult to imagine how other regions of the world can wield much influence on global issues unless the states that make them up group firmly together.

THE EU AND MERCOSUL

Mercosul has long held such a promise, and this explains not least the emotional (as opposed to the operational) support the EU has given to the enterprise. Here, many Europeans have hoped, was a group of like-minded countries, establishing similar structures of interdependence. This is not merely sentimentality. Generally the EU finds it easier to establish relations with regional bodies than with individual states. It has an inbuilt preference for regional entities that are capable of acting for their members and who are sufficiently efficient to implement agreements.

Regrettably, Mercosul's integration has fallen well short of these expectations. It is less its inability to 'formulate a foreign policy', as Helio Jaguaribe suggests, which has disappointed the EU. Europeans know that their own Union has some way to go before it can claim a foreign policy; they have learnt that the primary requirement of regional groupings, in regards to both their domestic and their international audience, is to function effectively within their declared mandate. Whenever the Union is able to get things done, its authority rises: whenever it is hindered by national rivalries or inefficient decision-making, popular support drops sharply.

For regional integration, internal cohesion is more important than the ability to 'speak with one voice' to the outside world; that voice will only be listened to if it comes from a strong mouth. The further advanced Mercosul is in internal cohesion, the more helpful the EU can be in encouraging its further development.

Yet, despite a tradition of close co-operation, Mercosul states are still wavering whether they prefer joining an extended NAFTA to building a stronger Mercosul. The test may come with the new US administration and its declared plans for greater hemispheric co-operation. If these plans materialise, the EU's chance of establishing a special trade and political relationship with Brazil and her partners could be lost, and the EU's prospects as the centre of a wider trade zone are dramatically weakened. That would be unfortunate for Europe and for the region, which would be deprived of the chance to organise itself before joining a group in which America will be by far the dominant power. However, it would primarily be the result of a lack of commitment and decisiveness on the part of the Mercosul nations, rather than EU indecision. Regional co-operation and organisation has to spring from the region itself, it cannot be born from the outside.

The vision of Mercosul corresponds to the world into which we are moving; the slowness of its integration highlights the weight of traditions from the world that is disappearing. The self-interest of nations demands a say in the shaping of the new, multilateral international order; the way to get it is for regional actors to group together. The Europeans were fortunate in their own multilateral effort. But when they embarked on integration, they had been sobered by a terrible war, were protected by the US and, thanks to the defeat of Hitler's Germany, firmly committed to democratic principles and values. The driving force for their coming together was the commitment never to relive the past.

Other parts of the world will have to establish regional structures with much less help from such outside events. Their integration will not result from the fear of the past, but from the hope to survive and prosper in the turbulence of globalisation. However, will these motives be powerful enough to overcome the many obstacles to regional unity, in Latin America as elsewhere? If they are not, their impact on the shape of the global regime for the twenty-first century will remain marginal.

FIVE

——◄◦►——

Mercosul: Beyond 2000

RICARDO ANDRÉS MARKWALD

INTRODUCTION

Despite a few hitches, until mid-1998, the regional integration process in the Southern Cone was generally viewed as making fairly good progress.In fact, after over three decades of frustrated attempts, the Mercosul South Cone Common Market was firming up as the first integration project in Latin America to achieve a reasonable level of success. Even within the broader context of the global economy, it was rated as an auspicious and original experiment in establishing an economic bloc linking economies that were still developing. Until recently, it was quite natural to look ahead towards a promising future for Mercosul, without this being dismissed as mere wishful thinking.

However, by year-end 2000, the circumstances are completely different. A best-case scenario – or even a fairly optimistic view – may no longer be appropriate as a working hypothesis underpinning a speculative exercise. This exercise was designed to describe the probable progress of this integration project during the first two decades of the new century. The range of options is currently far broader, and the probability of the occurrence of any specific scenario requires careful qualification.

This chapter is divided into three sections, in addition to this Introduction.The second section offers a brief analysis of the impacts of integration in the Southern Cone, highlighting the static effects, dynamic impacts and non-traditional gains arising from this process.The third section discusses the current deadlock in Mercosul, while avoiding a detailed examination of trade disputes flaring up among its members.To the contrary, stress is placed on the fact that Mercosul is not the only possible strategy for opening up the global economy to its two main members, as these clashes may be due to the existence of non-convergent alternatives running parallel to the integration drive. The fourth and final section focuses on Mercosul's external negotiations agenda, concluding with somewhat cautious forecasts for the future of this integration project.

OVERVIEW OF THE IMPACTS OF INTEGRATION

Regionalism is a phenomenon that has appeared over the past 40 years. In fact, through to early 2000 some 95 per cent of the 120 regional trade agreements notified to GATT/WTO were signed after 1960. During this period, the process of setting up free trade areas and customs unions saw two major upsurges: the first during the 1970s, when just over 60 agreements were notified to GATT, most involving the European nations; the second took place during the first half of 1990s, when some 30 initiatives were notified.

The collapse of the Soviet bloc was the main factor driving the more recent second wave of regionalism.[1] In fact, the break-up of the former Soviet Union spurred the countries of Central and Eastern Europe to seek trade agreements with the European Union (EU) and the European Free Trade Area (EFTA) as part of the process of restructuring their economies. Consequently, leadership of the integrationist process was once again taken over by Europe, which accounted for the largest number of trade agreements notified during the first half of the 1990s.

During this same period, regionalism posted significant advances in the Western Hemisphere that were few in number, but highly relevant in qualitative terms. The signing of the Treaty of Asuncion in 1991 launched the integration process in the Southern Cone, followed soon after by the introduction of the North American Free Trade Agreement. NAFTA sanctioned the establishment of a huge free trade area interlinking the three major economies in North America. Uncertainty and frustration over the outcome of the Uruguay Round (which apparently bogged down during the early 1990s) were key factors in the establishment of NAFTA, prompting the USA to explore other alternatives, moving away from multilateral negotiations. In the case of the Mercosul Southern Cone Common Market, the incentives were mainly political, particularly the almost simultaneous consolidation of the redemocratisation processes in the two main countries of this region: Argentina and Brazil.

In 1995, the importance of regionalism was unquestionable: intra-zone trade accounted for some 53 per cent of global trade, and the integration agreements actually in effect (just over 50 of the 109 notified to

GATT/WTO by that date) clearly proved the dynamic nature of this process, while also revealing significant potential for expansion.[2]

Rising concern over the proliferation of regional trade agreements within WTO and elsewhere consequently caused little surprise. In fact, from the mid-1990s onward, regional initiatives began to undergo increasingly stringent assessment and analysis processes, measuring their compatibility with the multilateral trade deregulation efforts stipulated in the GATT/WTO rules.

In general, these assessments focused initially on the static effects of preferential trade schemes, particularly on the discriminatory effects of integration agreements that adversely affected non-member countries. Not by chance, this approach is preferred by those adopting a critical stance to regionalism. More recently, however, closer attention has been paid to the dynamic impacts of integration. Together with a number of the 'non-traditional' gains associated with the sweeping integration processes, these impacts are stressed mainly by those who urge and support integrationist initiatives.

Despite their importance, dynamic impacts are not easy to identify or to quantify, which is why empirical evidence in favour of preferential trade agreements is rarely in generous supply.[3] Even in cases where identification of the benefits introduced by preferential trade liberalisation seems both feasible and convincing, regional schemes are challenged under the claim that unilateral liberalisation can produce even greater benefits. Consequently, assessments of regional trade agreements are always surrounded by much controversy.

The following summary presents the proof gathered from several examinations undertaken to analyse the *pros* and *cons* of the Mercosul Southern Cone Common Market. From many aspects, the situation is still far from conclusive, but in general, it indicates a favourable outcome for the integration process in the Southern Cone.

Static effects, dynamic impacts and non-traditional gains from integration in the Southern Cone

Static effects

The formation of free trade areas or customs unions may either increase or diminish members' welfare. The benefits generated by the integration process depend on the extent of the 'trade creation' effect, while its costs are associated with the scope of the 'trade diversion' effect.[4] The net balance of these effects decides whether or not a preferential trade agreement is beneficial or harmful to its members.[5]

In Mercosul, static effects have been analysed through a number of estimates. At least two relatively important studies concluded that the integration project had promoted trade diversion to a significant extent. Based on a gravity model, one of these studies showed that intra-zone imports were appreciably higher than those forecasted by the model, which would indicate the possible existence of trade diversion.[6] In the terminology enshrined by this type of model, Mercosul does not constitute a 'natural' trade bloc, but is rather a 'super-natural' arrangement.

Based on the joint use of regional intensity indexes for exports and revealed comparative advantages indexes,[7] the second study had an even greater impact. According to this analysis, both the re-orientation of export flows favouring the regional market and fostering a rapid upsurge in trade among its members, as well as the high share held by capital-intensive manufactured products in intra-zone trade flows, revealed the existence of significant trade diversion. In the view of Yeats,[8] preferential tariffs and discriminatory sectoral policies – particularly the common automobile regime – are key factors behind the impressive upsurge in intra-bloc exports, as well as their concentration in products where Mercosul does not exhibit any obvious comparative advantages. This becomes evident from the minor share held by these products in extra-zone trade flows.

This study prompted strong reactions, even at the diplomatic level. Critics questioned the fact that Yeats grounded his conclusions on the performance of exports rather than imports. In a later work, Nagarajan[9] adopted the same methodology developed by Yeats in order to examine trade diversion, but now the analysis was based on imports. Nagarajan noted that from this standpoint the results were not conclusive. The study also spotlighted two significant facts that run counter to the concerns expressed by Yeats: (i) extra-Mercosul imports also rose at very high rates, keeping pace with the upsurge in intra-zone flows; and (ii) extra-bloc imports continued to be heavily concentrated in high-technology products, even after the establishment of the Southern Cone Common Market. Both these observations would suggest that the extent to which trade flows are diverted might well not be too significant.

An examination of intra- and extra-Mercosul trade flows over the past decade ratifies these conclusions. The growth rate for extra-zone imports (11.9 per cent p.a.) was very high during the 1990s, and the difference in terms of the increase in intra-zone flows (16.3 per cent p.a.) is not expressive. In fact, Mercosul has grown into a highly dynamic importer market for *both* its regional members and its trading partners outside the bloc (see Table 5.1).

Ricardo Andrés Markwald

Table 5.1:
Mercosul: Intra- and extra-zone trade flows – 1990/1999 (US$ million)

Description	90	91	93	95	97	99	90/97	90/99
	Year						Growth (% per annum)	
Total exports	46,433	45,911	54,046	70,494	83,473	74,315	8.7	5.4
Intra-Mercosul (%)	*8.8*	*11.1*	*18.6*	*20.5*	*24.9*	*20.7*	26.0	15.7
Extra-Mercosul (%)	*91.2*	*88.9*	*81.4*	*79.5*	*75.1*	*79.3*	5.8	3.8
LAIA (%)	*7.1*	*9.1*	*10.3*	*9.7*	*9.9*	*9.4*	13.9	12.7
USA (%)	*20.7*	*17.0*	*17.6*	*15.3*	*14.2*	*18.4*	3.0	4.0
EU (%)	*31.1*	*32.2*	*26.7*	*25.5*	*23.2*	*25.6*	4.3	3.1
Others (%)	*32.3*	*30.6*	*26.8*	*29.0*	*27.8*	*25.9*	6.5	3.6
Total imports	27,367	32,328	46,178	75,708	98,992	80,039	20.2	14.9
Intra-Mercosul (%)	*15.0*	*15.8*	*19.6*	*18.5*	*20.9*	*20.0*	26.0	16.3
Extra-Mercosul (%)	*85.0*	*84.2*	*80.4*	*81.5*	*79.1*	*80.0*	18.9	11.9
LAIA (%)	*7.0*	*7.3*	*5.4*	*6.1*	*5.8*	*5.6*	17.1	9.8
USA (%)	*20.2*	*21.1*	*20.6*	*20.0*	*21.2*	*21.7*	21.0	13.5
EU (%)	*21.4*	*22.2*	*22.8*	*25.9*	*26.0*	*28.6*	23.6	16.4
Others (%)	*36.4*	*33.6*	*31.6*	*29.5*	*26.1*	*24.2*	11.1	4.8
Trade balance*	19,043	13,577	6,862	−5,682	−15,584	−5,096		

Source: International Economic Centre (CEI – *Centro de Economía Internacional*), Argentina.
Note: *Trade balance between extra-regional exports and imports.

More important still, both the European Union (EU) and the US (which are leading suppliers of industrialised products for this bloc) have increased their share in Mercosul's imports.[10] Consequently, concern over the possibility of trade diversion seems somewhat exaggerated.

The marked gap between the growth in intra-zone and extra-zone exports, which is stressed by Yeats, also warrants comments. Initially, it should be recalled that intra-regional exports and imports are the same thing. This means that the excellent performance of intra-regional exports (15.7 per cent p.a.) during the 1990s, merely mirrors the flip-side of the impressive expansion in Mercosul imports over the same period: a phenomenon that benefited both its members, as well as non-member nations, as mentioned above.[11] On the other hand, the poor performance of extra-regional exports (3.8 per cent p.a.) can be explained in various ways: over-valued foreign exchange rates, significant external barriers in important markets (EU and USA), and – no less important – undeniable difficulties in producing competitive goods that undermined Mercosul exports and still continue to do so.[12]

In addition to these 'Vinerian' aspects, two other static effects are also noteworthy. First, the impact of integration on transaction costs, which some studies estimate at up to 3 per cent of gross trade values. These costs include customs formalities, a lack of familiarity with the legal frameworks regulating destination markets, foreign currencies, etc. From this standpoint, there is no denying that the regional integration process in the Mercosul has made a positive contribution, pruning these costs despite frequent changes in the regulations and provisions regulating trade transactions among its members.

Finally, the impact of integration on terms of trade should also be mentioned. This may be relevant where extra-regional imports are replaced by imports from trading partners, with a significant reduction in extra-zone demands, leading to a decrease in external prices. Consequent changes in the terms of trade benefit the members of the integration scheme, but also adversely affect non-member countries.[13] In a recent study, Chang and Winters (1999) found strong evidence of changes in the terms of trade benefiting the Mercosul, concluding that '. . . the effects identified here are large enough to warrant serious consideration'.[14] This conclusion is surprising, as the Southern Cone integration process coincided with an increase rather than a drop in extra-zone demands, with no significant changes in its composition.

Dynamic effects
In contrast to static effects, the dynamic impacts of integration cannot be classified through an accurate taxonomy. For instance, Winters[15] adopts a broad-ranging of the concept of dynamic ('. . . anything that affects a country's rate of economic growth over the medium term') and basically lists three types of impacts: (i) those prompting spill-overs among the members of the integration scheme, fostering the convergence of *per capita* income growth rates among its members; (ii) those affecting the capital accumulation rate, prompting an increase in domestic investments and/or heavier inflows of direct foreign investments; and (iii) those deriving from the interaction of economies of scale with agglomeration economies and transaction costs, affecting decisions on where to locate industrial plants.

Along the same lines, Fernández and Portes[16] emphasise the impact of preferential integration on direct foreign investment flows, as well as the capacity of the extended market to heat up competition and improve efficiency in industry, boosting income. In turn, Bouzas[17] points out increases in resources aimed at R&D, because of well-known indivisibilities in this area, and the rationalisation of regulation tools as the potential dynamic impacts of integration. Finally, other authors stress economies of specialisation, as this results in an increase in intra-industry trade, as well as a learning curve that is particularly important for small and medium-size enterprises testing the water through their first experiences in internationalisation in an extended market.

There are few Mercosul studies undertaken with the specific objective of identifying or quantifying these effects. However, there is some evidence – even if indirect – illustrating the impact of integration on direct foreign investment flows, in addition to a number of analyses focused on detecting changes in the level of international integration among the Southern Cone economies.

Impacts on investment flows

The impact of the Southern Cone integration process on direct foreign investment flows is analysed by Blomström and Kokko,[18] as well as Castilho and Zignago.[19] The authors of the first study found some evidence that the sub-regional integration process encouraged an inflow of direct foreign investment, although they saw macro-economic stabilisation in the countries of this region as a far more significant factor. On the other hand, examining the relationship between the Mercosul and the OECD countries, Castilho and Zignago (2000) noted some complementarity between trade and investment flows, but failed to identify any significant association between the integration process and the inflow of direct foreign investment from the OECD nations. Macro-economic stabilisation and structural reforms are once again indicated as the main factors behind burgeoning flows of direct foreign investment during the 1990s, headed up by privatisation processes in Argentina and Brazil.

Data on the inflow of direct foreign investment tends to confirm the impression that Mercosul played a secondary role as a factor attracting these flows (Table 5.2).

From 1991 to 1995, the flow of direct foreign investment to Argentina largely outstripped flows channelled to Brazil, with the opposite noted from 1996 to 1999. This is explained by the fact that Argentina stabilised its economy and began to privatise its state-run enterprises early in the decade, while these processes began in Brazil only in the mid-1990s.

Despite these observations, there is some evidence that the creation of Mercosul had a positive effect on investment decisions in this region. Although less relevant in quantitative terms, intra-bloc investment flows and the expansion of local companies beyond their national borders constitute a trend that has been building up over the past few years. A good example of this process is the recent establishment of over 300 Brazilian

Table 5.2:

Mercosul: Net direct foreign investment – 1991/1999 (US$ million)

| Bloc/Country | Year | | | | | | | | | Accumulated 1991/1999 | |
	91	92	93	94	95	96	97	98	99	Amount	Share (%)
Mercosul	91	92	93	94	95	96	97	98	99	145.011	100.0
Argentina	2,439	3,218	2,059	2,480	3,756	4,937	4,924	4,175	20,000*	47,988	33.1
Brazil	89	1,924	801	2,035	3,475	11,666	18,608	29,192	26,500	94,290	65.0
Uruguay	32	58	102	155	157	137	113	164	145	1,063	0.7
Paraguay	84	118	75	137	155	246	270	235	350	1,670	1.1

Source: ECLAC (2000). Note: * Includes investment in YPF by REPSOL.

companies in Argentina. Additionally, from 1995 to 1999, direct Brazilian investments in Argentina topped US$5 billion,[20] ranking Brazil fourth among the leading foreign investors in this country.[21]

On the other hand, Argentine investments in Brazil have also risen appreciably over the past few years. According to surveys carried out in Argentina, companies in this country plan to invest some US$2.4 billion in Brazil from 1998 to 2000, more than fivefold the amount of investments between 1990 and 1997.[22]

Mapping the mergers and acquisitions taking place throughout Mercosul helps highlight the impacts of integration on the asset restructuring process of companies in this sub-region.[23] From 1992 to 1998, some 650 transactions were recorded, involving mergers and acquisitions among companies in the Southern Cone Common Market. Most of them (58 per cent) took place among companies in the same country, followed by transactions involving stakes held by the subsidiaries of multinationals already established in the country (24 per cent). The volume of cross-border transactions, meaning operations where the purchasers were companies located in other Mercosul countries, was nevertheless not negligible (18 per cent). More significant still, these transactions took place largely in important industrial sectors such as auto-spares and beverages.

In general, it may be said that both Brazilian and transnational companies, particularly those already operating with production bases established in more than one country in the region, have undertaken actions designed to rationalise their activities within Mercosul. They have redefined their production schedules and thus have ensured better economies of scale and greater specialisation, while reorganising their marketing structure. In brief, there is no lack of evidence that the Mercosul is playing a reasonably important role as a magnet for investment and modernisation processes, as well as asset restructuring in the region.

Impacts on the level of integration in the international economy

One of the main expectations of the architects and formulators of the integration project was that it would pave the way for the countries in the region to move into the international economy more smoothly. In fact, they believed that the integration process would foster the use of economies of scale, resulting in intra-industrial specialisation, and encouraging the rationalisation of regional production structures. This in turn fuels the establishment of bi-national companies, joint ventures or even multinationals based in Mercosul, and makes decisive contributions to reshape trade flows between this region and the rest of the world.

The industrial structure of this region has, in fact, been swept by major changes over the past decade. However, not all of them have resulted in the desired directions or scales, due mainly to the widely varying response of industrial companies to the new macro-economic and regulatory context of the 1990s.

The industrial reorganisation process sweeping through countries in this region can be exemplified by the case of Argentina. Examining the response of its industries to the opening-up of the import substitution model, Kosacoff and Gómez[24] basically identified two types of conduct: offensive strategies and defensive or survival restructuring. Offensive strategies were adopted by corporations investing heavily in machinery and equipment, while also introducing deep-rooted organisational changes into their production models. These companies chalked up notable increases in productivity for their industrial plants, reaching levels close to international standards. However, the level of dissemination achieved by these offensive restructuring processes was somewhat limited. In fact, no more than 400 cases were found that could clearly be ranked under this type of strategy, although producing some 40 per cent of Argentina's industrial output.

Defensive restructuring was the response adopted by some 25,000 companies accounting for the remaining 60 per cent of Argentina's industrial output. This obviously includes countless firms that failed to survive, as well as a few new enterprises. On average, the companies in this group posted notable increases in productivity and, from an evolutory standpoint, their current situation compares favourably with their status some 10 or 20 years ago. However, these companies still preserve many of the characteristics of the import substitution stage: low levels of productive specialisation, widespread vertical integration, limited development of specialised suppliers, and sizes that reach only 5 per cent or 10 per cent of the optimum scale. In brief, these companies lag well behind international standards and are unable to compete in an open economy.[25]

This brief overview of the reaction of Argentine industries to the new macro-economic setting of the 1990s, can be extended to other countries in the region. Consequently, it is not surprising that no Mercosul members have recorded any more dramatic changes in their trading levels with the rest of the world. There is much evidence outlining extra-regional export flow profiles, with export listings clustered tightly around a limited number of products. This reflects the limited market share held by Mercosul in the more developed countries, low technological content of exported goods, and the incipient nature of intra-industrial trade.

Table 5.3:
Argentina and Brazil: Total exports divided into categories of goods and
destination markets (%)

Description	Export structure				Export destination (1997)			
	Argentina		Brazil		Argentina		Brazil	
	1990	1997	1990	1997	LAC*	ROW	LAC*	ROW
Primary Goods	**28.9**	**31.3**	**19.7**	**19.7**	**29.1**	**33.5**	**4.6**	**25.3**
Agriculture	27.4	22.1	10.8	13.6	15.9	28.3	2.8	17.6
Ores	0.2	0.4	8.9	6.1	0.2	0.7	1.8	7.7
Energy	1.3	8.8	0.0	0.0	13.0	4.5	0.0	0.0
Industrialised Goods	**71.0**	**67.7**	**79.1**	**78.8**	**70.8**	**64.5**	**95.2**	**72.6**
Traditional	33.2	29.5	28.7	30.3	20.0	39.0	21.5	33.7
High economies of scale	31.3	21.4	30.8	24.4	21.0	21.9	26.6	23.5
Durables	1.7	10.5	6.8	9.8	19.7	1.2	23.5	4.7
Technical progress disseminators	4.8	6.3	12.8	14.2	10.0	2.4	23.5	10.7
Others	**0.1**	**1.0**	**1.2**	**1.5**	**0.1**	**2.0**	**0.2**	**2.1**
Total	**100.0**	**100.0**	**100.0**	**100.0**	**100.0**	**100.0**	**100.0**	**100.0**

Source: ECLAC (1999). *Note*: * LAC = Latin America and Caribbean/ROW: Rest of the World.
Note: *Traditional*: Foods, beverages, tobacco, footwear, hides and leather, fabrics.
    Economies of scale: petrochemicals, paper, pulp, cement, base metals.
    Durables: Household appliances, consumer electronics, vehicles.
    Technical progress disseminators: Machinery, instruments, fine chemicals.

From 1990 to 1997 (Table 5.3), Argentina managed to introduce some
remarkable changes in the composition of its industrialised exports, reducing the share held by traditional manufactured products and intermediate
goods (industrial commodities produced in sectors with high economies of
scale), while boosting the share held by goods with higher added value
(durable goods and disseminators of technical progress).[26]

It should be noted, however, that these changes do not affect trade flows
outside Latin America, which remain heavily concentrated on primary
products and traditional manufactured goods.

In contrast, Brazil's performance is somewhat more disappointing, with
only limited changes in the composition of its export listings from 1990 to
1997. Compared to Argentina, Brazil's extra-regional trade flows are certainly less tightly concentrated on traditional products. Nevertheless, the

share in extra-regional Brazilian exports (15.4 per cent) held by goods with high added value remains somewhat negligible, excluding Latin America.

There is other evidence pointing in this same direction. For instance, Pereira[27] shows that the Brazilian export concentration index for Asia and the EU is six to seven times higher than exports to the Mercosul and Latin American Integration Association (LAIA) nations. More specifically, just ten products account for over 70 per cent of Brazilian exports to Asia, and 50 per cent to 70 per cent of exports to the EU. For the USA, this figure hovers between 40 per cent and 50 per cent, dropping to under 40 per cent for the Mercosul and LAIA nations. In turn, Motta Veiga[28] shows that over 47 per cent of Brazilian exports to Mercosul in 1998 consisted of medium and high technology-intensive products, shrinking to under 28 per cent for the extra-regional flows. This gap has been narrowing very slowly: in 1990, these figures stood at 44 per cent and 22 per cent respectively. Finally, Markwald and Machado[29] noted that 61 per cent of the trade in industrialised products between Brazil and Argentina was intra-industrial. This share drops to 30 per cent, 25 per cent and 17 per cent respectively for trade between these two countries and the North American Free Trade Agreement (NAFTA), the EU and Asia. Overall, the assistance offered by Mercosul in paving the way to closer integration between the countries in this region and the international economy, has been almost negligible so far.

However, there are some bright spots in this somewhat gloomy picture, as Mercosul seems to be playing a relatively relevant role in the internationalisation process of companies in this region. This comment is valid for both micro-enterprises, as well as the select group of Argentine and Brazilian multinationals. In the case of Brazilian micro-enterprises, for instance, the share of Mercosul in exports rose almost sixfold during the 1990s, up from 4.3 per cent to 24.9 per cent. For Brazilian companies as a whole, the Mercosul share rose from 4.2 per cent to 14.2 per cent over the same period. The contribution of the extended market to the internationalisation process of smaller companies consequently seems quite undeniable.

At the other end of the economic spectrum are the Southern Cone multinationals. These are large Brazilian or Argentine corporations or economic groups that provide direct foreign investments. Consisting of fewer than 30 companies with annual revenues that rarely top US$4 billion,[30] their activities are concentrated in only four or five sectors: oil and petrochemicals (Petrobrás, Repsol-YPF and Pérez Companc); food and beverages (Arcor, Sancor, SOCMA, Arisco, Garantia, Brahma and Bemberg); steel (Techint, CVRD and Gerdau); engineering services (Odebrecht, Andrade Gutierrez, Techint and IMPSA); and finance (Itaú).

Most investments by Brazilian and Argentine multinationals are channelled to their respective neighbour nations (Mercosul countries and other LAIA countries), although the USA, Europe and some of the less developed countries of Asia have also occasionally benefited from flows of investment from these corporations. Well aware of this trend, Chudnovsky and López[31] noted that the specialisation levels of Argentine and Brazilian multinationals reflect dense clustering in activities that are already mature from the product cycle standpoint.[32] Internationalised corporations operate in the services sector (finance, engineering and construction); traditional manufacturing activities (food and beverages); commodities (steel, petrochemicals, paper); or natural resources (oil). There are only a few cases of internationalisation in sectors requiring heavier investments in technologies or skills: pharmaceuticals (Bagó), telecommunications (IMPSAT) and information technology (SOCMA) in Argentina; autospares (Iochpe-Maxion) and transportation materials (Randon) in Brazil.

The outcome of the internationalisation process for Brazilian and Argentine economic groups is still hazy. Nevertheless, there is some consensus that the establishment of Southern Cone Common Market represents a clear incentive for the development of this process, as it encourages the expansion of Brazilian groups and corporations striving to consolidate their leadership on the extended market. Despite some disappointments, internationalisation has ushered in many appreciable advantages for the companies involved, as well as their countries of origin: expanding exports, higher added value for foreign sales, increased production scales, access to international sources of financing, and streamlined corporate restructuring processes, among others.[33]

Final comments

The outcome of the Southern Cone integration process is unquestionably favourable. Intra-zone total trade rose from 11 per cent in 1990 to over 20 per cent in 1999, peaking at 23.7 per cent in 1997. To a large extent, this growth is due to domestic supplies being displaced by competitive imports from regional members, rather than to the diversion of trade flows with adverse effects on more efficient producers in third-party countries. Consequently, concern over the static effects of integration lacks any solid ground. This impression is confirmed by flourishing flows of extra-Mercosul imports, added to the lack of any appreciable changes in the market share of the countries involved or the composition of imports from these same suppliers.

Nevertheless, there is no denying that the dynamic impacts of integration have not measured up to expectations. Although it is possible to pick out some examples of intra-industrial specialisation and increases in production scales, as well as a number of cases of productive, organisational and asset restructuring prompted by the establishment of an extended market, these phenomena are not widespread. More serious still, there has been little change in the pattern of extra-regional trade of Mercosul economies over the past decade. This is a statement of fact, despite the impressive inflow of direct foreign investments and some far from spectacular advances in the internationalisation process of regional firms.

However, drawing up balance sheets for preferential trade agreements requires more than just assessing the static and dynamic effects of integration. Other benefits must be taken into consideration, related to various non-traditional gains ushered in by this process. By lowering transaction costs among the member countries, integration schemes may effectively increase the bargaining power of trading partners in international negotiations, for instance.[34] In the case of Mercosul, the importance of extra-zone trade – over 75 per cent of its total commerce – has proved a particularly powerful incentive for partners in the bloc to co-ordinate their foreign trade policy, as potential gains beckon promisingly. Mercosul has already made good use of this aspect, both in the process of establishing the Free Trade Agreement of the Americas (FTAA) as well as during inter-regional negotiations with the EU. During the FTAA negotiations, the Mercosul nations were able to withstand US pressures pushing for a faster-track liberalisation time schedule, in addition to guaranteeing their participation in the negotiations as an economic bloc. Additionally, it successfully urged that a specific negotiating group be set up to deal with agricultural trade liberalisation. During preliminary discussions over setting up a free trade area with the EU, Mercosul successfully blocked all attempts to exclude agriculture from the talks agenda.

Preferential trade agreements can also provide a safety net against future events. This is the case with integration systems whose members waive contingent trade protection measures, such as anti-dumping and countervailing duties. Mercosul cannot yet be slotted into this category of agreement, because some of its members – particularly Argentina – have been enthusiastically wielding trade protection instruments, with adverse effects on its regional trading partners. However, the harmonisation competition policies for the member nations and reviews of their export subsidy mechanisms are already on the talks agenda for this bloc.

More important still from the political standpoint is the commitment undertaken by the four members to sign the Democracy Clause. This provision imposes severe sanctions on any break-away from the constitutional democratic order in any of the member countries, up to and including the possible future exclusion of the offender from the Mercosul.[35] On the other hand, by supporting a deep-rooted integration project, the Southern Cone countries ratified their option for a new style of political relationship based on co-operation, definitively leaving behind the conflict-based approaches that characterised the relationships among its partners through to the mid-1980s.[36]

The problem with the 'non-traditional' benefits of integration is that to a large extent they depend on the credibility and stability of the agreements negotiated. This means they may rapidly turn into shortcomings whenever relationships among the partners begin to crumple, or when undermined by crises triggering doubts about the solidity of previously undertaken commitments. Mercosul is currently suffering a crisis of this type. Its origins and consequences are discussed in the next section.

DEADLOCKS IN MERCOSUL

After four months of a steady outflow of its international reserves, Brazil gave up on its foreign exchange band policy in January 1999, opting for the free fluctuation of its currency. This resulted in a sudden, sharp devaluation of the real against the dollar. For the other members of the integration scheme, the reformulation of Brazil's foreign exchange policy represented a dramatic shift in the rules of the game and an about-turn in the intra-bloc conditions in terms of competitiveness, benefiting the country leading Mercosul. The deterioration of the international scenario helped make this crisis even more severe. In fact, the shift in Brazil's foreign exchange policy spurred on other adverse factors that undermined the performance of all members of the bloc: shrinking international credit supplies, the simultaneous decline of economic activities in other parts of Latin America, weak commodity prices on the international market, and the widespread slowdown in global trade. Additionally, the competitive stance between the two main partners in this bloc was swayed by yet another factor: less than two weeks prior to Brazil's foreign exchange crisis, Argentina and Brazil lifted the last tariff constraints on intra-zone trade, with the only remaining exceptions being automobiles and sugar.[37] Consequently, for Argentina, the Brazilian crises took place at a particularly unfortunate time, as it coincided with the removal of the remaining tariff protection for industrial sectors rated as sensitive. In brief, these were the factors that fuelled the most serious crisis in Mercosul since the start of the integration project.

Two years after the start of the crisis, the regional macro-economic scenario is still causing concern, particularly the precarious state of the

Argentine economy. However, the relationship between the partners has shown some progress. The devaluation of the Brazilian currency shrank to around 18 per cent in real terms, compared to pre-crisis levels, easing the competitive disadvantage of the other members of the bloc. On the other hand, Brazil should grow 3.5 per cent to 4.0 per cent in 2000, with its imports up more than 10 per cent, making a positive contribution to the expansion of intra-regional trade. Additionally, the balance of trade between Brazil and Argentina remains favourable to the latter, due to the rising value of Argentine oil sales to the Brazilian market. Finally, the new government in Argentina has helped – even if moderately – to make political dialogue with Brazil more fluid. Thus, in turn, Argentina has taken up a more flexible stance in its relationship with Brazil.

Despite the relatively favourable development of the relationship between the partners, the process of 'relaunching' Mercosul has proven excessively sluggish and difficult. The agenda for extending the Customs Union has posted few advances, while a variety of disputes continue in the commercial area. Lacking real effective progress in settling domestic issues, diplomatic efforts are tending to focus on the external agenda of the bloc, eager to make Chile a full member and establish a free trade agreement with the countries in the Andean Community. Nevertheless, it is obvious that the crisis in the bloc has not yet been resolved, and a solution is not prompted merely by changes in the competitive conditions ushered in by the devaluation of the Brazilian currency. There are many other broader-ranging issues now threatening the future of this integration project. These issues warrant further examination.

Political and economic issues

Initially, this deadlock has a clearly political aspect that can be described very simply: Mercosul is not the only possible strategy for moving into the international economic scenario for either Brazil or Argentina. In fact, despite official rhetoric that insists on proclaiming that Mercosul is a genuine 'politique d'État', both these countries are considering alternative options and strategies that are not necessarily convergent. At times of crisis, these alternatives obviously move upstage to appear more clearly and firmly. However, it would be naive to believe that they are prompted merely by today's delicate economic situation. Much to the contrary, the existence of strategies other than the sub-regional integration project is the outcome of more permanent factors of a structural nature, such as the size of each country, the specific characteristics of each country's production structure, and their individual history.[38]

Brazil

Brazil has at least two reasonably firm options: the first is to try to move into the world in an autonomous manner, which some more sceptical observers have called the 'Lonely Runner' strategy. The second is to urge a strategic alliance with its neighbours, in order to affirm its leadership in the region and ensure a higher profile on the international scene. However, this latter alternative is subject to the following conditions: (i) its leadership should include the whole of South America and not merely Mercosul; (ii) the costs deriving from the exercise of this leadership should be low; and (iii) its foreign policy should preserve a reasonable level of autonomy.

The option for autonomous entry expresses a view of the national interest that has never ceased to be present in the paradigm of Brazil's foreign policy. In fact, Brazil has always believed that the size of both its populace and territory, together with the complexity of its industrial structure and the clout of its GDP, are sufficient credentials for it to claim a leading role on the international scene, even with 'Lonely Runner' status. This is not a completely groundless ambition for a country whose economy rates ninth world-wide, backed by a network of broadly diversified relationships that rank it as a legitimate global trader. In fact, Brazil is often lined up with India, Russia and Indonesia as a pivot country: regional powers with their own specific weight on the global scene.

On the other hand, the strategy based on promoting Brazilian leadership in South America should also be considered as an alternative to the sub-regional integration project. This certainly does not exclude Mercosul, but rather, bypasses it. Within the framework of this alternative, the preservation of Mercosul in fact constitutes a necessary, but not sufficient condition in itself. This is because, without the support of the other countries in South America, the incentives to promote a deepening of the sub-regional scheme are extremely weak. Consequently, this is not an incremental foreign policy that starts with a hard core (Brazil–Argentina relationship) and extends outwards in concentric circles. It is the outer circle that shapes the inner, rather than the other way around. This results in somewhat tepid enthusiasm for consolidating this core, in parallel to a clear preference for more informal leadership, with lower costs and few rules and institutions.

The conditioning factors behind this latter alternative can be easily understood in the light of a few indicators (Table 5.4).

For instance, in aggregate terms, the Mercosul members are equivalent to only 27 per cent of the area, 39 per cent of the populace and 44 per cent of the GDP of Brazil. On the other hand, the share of the three partners together in Brazil's trade flows hovers at just under 16 per cent. From the

Table 5.4:
Brazil in South America

Countries in South America	Population* (10⁶ inhab.)	Index	Area* (10³ Km²)	Index	GDP* (US$ 10⁹)	Index	GDP (PPP)* (US$ 10⁹)	Index	GDP per capita (PPP)* (US$)	Index
Brazil	**165.9**	**100**	**8,547**	**100**	**767.6**	**100**	**1,070.0**	**100**	**6,460**	**100**
Rest of Mercosul (A)	*44.6*	*27*	*3,364*	*39*	*319.5*	*42*	*475.0*	*44*	*10,628*	*164*
Argentina	36.1	22	2,780	32	290.3	38	424.0	40	11,723	182
Uruguay	3.3	2	177	2	20.0	3	28.0	3	8,541	132
Paraguay	5.2	3	407	5	9.2	1	23.0	2	4,312	67
Mercosul Associates (B)	*22.7*	*14*	*1,856*	*22*	*81.9*	*11*	*144.0*	*14*	*6,314*	*98*
Chile	14.8	9	757	9	73.9	10	126.0	12	8,507	132
Bolivia	7.9	5	1,099	13	8.0	1	18.0	2	2,205	34
Andean Community (C)	*101.0*	*61*	*3,620*	*42*	*261.7*	*34*	*513.0*	*48*	*5,067*	*78*
Colombia	40.8	25	1,139	13	100.7	13	239.0	22	5,861	91
Venezuela	23.2	14	912	11	82.1	11	133.0	12	5,706	88
Peru	24.8	15	1,285	15	60.5	8	104.0	10	4,180	65
Ecuador	12.2	7	284	3	18.4	2	37.0	4	3,003	47
Subtotal (A+B+C)	**168.3**	**101**	**8,840**	**103**	**663.1**	**86**	**1,132.0**	**106**	**6,709**	**104**

Source: World Development Indicators (World Bank, 2000). Note: *Data from 1998.

Brazilian standpoint, these asymmetries constitute an undeniable stumbling-block to any extension of the regional integration scheme, particularly for issues involving constraints on its national sovereignty.

The inclusion of the other countries in South America in this comparison undoubtedly changes this situation. Nevertheless, the weight of Brazil is still equivalent to that of the nine partners together. The trade between Brazil and the countries in the Andean Community and the associate members of Mercosul is still relatively modest, with the global share held by South America in Brazil's trade flows barely topping 22 per cent. On the other hand, Brazil's unwillingness to bear the costs of more formal leadership of either Mercosul or even South America, within a broader context, can be better understood through an examination and comparison of its *per capita* GDP: Brazil ranks well below Argentina, Uruguay and Chile, and only just above Colombia and Venezuela. In fact, Brazil is above only Bolivia, Ecuador, Peru and Paraguay, and even so, its income distribution profile is more jagged than most of these latter countries.

The fact that Brazil's foreign policy simultaneously includes alternative strategies for moving into the global economy, lies at the root of the lack of definition and the ambiguities permeating its economic and commercial relationships with its partners in Mercosul. First, unilaterism is particularly noteworthy, reflected in the use of economic policy tools that rarely take into account the impact of domestic policy measures on the economies of its regional partners. In fact, Brazil took over as the natural leader of this bloc and assumed that the other partners would passively implement policies tailored to Brazil's activist approach.[39] However, there is no clear perception of the limits to be respected by this leadership. They cannot be either hegemonic or the outcome of coercive dynamics, as this would run the risk of incompatibility with the intention of fostering a strategic alliance.[40]

Another element to be stressed is the lack of a community vision, understood as a genuine concern that Mercosul should make effective contributions to the industrial development of the other regional members. This concern was in the fore prior to the formal establishment of Mercosul (1985–90), but faded during the 1990s. In fact, the explicit objective guiding talks on the initial bilateral agreement between Brazil and Argentina was to usher in an intra-industrial specialisation and complementation scheme within the framework of reasonably well-balanced and symmetrical trade. This was intended to avoid the possibility of any type of intra-industrial specialisation among the countries. For Argentina, this was in fact the only acceptable basis for an integration agreement with Brazil, as both government and business reject any project that might relegate

Argentina to the role of a mere supplier of agricultural raw materials or industrial commodities.[41]

The idea that the regional partners could specialise in producing primary goods with low added value and develop into markets for Brazil's industrial output, still shapes many of its attitudes. Quite correctly, Lavagna[42] stresses that the Argentine interest in this type of proposal is nil. If Argentina decided to enter the global economy solely on the basis of its static advantages, its target would not be just the Brazilian market, but rather the entire world. In turn, Motta Veiga[43] stresses that one of the driving ideas behind Brazil's foreign policy is to help build up the conditions for the development of Brazilian industry. This would be why Brazil does not support integration based on liberal policies. However, according to Motta Veiga, Brazil is also reluctant to support integration based on policies that would foster the industrial development of the region as a whole, as its industrialisation project is domestic rather than community-based. This explains its aggressively competitive stance in terms of its policy for attracting foreign investments, as well as its lack of interest in setting up a regional bank to finance development projects within Mercosul. Furthermore, it also explains its opposition to *maquilas* in Paraguay, as well as its utterly intransigent position during the crisis that swept through the first six months of 1999, when it refused to discuss any type of measure – even temporary – with Argentina in order to cushion the dramatic shift in competition conditions resulting from the devaluation of its currency.

Briefly, unilateralism and the lack of a community-based vision – as well as a certain unwillingness to incur the costs deriving from the exercise of leadership – are the results of the Brazilian stance, which is based on a foreign policy that is still reluctant to opt definitely for an integration project through Mercosul.

Argentina

Like Brazil, Argentina is also analysing the possibility of an autonomous global economy as a strategic alternative to Mercosul. In this case, its options are not very different from the strategy already adopted by Chile, whose economy is supported on an industrial base that is far narrower, and three to four times smaller than that of Argentina. The options are: (i) lower import costs; (ii) encourage specialisation in limited groups of sectors; (iii) exploit market niches that require intensive use of skilled labour; (iv) sign free trade agreements with the largest possible number of partners; and (v) try to preserve preferential access to the Brazilian market, in order to enhance its attractions and streamline the inflow of direct foreign investments.

If Brazil's strategy for autonomous entry to the global market may be restricted by over-confidence in its true possibilities, the Argentine strategy errs the other way: it may underestimate the potential of the Argentine economy and propose a development model whose capacity to guarantee the balance of its foreign accounts and underpin full domestic employment may be uncertain.[44]

The option for a Chilean-style strategy reflects an ongoing discussion in Argentina that picks up momentum whenever conflicts flare up with Brazil. This was the case in 1993, when the bilateral trade balance was highly favourable to Brazil, and discussions over the establishment of the Common External Tariff (CET) were dragging, due mainly to protectionist demands from a variety of industrial sectors in Brazil. This reappeared in 1995, when Brazil introduced its own automotive system that, although inspired by a similar scheme in effect in Argentina since the start of the decade, ran counter to the provisions of the Treaty of Ouro Preto. Soon after, Brazil decided to offer tax incentives to foreign auto-assemblers setting up plants in Northeast Brazil, once again fuelling discussions over the flimsy trustworthiness of the major partner and the convenience of reformulating the entire integration project. Since mid-1998, when the first signs of the Brazilian crisis became apparent, open discussions have been under way in Argentina over the possibility of turning Mercosul into a simple free trade area. Downsizing this regional integration project would allow Argentina to take back the reins of its own trade policy, opening up a new round of tariff reductions and establishing trade agreements with new partners – in brief, opting for a strategy similar to that of Chile.

From the political point of view, opting for this alternative would officially firm up the triangular relationship between Argentina, the USA and Brazil, with the former as its main ally and the latter as its principal market. This strategy was clearly explained by Escudé (1998):

> The alliance with the USA has three functions: Eliminating barriers to Argentine development due to useless political clashes that have taken place for decades; discouraging the potential buccaneering spirit of certain military sectors in Chile without earmarking funds to purchase weapons, and curbing the expectations of Brazil, as the alliance between Argentina and USA shows that Argentina is not willing to face up to the USA through Third World utopias remote from the immediate interests of the Mercosul nations. In turn, the alliance with Brazil meets three main objectives; encouraging economic integration at the subregional level, which is vital for the development of

Argentina; imposing limits on its alliance with the USA and clearly indicating that Argentina would not tolerate any US attempt to intervene in the domestic affairs of Brazil (for instance, claiming the need to protect the eco-systems of Amazonia), while also helping discourage the potential bucca-neering spirit of some military sectors in Chile.[45]

By considering a strategy offering an alternative to Mercosul, Argentina has also heaped coals on other disputes and irritated Brazil. However, this irritation has been caused far more by the consequences of the political emergencies of the alternative Argentinean project than by its outcome at the economic level. In fact, the strategic dependence of this partner on a power outside South America is more threatening for Brazil than the weak-ening of its preferential status on the Argentine market. As a matter of fact, suggestions of 'shrinking' Mercosul into a free trade area have been backed by some segments of the Brazilian public opinion as well. However, the Argentine initiative of negotiating its status as an ally outside NATO was rated as far more provocative, as at the same time it refused to support Brazil's claim to a Permanent Seat on the UN Security Council.

The new government, which took office at Argentina in late 1999, boosted optimistic expectations in Brazil. In fact, it was believed that an effective shift would take place in the policy of alignment with the US. However, the new administration introduced only moderate adjustments to the guidelines shaping Argentina's foreign policy, reflecting a diplomatic style that is both undefined and defensive. Its financial fragility and heavy dependence on international capital markets have undoubtedly helped prune its negotiating power. The fact is that – despite some discomfort – Argentina seems resigned to clinging on to the US bandwagon.[46]

Legal and institutional issues

Mercosul suffers from legal and institutional shortfalls. This diagnosis is generally agreed, prompting little dispute. However, the relevance of the problem and its implications for the future of Mercosul – as well as which members benefit, which are adversely affected, and what solutions should be adopted – are all subjects where widespread disagreement prevails. Consequently, it is worthwhile attempting to offer a brief overview of these issues.

There are three main problems: (i) the rules approved by Mercosul enti-ties do not constitute community law *strict sensu*, but are merely interna-tional law in the classic sense, consequently requiring prior inclusion in the

domestic legal arrangements of the member countries through the procedures defined by constitutional rules or laws in each of them; (ii) Mercosul
lacks an effective system for settling disputes, and has no juridical entity
that is empowered to interpret and apply the agreements and; (iii) the
organs established by Mercosul are all intergovernmental and consequently
political in nature, implying mechanically analogous negotiations for political and technical matters, with obviously adverse effects for the latter.[47]

With regard to the problem of the juridical status of Mercosul in the
member countries, it should be stressed that there are marked differences
among its members. For instance, Argentina acknowledges the hierarchy of
the international treaties as being superior to national law and even constitutional provisions.[48] Paraguay also accepts a supra-national juridical order,
although in a more restricted manner, as international rules are subject to
later control by its Supreme Court of Justice.[49] There is far more uncertainty over the judicial status of integration law in Brazil and Uruguay,
where: 'international treaties do not prevail over the Constitution, or even
over domestic infraconstitutional law, and are merely equivalent to domestic law, by which they may be modified'.[50] In realistic terms, this means that
a national law sanctioned by the Legislative Authority in Brazil or Uruguay,
may at any time refuse to acknowledge the matters agreed through the
Treaty of Asuncion. In the case of Brazil, it is worthwhile emphasising that
in 1995 there was an attempt to introduce a constitutional provision similar
to that of Argentina, which was swiftly dismissed by Congress.[51] The political implications of this fact are undeniable, as it illustrates the resistance
built up in Brazil to proposals that involve curbs on its sovereignty.
Consequently, it is not surprising that Argentine observers feel that the
current situation breaches the reciprocity of rights and obligations
enshrined in the Treaty of Asuncion.[52]

On the other hand, the need to move ahead with including these rules
in national juridical arrangements, makes the decisions of Mercosul entities void in juridical terms. This results in asymmetrical or muddled situations in cases where the rules are already incorporated in one country but
not in another. The process of including these rules is also extremely time-
consuming, depending solely on the will of the member countries.[53] Not
without good reason, the fragility of the juridical arrangements of
Mercosul has been blamed on the fact that the states have deliberately side-
stepped rigid legal obligations that could curtail their room for manoeuvre.[54]

With regard to the system for the settlement of disputes, Mercosul has
established reasonably complex procedures stipulating that disputes should
be initially dealt with by inter-governmental entities, and if no agreement

is reached, they should then be subject to the decision of an *ad-hoc* Arbitration Court. This consequently avoids establishing a supra-national Court of Justice, or even a permanent Court of Arbitration.

There are many criticisms of this system. Initially, it discourages the use of formal mechanisms and encourages the political solution of disputes, as if they must be handled initially at the inter-governmental level. The settlement of trade disputes through diplomatic means has a negative effect, as every dispute seems to be vital for the continuity of the regional project.[55] Secondly, the *ad hoc* nature of the Court hampers the accumulation of jurisprudence, as changes in its composition eliminate the moral constraints imposed on a Court by its own precedents.[56] Thirdly, without a Permanent Court, there is no juridical entity empowered to interpret and apply the agreements or reply to queries.

The possibility of establishing a Permanent Court has been under discussion by the member countries for at least two years. But this step is meeting resistance, mainly from Brazil. Paradoxically, the members of Mercosul have promptly accepted the system for the settlement of disputes introduced by the World Trade Organisation (WTO). This system regulates their trade relationships with partners all over the world, while refusing to establish a similar mechanism for settling their own disputes, despite their common project.[57]

However, the most serious problem is the essentially political nature of Mercosul entities, and the lack of any technical organisation. Mercosul institutions are staffed by civil servants, not necessarily permanent and appointed by their respective governments. They act according to the instructions received from their superiors, quite naturally complying with the existing hierarchy in the government area to which they belong. Interaction among decision-taking entities occurs after each country has filtered these issues through the mesh of its domestic interests. Consequently, each government arrives at the negotiating table urging its own specific interests, which may run counter to those of the Customs Union.[58] Consequently, the strategic vision is lost, as there is no one to present the common interest (i.e. the interests of Mercosul). This spotlights an obvious need to establish independent entities staffed by civil servants working for Mercosul rather than its member states, with the sole function of urging policies that will help fine-tune the Customs Union. Although these entities will naturally be assigned only pro-positive powers, they are nevertheless of the utmost importance.

The legal and institutional shortfall outlined above is causing concern, as it fuels disputes and makes doubts worse, while delaying the resolution of problems. In keeping with the viewpoints of the smaller members, including Argentina, the current juridical and institutional framework undermines the trust inspired individually by the countries to which investors channel their resources. This results in a situation that favours the largest market – i.e. Brazil. The lack of standards and the prevalence of slap-on-the-wrist rules also tend to favour Brazil due to its greater capacity to force decisions, or delay the settlement of disputes.

However, from the Brazilian point of view, the current decision-taking system, based on consensus, deserves criticism, as it leads to a fictional equality among the partners, granting the smaller nations excessive power.[59] Nevertheless, Brazil refuses to accept any proposal that includes the settlement of certain issues by a qualified majority. This is because it would result in a discussion of the 'thorny' and presumably insoluble issue of the distribution of voting power among the member countries. In fact, given the current configuration of Mercosul, with only four members (and bearing in mind differences in size among its members), it is difficult to imagine any type of voting power share-out that would be acceptable to Brazil, while at the same time preserving the political identity of the other members.

Despite these comments, it is obvious that there is ample room for introducing changes in the current institutional framework of Mercosul. Outstanding among the solutions already presented are: (i) setting up Technical Committees; (ii) introducing an Arbitration Court endowed with greater independence and endowing its officers with a certain stability, or alternatively, the introduction of a juridical entity empowered to interpret agreements, reply to queries, and guide national courts in the application of the law emanating from the Mercosul rules; (iii) establishing fast-track procedures or deadlines for the inclusion of the rules in national juridical arrangements; and (iv) the introduction of a common anti-trust bureau to protect competition and ensure fair trade practices.

The current halt in institutional discussions cannot be blamed solely on the attempts to prevent the 'issue of supra-nationality' from even being approached. The lack of an effective strategic commitment to the integration project, as outlined above, constitutes a more plausible reason explaining this real instructional phobia.

NOTES

1. Serra, J. *et al. Reflections on Regionalism. Report of the Study Group on International Trade*, Carnegie Endowment for International Peace, Washington, 1997.
2. Ibid.
3. Winters, L.A. stresses this point critically: 'Having found that the static benefits are usually rather small or possibly even negative, advocates of regional integration arrangements typically appeal to

the dynamic effects. However, what these constitute and how they come about are frequently rather vague and the evidence linking dynamic benefits to particular instances of integration very difficult to pin down', 'Assessing Regional Integration Agreements' (draft), Montevideo, 1997, p. 22.

4. Trade creation occurs when imports from member countries – meaning the trading partners dis place less efficient domestic supplies as a result of a preferential tariff reduction. In this case, there will be benefits for the local economy, as domestic consumption will be met with less expenditure of real resources. Alternatively, should the imports from the member countries help to edge out lower-cost imports from non-member countries – meaning third party countries not benefiting from the preferential tariff concession – then trade diversion will take place. In this case, there will be losses for the local economy as domestic consumption will be met through higher expenditures of real resources.

5. Fernández, R. and Portes, J. Returns to Regionalism: An Analysis of Nontraditional Gains from Regional Trade Agreements, *The World Bank Economic Review*, Vol. 12, No. 2, May, Washington, 1998.

6. Viner, J. *The Customs Union Issue*, Carnegie Endowment for International Peace, New York, 1950.

7. Frankel, J.A., Stein, E. and Wei, S.J. *Trading blocs: The Natural, the Unnatural and the Super-Natural*, WP. 034, University of California at Berkeley, 1994.

8. Yeats, A.J. Does Mercosul's Trade Performance Raise Concerns about the Effects of Regional Trade Agreements? *The World Bank Economic Review*, Vol. 12, No. 1, January, Washington, 1998.

9. Nagarajan, N. On the evidence of trade diversion in MERCOSUL. European Commission. Technical Paper, 1998.

10. Winters, L.A. Even if import's share of more efficient non-member countries increases, this does not exclude the possibility of trade diversion, because such an approach fails to take account of changes in the relative sizes of economies as they grow at different rates. He is surely right, but there is no denying that this fact offers very strong proof that trade diversion is not too relevant. Montevideo, 1997.

11. Commenting on the increased trend towards intra-Mercosul trade between 1986/1988 and 1995/1996, Soloaga and Winters reached the same conclusion: 'The positive trend in the estimated coefficients for bloc member's imports . . . presumably reflects the unilateral trade liberalization that swept Latin America in the late 80's and early 90's.' In *Regionalism in the Nineties: What effects on Trade?* WPS, World Bank, Washington. 2000, p. 11.

12. Soloaga and Winters ibid., do not disagree with this interpretation: 'The increases in CACM and ANDEAN members' overall export coefficients also reflect liberalization, while the opposite trend in Mercosul suggests that its members' trade performance was dominated by currency overvaluation rather than trade policy', p. 11. Or even: 'The exception was the Mercosul, for which import and export propensities displayed opposite movements. While Mercosul members have undoubtedly liberalized since the mid-1980's, these results suggest that their trade performance has been influenced more by competitiveness than by trade policy', p. 13.

13. Once again, concern is noted over the impact of discriminatory liberalisation on non-member countries.

14. Chang, W. and Winters, L.A. *How Regional Blocs Affect Excluded Countries: The Price Effects of Mercosul*, World Bank, 1999.

15. Winters, L.A., 'Assessing Regional Integration Agreements'.

16. Fernández, R. and Portes, J., 'Returns to Regionalism'.

17. Bouzas, R. Las perspectivas del Mercosul: desafíos, escenarios y alternativas para la próxima década, J. Campbell (ed.) *Mercosul, entre la realidad y la utopía*, Nuevo Hacer, Buenos Aires, 1999.

18. Blömstrom, M. and Kokko, A. *Regional Integration and Foreign Direct Investment: A conceptual framework and three cases*, WPS No. 1750, World Bank, 1997.

19. Castilho, M. and Zignago, S. *Commerce et IDE dans un cadre de régionalisation: le cas du Mercosul* (Mimeo), Rio de Janeiro, 2000.
20. ECOLATINA *Mercosul Insights*, No. 349, June, Buenos Aires, 2000.
21. Instituto para la Integración de América Latina y el Caribe – INTAL, *Informe Mercosul No. 5*, Año 4, Buenos Aires, 1999.
22. Centro de Estudios para la Producción – CEP. *Mercosul-Unión Europea:Análisis del comercio en los noventa*, *Sintesis de la Economía Real*, March, Buenos Aires, 2000.
23. Bonelli, R. *Fusões e Aquisições no Mercosul. Texto para Discussão No. 718*, IPEA, Rio de Janeiro, 2000.
24. Kosacoff, B. and Gómez, G. 'Industrialización em um contexto de estabilización y apertura externa. El caso argentino em los noventa', B. Kosacoff (ed.) *El desempeño industrial argentino. Más allá de la substitución de importaciones*, CEPAL, Buenos Aires, 2000.
25. Ibid.
26. A rapid increase is also noted in primary energy products (oil and oil products). To a large extent, this is the result of the privatisation of the state-owned YPF oil company.
27. Pereira, 2000
28. Motta Veiga P. 'Brasil en el Mercosul: política y economía en un proyecto de integración', J. Campbell (ed.) *Mercosul, entre la realidad y la utopía*, Nuevo Hacer, Buenos Aires, 1999a.
29. Markwald, R. and Bosco Machado, J. 'Hacia una política industrial para Mercosul', R. Roett (ed.) *Mercosul: Integración regional y mercados mundiales*, Nuevo Hacer, GEL, Buenos Aires, 1999.
30. This limit is outstripped by five Brazilian companies or groups (Petrobrás, Itaú, Garantia, Companhia Vale do Rio Doce and Odebrecht) and two Argentine groups (Repsol-YPF and Techint). For the purposes of comparison, leading Korean groups post revenues of US$30 million to US$60 billion a year.
31. Chudnovsky, D. and López, A. 'Las Empresas multinacionais de América Latina. Características, Evolución y Perspectivas', Chudnovsky, D., Kosacoff, B. and López. A. (eds) *Las Multinacionales latinoamericanas: sus estrategias en un mundo globalizado*, Fondo de Cultura Económica, Buenos Aires, 1999a.
32. Ibid.
33. Ibid.
34. Fernández and Portes, 1998.
35. The strength of this device was recently tested successfully during the political crises in Paraguay.
36. Quite correctly, García Peluffo stresses the importance of this political change for increasing links among neighbouring transportation infrastructures: 'One of the most noticeable consequences of the chronic clashes among the countries in the region has been the complete lack of connection among transportation infrastructures. Quite certainly the lowest-cost protection against any neighboring country was a physical gap which avoided building up troops on the border, as well as other similar war-like steps. Once the possibilities of conflict had shrunk, it was quite logical to launch a dynamic process of physical interconnection among the neighboring countries', in 'Algunos aspectos relevantes en la profundización del Mercosul', Celia Barabato (ed.) *Mercosul, una estrategia de desarrollo. Nuevas miradas desde la economía poítica*, Edicones Trilce, Montevideo, 2000, p. 60.
37. In 1995, when the Customs Union came into effect, the members of the Mercosul agreed on national product lists that would constitute temporary exceptions to intra-regional free trade for these products, covered by a special system (*Regime de Adequação*). An automatic step-down tariff schedule was agreed which ended on 1 January 1999 for the Argentine and Brazilian national listings. The Argentine list consisted of 211 products, concentrated mainly in sensitive industrial sectors: textiles, footwear, steel and paper. Consequently, in early 1999, these sectors cut their tariff protection for intra-regional trade from an average of 7 per cent to zero. Two weeks later, Brazil devalued its currency by some 60 per cent.

38. Garcia Peluffo, 2000.

39. Lavanga, R. *Zona de livre comércio ou área de decisão brasileira? Fim da integração ou a insuportável leveza das propostas*, RBCE- *Revista Brasileira de Comércio Exterior*, No. 51, FUNCEX, Rio de Janeiro, 1999.

40. Hirst, M. *Atributos y dilemas políticos del MERCOSUL*, em *Escenarios Alternativos*, Año 4, No. 9, Winter, Buenos Aires, 2000.

41. Campbell *et al.* describe the principles that guided these agreements: '. . . right from the start, it was agreed that the integration process would have to move ahead on the basis of integrated selective projects, and at different speeds. Consequently, efforts were made to move towards industrial and commercial complementation in different production segments, trying to minimize the possibility of any destructive effects on either of the two economies, while encouraging each of them to specialize in certain market niches or production lines within a given sector. The idea was not only to upgrade the production performance of both economies (based on intra-regional complementation and economies of scale), but also to underpin the evenly-balanced expansion of bilateral trade within a context of tight foreign financial constraints' (pp. 82–3).

42. Lavanga, *Zona de livre.*

43. Motta Veiga, 1999a.

44. Lavanga, *Zona de livre.*

45. Escudé, C. *La Argentina y sus alianzas estratégicas*, *Archivos del Presente*, Año, Número, Buenos Aires, 1998.

46. Tokatlián, J.G. *De Menem a De La Rúa: La diplomacia del ajuste*, em *Escenarios Alternativos*, Año 4, No. 9, Buenos Aires, 2000.

47. Redrado, M. *Desarrollo institucional en el Mercosul: Un aporte para la consolidación del bloque regional* (Mimeo), Buenos Aires, 1999.

48. This principle was enshrined by the 1994 Constitutional Reform (Article 75 of the current Argentinian Constitution).

49. Jimenez, 1997.

50. Abreu Dallari, P.B. 'O Mercosul perante o Sistema Constitucional Brasileiro', Maristela Basso (ed.) *Mercosul: seus efeitos jurídicos, econômicos e políticos nos Estados-membros*, Livraria do Advogado Editora, Porto Alegre, 1997.

51. In fact, the draft bill submitted by a Congressman in Rio Grande do Sul State needed 293 votes to pass; however, it was rejected with 168 votes in favour, 144 votes against, and 7 abstentions. Abreu Dallari, 1997.

52. De la Balze, F.A.M. 'El destino del Mercosul: Entre la Unión Aduanera y la "integración imperfecta"', F. de la Balze (ed.) *El futuro del Mercosul. Entre la retórica y el realismo*, Cari-Aba, Buenos Aires, 2000.

53. From 1995 to 1998, the Common Market Group issued 280 Resolutions, but only 88 had been effectively incorporated by the four members through to year-end 1988 Redrado, 1999.

54. Gonzalez, F.F. *Mercosul: incompatibilidad de sus instituciones con la necesidad de perfeccionar la Unión Aduanera*, *Integración & Comercio*, Bid-Intal, No. 9, Año 3, Buenos Aires, 1999.

55. Redrado, M. 'De la institucionalidad a la convergencia', F. de la Balze (ed.) *El futuro del Mercosul. Entre la retórica y el realismo*, Cari-Aba, Buenos Aires, 2000.

56. Gonzalez, F.F. *Mercosul:*, 1999.

57. Torrent, R. *Tres ideias sobre a institucionalizacao do Mercosul*, RBCE- *Revista Brasileira de Comercio Exterior* No. 62, FUNCEX, Rio de Janeiro, 2000.

58. Gonzales, F.F. *Mercosul:*, 1999.

59. Baptista, L.O. *Pautas viáveis para um desenvolvimento institucional do Mercosul* (Mimeo), Buenos Aires, 1999. However, it should be noted that consensus is not synonymous with unanimity. Consensus accepts abstentions, but not votes against.

BIBLIOGRAPHY

Abreu Dallari, P.B. (1997) 'O Mercosul perante o Sistema Constitucional Brasileiro', in Maristela Basso (ed.), *Mercosul: seus efeitos jurídicos, econômicos e políticos nos Estados-membros*, Livraria do Advogado Editora, Porto Alegre.

Abreu, M.P. (1997) *O Brasil e a Alca: Interesses e Alternativas*, Texto para Discussão No. 371, PUC, Rio de Janeiro.

Araujo Jr, J.T. (1999) 'O futuro do Mercosul' (mimeo), November, Washington, DC.

Baptista, L.O. (1997) 'A solução de controvérsias no Mercosul', in Maristela Basso (ed.), *Mercosul: seus efeitos jurídicos, econômicos e políticos nos Estados-membros*, Livraria do Advogado Editora, Porto Alegre.

Baptista, L.O. (1999) 'Pautas viáveis para um desenvolvimento institucional do Mercosul' (mimeo), Buenos Aires.

Bevilaqua, A., Talvi, E. and Blanco F. (1999) 'Brazil dependence in Mercosul: Is it real?' (mimeo), July, Rio de Janeiro.

Blömstrom, M. and Kokko, A. (1997) *Regional Integration and Foreign Direct Investment: A conceptual framework and three cases*, WPS No. 1750, World Bank.

Bonelli, R. (2000) *Fusões e Aquisições no Mercosul*, Texto para Discussão No. 718, IPEA, Rio de Janeiro.

Bonvecchi, C. (2000) 'Uma evaluación del desempeño de la industria argentina en los años noventa', in B. Kosacoff (ed.), *El desempeño industrial argentino. Más allá de la substitución de importaciones*, Cepal, Buenos Aires.

Bouzas, R. (1999a) 'Las perspectivas del Mercosul: desafios, escenarios y alternativas para la próxima década', in J. Campbell (ed.), *Mercosul, entre la realidad y la utopía*, Nuevo Hacer, Buenos Aires.

Bouzas, R. (1999b) 'Las negociaciones comerciales externas del Mercosul: Administrando una agenda congestionada', in R. Roett (ed.), *Mercosul: Integración regional y mercados mundiales*, Nuevo Hacer, GEL, Buenos Aires.

Carvalho, A. and Parente, A. (1999) *Impactos Comerciais da Área de Livre Comércio das Américas*, Texto para Discussão No. 635, IPEA, Brasília.

Castilho, M. and Zignago, S. (2000) 'Commerce et IDE dans un cadre de régionalisation: le cas du Mercosul' (mimeo), Rio de Janeiro.

CEP – Centro de Estudios para la Producción (2000) *Mercosul-Unión Europea: Análisis del comercio en los noventa*, Sintesis de la Economía Real, March, Buenos Aires.

CEP (1998) 'La inversión extranjera en la Argentina de los años 90: tendencias y perspectivas, *Estudios de la Economía Real*, No. 10, October, Buenos Aires.

Chang, W. and Winters, L.A. (1999) *How Regional Blocs Affect Excluded Countries: The Price Effects of Mercosul*, WPS, World Bank.

Chudnovsky, D. and López, A. (1999a) 'Las Empresas multinacionais de América Latina. Características, Evolución y Perspectivas', in Chudnovsky, D., Kosacoff, B. and López. A. (eds), *Las Multinacionales latinoamericanas: sus estrategias en un mundo globalizado*, Fondo de Cultura Económica, Buenos Aires.

Chudnovsky, D. and López, A. (1999b) 'La Evolución del debate sobre el papel del Mercosul en la estrategia de desarrollo económico de la Argentina', in J. Campbell (ed.), *Mercosul, entre la realidad y la utopía*, Nuevo Hacer, Buenos Aires.

CEPAL – Comisión Económica para América Latina y el Caribe (1998) *Expectativas empresariales frente a las negociaciones del ALCA*, Buenos Aires.

CEPAL – Comisión Económica para América Latina y el Caribe (2000) *Balance preliminar de las economías de América Latina y El Caribe-1999*, Santiago de Chile.

De La Balze, F.A.M. (1994) *La estrategia de inserción argentina en el comercio internacional: Los casos del Mercosul y Nafta*, Documento de Trabajo No. 3, Instituto del Servicio Exterior de la Nación – ISEN, Buenos Aires.

De La Balze, F.A.M. (2000) 'El destino del Mercosul: Entre la Unión Aduanera y la 'integración imperfecta', in F. de la Balze (ed.), *El futuro del Mercosul. Entre la retórica y el realismo*, Cari-Aba, Buenos Aires.

Devlin, R., Estevadeordal, A. and Garay, J.L (1998) 'Some Economic and Strategic Issues in the Face of the Emerging FTAA' (mimeo), Brasília.

ECOLATINA (2000) *Mercosul Insights*, No. 349, June, Buenos Aires.

Escudé. C. (1998) 'La Argentina y sus alianzas estratégicas', *Archivos del Presente*, Buenos Aires.

Fernández, R. and Portes, J. (1998) 'Returns to Regionalism: An Analysis of Nontraditional Gains from Regional Trade Agreements', *World Bank Economic Review*, Vol. 12, No. 2, May, Washington.

Frankel, J.A., Stein, E. and Wei, S.J. (1994) *Trading Blocs: The Natural, the Unnatural and the Super-Natural*, WP. 034, University of California at Berkeley.

García Peluffo, J.G. 'Algunos aspectos relevantes en la profundización del Mercosul', in Celia Barabato (ed.), *Mercosul, una estrategia de desarrollo. Nuevas miradas desde la economía poítica*, Edicones Trilce, Montevideo.

Gonzalez, F.F. (1999) 'Mercosul: incompatibilidad de sus instituciones con

la necesidad de perfeccionar la Unión Aduanera', *Integración &
Comercio*, Bid-Intal, No. 9, Año 3, Buenos Aires.

Guimarães, S.P (1999) 'Argentina e Brasil: integração, soberania e ter-
ritório' (mimeo), Brasília.

Heymann, D. (1999) 'Interdependencias y políticas macroeconómicas:
reflexiones sobre el Mercosul', in J. Campbell (ed.), *Mercosul, entre la
realidad y la utopía*, Nuevo Hacer, Buenos Aires.

Hirst, M. (2000) 'Atributos y dilemas políticos del Mercosul', *Escenarios
Alternativos*, Año 4, No. 9, Winter, Buenos Aires.

Institute for European-Latin American Relations – IRELA (1999a)
*Prospects for an EU–Mercosul free trade agreement and the US policy
options*, Special Report, November, Madrid.

Institute for European-Latin American Relations – IRELA (1999b)
*Economic relations between Mercosul and the EU: Prospects for the coming
decade*, Special Report, November, Madrid.

Instituto para la Integración de América Latina y el Caribe – INTAL (1999)
Informe Mercosul No. 5, Año 4, Buenos Aires.

Kosacoff, B. and Gómez, G. (2000) 'Industrialización em um contexto de
estabilización y apertura externa. El caso argentino em los noventa', in
B. Kosacoff (ed.), *El desempeño industrial argentino. Más allá de la substitución de importaciones*, Cepal, Buenos Aires.

Laplane, M. and Sarti, F. (1999) *Investimento Direto Estrangeiro e o impacto na
balança comercial nos anos 90*, Texto para Discussão No. *629*, IPEA, Brasília.

Lavagna, R. (1991) 'Integração Argentina-Brasil: Origem, resultados e
Perspectivas', in P. Motta Veiga (org.), *Cone Sul: A Economia Política da
Integração*, FUNCEX, Rio de Janeiro.

Lavagna, R. (1999) 'Zona de livre comércio ou área de decisão brasileira?
Fim da integração ou a insuportável leveza das propostas', *RBCE-
Revista Brasileira de Comércio Exterior*, No. 51, FUNCEX, Rio de
Janeiro.

Lavagna, R. (2000) 'Integração e gestão de crises financeiras. Impacto sobre
o Mercosul', *RBCE- Revista Brasileira de Comércio Exterior*, No. 63,
FUNCEX, Rio de Janeiro.

Markwald, R. and Bosco Machado, J. (1999) 'Hacia una política industrial
para Mercosul', in R. Roett (ed.), *Mercosul: Integración regional y mercados mundiales*, Nuevo Hacer, GEL, Buenos Aires.

Markwald, R. and Iglesias, R. (2000) *A Política econômica externa da
Argentina: uma visão dos anos 90*, IPRI, Brasília.

Motta Veiga, P. (1999a) 'Brasil en Mercosul: Influencias recíprocas,' in R.
Roett (ed.), *Mercosul: Integración regional y mercados mundiales*, Nuevo
Hacer, GEL, Buenos Aires.

Motta Veiga, P. (1999b) 'Brasil em el Mercosul: política y economía en un proyecto de integración', J. Campbell (ed.), *Mercosul, entre la realidad y la utopía*, Nuevo Hacer, Buenos Aires.

Nagarajan, N. (1998) *On the evidence of trade diversion in MERCOSUL*, European Commission Technical paper.

Puga, D. and Venables, A. (1998) 'Trading Arrangements and Industrial Development', *World Bank Economic Review*, Vol. 12, No. 2, May, Washington, DC.

Redrado, M. (1999) 'Desarrollo institucional en el Mercosul: Un aporte para la consolidación del bloque regional' (mimeo), Buenos Aires.

Redrado, M. (2000) *De la institucionalidad a la convergencia*, in F. de la Balze (ed.), *El futuro del Mercosul. Entre la retórica y el realismo*, Cari-Aba, Buenos Aires.

Serra, J. *et al.* (1997) *Reflections on Regionalism. Report of the Study Group on International Trade*, Carnegie Endowment for International Peace, Washington, DC.

Soloaga, I. and Winters, L.A. (2000) *Regionalism in the Nineties: What effects on Trade?* WPS, World Bank, Washington, DC.

Tokatlián, J.G. (2000) 'De Menem a De La Rúa: La diplomacia del ajuste', *Escenarios Alternativos*, Año 4, No. 9, Buenos Aires.

Torrent, R. (2000) 'Tres ideias sobre a institucionalizacao do Mercosul', *RBCE- Revista Brasileira de Comercio Exterior*, No. 62, FUNCEX, Rio de Janeiro.

Vamvakidis, A. (1998) 'Regional Integration and Economic Growth', *World Bank Economic Review*, Vol. 12, No. 2, May, Washington, DC.

Viner, J. (1950) *The Customs Union Issue*, Carnegie Endowment for International Peace, New York.

Winters, L.A (1997) 'Assessing Regional Integration Agreements' (draft), Montevideo.

Yeats, A.J. (1998) 'Does Mercosul's Trade Performance Raise Concerns about the Effects of Regional Trade Agreements?', *World Bank Economic Review*, Vol. 12, No. 1, January, Washington, DC.

SIX

————◄◦►————

The International Political Role of Mercosul II

SAMUEL PINHEIRO GUIMARÃES

THE WORLD SCENE

Mercosul is presented in academic articles and diplomatic speeches as a political instrument for Brazil and Argentina (and Uruguay and Paraguay). It is used to defend their interests and to promote their objectives in a new (hostile, dangerous or benign, as one may prefer) world order. In those articles and speeches, no detailed explanation is given of how this happens, or may happen in a complex international scene. The importance of the political role of Mercosul, especially if it comes to include other regional countries, seems to be considered as a natural consequence of size of its GDP, territory and population. In addition there are other factors which, according to Mercosul enthusiasts (even when they are inferior as is the case with GDP), could be compared to the corresponding figures for the European Union (EU) and NAFTA.

The analysis of the conditions, strategy and tactics of the political role of Mercosul should be preceded by the presentation of a view of the world system, inside which the political role has to take place. The world view presented here is certainly not the only one that can be imagined. Therefore it is open to dispute and contradiction and may be replaced by other plausible views. However, some comprehensive view of the world has to be presented and discussed before dealing with the political role of Mercosul.

The world system can be described as marginally co-operative, essentially competitive and eventually conflictive, to the point of confrontation and war. Due to the dynamism of the characteristics of the world system, there is no discernible trend towards peace and stability, no matter how much these positive aims are sincerely wished for. The six main characteristics and trends of the world system are the following:

1. acceleration of scientific and technological progress;

2. widespread and deep production restructuring;

3. concentration of power;

4. territorial reorganisation;

5. reincorporation of areas into the global capitalist economy; and

6. *normatisation* of international relations.

These six characteristics and trends are interlinked in complex, simultaneous and two-way circular relationships of cause and effect. However, it would be reasonable to identify the acceleration of scientific and technological progress as the most powerful factor influencing the other five characteristics, and trends and their mutual relationships.

According to some imprecise estimates, the world stock of *scientific and technological knowledge* doubles every seven to ten years. However, these estimates merely have the merit of calling attention to this awesome fact, whose complete (and perhaps ominous) consequences are difficult to foresee. Research and development has become an activity heavily financed by powerful governments and very large businesses. It is organised in an extremely careful and detailed industrial and scientific way, congregating thousands of scientists and engineers from the most diverse fields. The laboratories where they work are equipped with extremely sophisticated machines, their activities shrouded in secrecy and the results protected by law. The activities of the Echelon, the extremely sophisticated and secret 'surveillance' system organised by the US, reveal the crucial importance of science and technology and the 'extreme' methods employed by Great Powers to illegally appropriate business and secret scientific information.

The innovations that result from the intense research effort in the central fields of information technology, biotechnology and communications, are the main driving forces behind the wide and deep *restructuring of production and managerial practices* in all sectors of society. This restructuring permits and provokes business mergers and the organisation of extremely large companies, which may be called mega-multinational companies, that oligopolise markets at national and world scale. This restructuring of production and managerial practices facilitates the globalisation of some industrial and service sectors, especially financial activities, and generates severe and persistent imbalances in all labour markets. Finally, the huge scientific and technological research effort revolutionises the art of war, in all its aspects, from espionage, propaganda and subversion to open violence.

Territorial reorganisation runs a gamut of structures from one extreme of political and economic integration to the other extreme of complete territorial, political and economic disintegration. We may observe a range of increasingly complex economic integration schemes, more or less successful, to the point of territorial unification. However, increasing demands of local autonomy may also be found in all regions, leading eventually to social disturbances, and from there to civil war and political disintegration. The most important case of recent territorial disintegration, due to its political and military consequences, took place in the former Soviet Union, resulting in the emergence of fifteen new sovereign states.

Separatist and autonomist movements take place all over the world. They are a delayed effect of the subordination and oppression of ethnic and religious groups. In the past, autonomy claims were covertly stimulated, but nowadays, with the loss of prestige of the non-intervention principle, powerful governments become increasingly outspoken in their support of separatist or autonomist movements in other countries. Separatist movements and local claims for different degrees of autonomy take place with greater or smaller intensity in Europe (Italy, Spain, United Kingdom and Russia), in the Middle East (Kurds), in Africa (Eritrea), in Asia (Indonesia, India) and in the Americas (Canada), just to mention some of the most publicised cases.

Economic (and political) integration schemes, that may or may not lead to territorial integration, have been mushrooming all over the world. To a certain extent, they are a response to technological developments leading to profound and quick restructuring of production practices, which increase the optimum size of plants and demand larger and more secure markets. Sometimes, these integration initiatives appear as an attempt to replicate the successful integration experience of the EU, where a new and powerful state is taking shape.

Mercosul is an episode in the long history of Latin American economic integration initiatives. It is properly classified as a new type of economic integration scheme among developing countries, named *open integration*. These new schemes obtained acceptance from orthodox trade economists, powerful states, conservative politicians and international agencies such as the World Trade Organisation (WTO). This was because they were presented as a 'right step' towards the achievement of complete integration of the participant countries in the global economy, without harming the exporting interests of the great trading nations.

Concentration of power is taking place in all fields – scientific, technological, economic, political, military and ideological – in favour of highly developed states in the centre of the international system, as well as inside each country, be it developed, developing or poor.

Scientific concentration of power can be measured by the number of scientific papers published and quoted according to the author's country of work, and by the number of scientific awards, such as the Nobel Prize, according to the country where the winners were working at the time of the prize. Technological concentration of power is revealed by the number of patents awarded by the country of origin, by the number of computers *per capita* and by the percentage of exports of technologically sophisticated products. All these indices that reveal concentration, are a consequence of relative GDP amounts of resources invested, and especially of absolutely enormous funds allocated by governments and business for R&D, and for the scientific education of their own population. Some developed countries, such as Canada and the US, organised programmes to stimulate the immigration of qualified scientists and engineers from the periphery to the centre, increasing the concentration of power in this field.

Economic concentration of power can be measured easily by the increasing difference in income *per capita*, between highly developed countries and poor countries. They are separated by differences among them in physical indices of well-being such as life expectancy, illiteracy, sanitation, daily calories intake and the percentage of population below the poverty line. The economic concentration of power also takes place inside each developed or developing country, and it can be measured by similar indices.

Political concentration of power accelerated with the demise of the Soviet Union and the subsequent economic and political disorganisation of Russia. Two of its consequences were the disarray that took over the Non-aligned Movement, and the almost total irrelevance of the United Nations General Assembly and the overwhelming presence and increasing 'interpretative' power of the Security Council. The exercise of arrogant and almost hegemonic crude power by the US, directly or through international agencies under its control (such as NATO), indicates the extent of this concentration.

Military concentration of power is also a consequence of the demise of the Soviet Union, but in this case, differential rates of technological progress in microelectronics and information and communications technology among countries played an important role. Technological innovations permit the production of highly sophisticated and very expensive automated, orbital, miniaturised and intelligent weapons. War is being dehumanised and it increasingly becomes just an aseptic game in carefully chosen theatres of conflict, such as Kosovo. The disarmament of peripheral countries through strong pressure, skilful persuasion, media manipulation and domestic political elite co-optation increases the relative power of already powerful states even more.

Concentration of ideological power is the result of the transformation of the press into a highly technical, capital-intensive business, in the hands of few mega-multinational companies. These companies control the world of electronic media, in its increasingly interconnected forms of public and cable television, broadcast, movies, video, press, Internet, publicity and news agencies. These mega-companies have the power to promote 'ways of life' and the international agenda, defined by the Superpower. The Superpower determines events that are important, which ones are not, and how they should be interpreted. Therefore, they exercise huge political, economic and social influence, and this influence is not unrelated to the interests of the governments of the countries in which they have their head-quarters. This is one of the most sensitive and less examined aspects of international affairs.

Reincorporation of areas into the global capitalist economy and the corresponding political-military system, is a phenomenon of special importance for the political role of Mercosul, and therefore deserves a more detailed discussion. The long period of gradual and successful globalisation of the world economy (and political system) that started with the Age of Discoveries in its last stage under the hegemony of the United Kingdom, was succeeded by a period of turmoil, from 1914 to 1989. This period was characterised by two central conflicts. The first was the leadership struggle inside the capitalist system between Germany and Japan, and England, France and the US, which led to the Second World War. The second conflict was between capitalism and socialism. The leadership dispute ended with the overwhelming victory of the US and its Allies over the Axis Powers in 1945. The second conflict finished with the victory of the United States and the 'Free World' over the USSR and the 'Evil Empire' in 1989.

However, during the long period from 1917 to 1989, the final victory of capitalism (and of the US) could not be taken for granted, and there was a gradual reduction of territories and populations under capitalism. The emergence of the Soviet Union, the establishment of Eastern Europe socialist regimes, the victory of the Chinese Revolution, the partition of Korea, the victory of the Cuban Revolution and the unification of Vietnam, were all moments of this process that brought great anxiety to the political, economic and military elites of the West.

On the other hand, Latin America's relative isolation from 1929 to 1945, the rise of new African and Asian states, the East–West political competition in the Third World, the efficiency of war planning and the success of Soviet development, and finally, the hegemony of Keynesian thought created a special ideological, political and economic environment. This special environment permitted the emergence of governments in the periphery of the capitalist system, intent on overcoming the economic backwardness and international dependence of their countries. Those governments were determined to accelerate economic development, especially through industrial and import substitution policies. Furthermore, their legal systems reserved some economic sectors of activity for local state or private companies, with the tacit tolerance of the great industrial, trading and capital exporting countries.

Oil crises, petrodollar recycling by international banks and skyrocketing interest rates, led to a rapid accumulation of foreign debt, then to foreign exchange crises, then to capital flight and to stagflation in the periphery. Military regimes, which had previously been supported and applauded by native and Western elites as barriers against subversion and as promoters of modernisation, after the eruption of the crises, were made responsible for stagnation and inflation. Political claims for the restoration of democracy and for economic liberal policies became common in the Third World.

In ex-socialist and peripheral areas, the need to renegotiate asphyxiating foreign debt and the internal desire to reform the economy and reduce state intervention (which now presented as much a result, as a cause, of military and authoritarian regimes) became increasingly stronger. The renegotiation of foreign debt gave the opportunity to international banks, creditor countries and international financial agencies to impose as conditions for debt renegotiation the implementation of 'structural reforms'. These reforms were to take place in the fields of trade, finance, privatisation and deregulation. Included in those economic negotiation packages were the political principles of transparency and democracy, and developing and ex-socialist countries were strongly urged to adopt (at least formally) democratic regimes.

The situation after 1989 was seen as a unique opportunity to guarantee the consolidation of the opening and deregulation (for the benefit of mega-multinational companies) of socialist and peripheral economies and their democratisation through mechanisms that would *lock in* the reforms and prevent 'retrogression'. The objective was to preserve the impulse towards the reconstitution of the global economy, under the political and military control of developed countries. These countries were faced with a foreseeable increase in world population imbalances, instability, social unrest, and the spread of local and regional conflicts.

The strategy adopted was to negotiate international agreements that would consolidate reduction and even eliminate barriers to trade and capital flows, and establish parameters for 'legitimate' domestic economic policies in developing and ex-socialist countries. In the political and military sphere, the main objective was to guarantee horizontal non-proliferation of weapons of mass destruction, while permitting vertical proliferation through the development of sophisticated military technology. The secondary objective was to stimulate conventional disarmament in the periphery, under the guise of promoting confidence-building measures, in order to reduce regional tensions.

This process of *normalisation of international relations* is perhaps the main aspect of today's international system. However, negotiations, legal rules elaboration and the development of international law are not good, in themselves, for the peripheral countries. The active negotiations of rules impelled by the Great Powers do not lead to a democratic organisation of the world. This democratic organisation is based on the principles of 'one citizen one vote', representativeness, rule of law, absence of violent imposition of will, separation of powers and 'checks and balances', and a peaceful legal solution to conflicts. (These areas are presented as the basis of domestic democracy in the US.) The democratic organisation of the world cannot be accepted by the Great Powers because they would not necessarily be in control of it. Furthermore, this organisation would have to promote redistribution of their own power. Today, they concentrate more than 80 per cent of world wealth (in all its manifestations, such as production, trade, investments, etc.), technology generation, capacity and military power in less than 20 per cent of world population and territory. However, these central countries are already promoting the political organisation of the world through the organisation and close control of 'hegemonic structures of power'. These structures are essentially non-democratic, and perpetuate the asymmetries of power and the enjoyment of benefits between centre and periphery, to be guaranteed by the use of force, 'legally' authorised by the same structures they control.

A system of global political governance to complement the globalisation of the world economy is therefore already evolving in an informal Anglo-Saxon style. Gradual and extensive negotiation and interpretation of existing treaties, such as in the case of the informal expansion of the competence of the United Nations Security Council, takes place in a haphazard way. This creates a web of understandings, agreements, treaties, regimes and informal arrangements, consolidating the power of 'hegemonic structures' in a world characterised by instability, by growing disparities inside and between countries, and by the arbitrary use of force. This 'web' consolidates the power of the hegemonic structures and crystallises the subordinated position of the periphery of ex-colonies, which are now formally independent states. It permits the growing interference of international agencies in the domestic, economic and political affairs of the peripheral countries. Everyday, new legal obstacles are created and 'accepted' by the great peripheral states, making it more difficult to promote their own development and to fight for a democratic redistribution of world power. While academics and politicians of Kantian inclination argue, unendingly, about the urgent need for global governance, the formal ways to organise it and the strategies to achieve this goal, this global governance system is already being organised and put quietly into place.

After this overview of the characteristics and trends of the international system as a whole, it is necessary to synthesise the situation and perspectives of South America, which is the natural and immediate region for the exercise of the Mercosul political role. It is also essential to review some aspects of the foreign policies of the central actors in the world strategic game as they affect South America and Mercosul.

THE SOUTH AMERICAN SCENE

After long and arduous foreign debt renegotiation according to the 'rules' of the Washington Consensus, the dutiful implementation of the 'suggested' policies resulted in a great inflow of foreign capital. However, despite this, the structural situation of South American countries stays basically the same, if not slightly deteriorated. South America presents an increasingly poor population, extreme concentration of income and wealth, state fragility and inefficiency, high unemployment rates, slow expansion of exports, increasing foreign and internal public and private debt, growing outflow of resources, economic denationalisation, accelerating internal instability and external vulnerability and, more recently, stagnation of promising integration schemes, especially Mercosul.

On the political side, South America, which had been considered a 'Continent of Peace', has been suffering from escalating social unrest, heavily armed urban violence, organised crime and organised corruption, drug production as well as widening consumption and trafficking, guerrilla movements, fragile formal and 'mediatic' democracies, undemocratic attempts to topple governments, and continuous tensions. (Even though only latent between states, such as are the cases of Peru-Ecuador, Venezuela-Colombia and Venezuela-Guyana.)

Social and political instability generates a growing risk for foreign interests in South America. The population increasingly identifies the informal, but real, alliance between national traditional or new oligarchies and foreign business, and the neoliberal policies implemented by domestic ruling elites. These policies are strongly believed, by foreign governments and agencies, to be responsible for the worsening of its social and political situation and for the non-delivery of the Earthly Paradise that had been promised by the neoliberal governments of the 1990s and their 'economic teams'.

The concern for the drug economy and political influence, for the guerrilla movements and the possible military coups, presents an opportunity and an excuse for the celebration of agreements between the US and certain South American countries. The consequences of these agreements are: the sale of weapons and the resulting tensions; the presence of American 'advisers'; and the organisation of military training 'joint' operations, which many times take place near the Brazilian borders and use their military bases. At the same time, for geographical and political reasons, the other members of Mercosul do not share the same degree of Brazilian concern with this increasingly unstable and tense military and political situation in the region. Furthermore, they sometimes contribute to its increase.

Much to the contrary of Panglossian views, the domestic and external environment in which Mercosul has had to build its political basis for international action beyond the continent, is not a stable and prosperous one. The immediate regional environment in which Mercosul would have to exercise its political role is characterised by growing economic and political instability and escalating military tensions. This is in spite of the wishful thinking and sincere desires of the promoters of neoliberal economic policies and aligned political strategies.

UNITED STATES FOREIGN POLICY

US foreign policy is by nature and need global, and its South American policy is only a part of its general strategic approach. The strong trade, financial, military and political links between each Mercosul country and the US makes a general presentation of US foreign policy, strategies and tactics essential, before examining the political role of Mercosul.

The most important factor to consider when trying to discern US foreign policy objectives and to understand its tactics, is that the US considers itself the most perfect, advanced and successful human society and state in the modern history of mankind. This is a genuine conviction of the American elite and population at large, and it has a profound effect on the foreign policy of the US, its conduct and its attitude in relation to all other nations.

American policymakers and the foreign policy establishment tend to view the world as archaic and unstable. They consider even some advanced European countries as tradition bound, unequal, less than democratic societies and, to some extent, envious in relation to the American 'success story', ungrateful to its benevolent and farsighted policies and hostile to vital American interests. The 'inherent' instability of the world and the belief that the world has to be reformed in the image of American institutions, as the only way to become progressive, peaceful and prosperous, is at the core of the idea that the US is 'the' country responsible for world peace and progress and therefore has special obligations and 'rights'.

A second factor is that the well-being of American society is highly dependent on foreign markets for goods and capital, on the side of exports, as well as imports. The access to essential strategic inputs such as oil and rare minerals, the need to attract foreign capital, the control of markets and the access to cheap imports are just some of the aspects of the close interconnections between the American economy and the world. Therefore, the profound dependence of the American economy in relation to the world economy, and the idea that American economic success was due to unfettered capitalism are the foundations of American permanent and consistent foreign economic strategy. This strategy is to open, and keep open, markets for American imports and exports of goods, and for American exports (direct investments, loans, etc.) and imports of capital (such as the purchase of United States Treasury bonds by foreigners), and to protect the American economy against so-called 'unfair' competition. This strategy is pursued bilaterally, through political and economic pressure; unilaterally, by the denial of access to the American domestic market; regionally, through trade negotiations such as the FTAA, and multilaterally, through WTO and OECD negotiations to reduce economic barriers and regulate economic domestic policies.

The creation and perpetuation of an international organisation such as the UN, which would make illegal the use of force by powerless countries who are not permanently represented in its Security Council, and to establish the Council as a condominium of 'legitimate users of force' has been a central objective of American policy since the end of the Second World War. The principles adopted in the UN Charter froze territorial borders, prohibited foreign interference in domestic affairs, guaranteed auto-determination and choice of political and social regimes. All these principles, and the system of global collective security, are now in a state of flux due to the disappearance of the Soviet Union and the fragilisation of Russia. Auto-determination has been in practice abolished, and democracy under the novel dress of 'market democracy' is now, for the US (and for the UN in spite of not being mentioned in the Charter), the only 'legitimate' form of social organisation. However, and paradoxically, American political strategy promotes and supports regimes regardless of their democratic nature and according only to their friendliness towards American interests. The US actively fights and undermines regimes considered hostile, or 'rebellious', regardless of their democratic or dictatorial nature. Obviously, the destabilisation operations, whenever denounced, are emphatically denied. Its details, however, became public only 20 years later, with the partial publication of US government documents and after its consequences took place, such as with the overthrow of democratic regimes in Latin America in the 1960s.

The US foreign policy elite is aware that a process of concentration of power is taking place all over the world, and that it would be impossible to generalise to all countries, present-day consumption and pollution patterns now 'enjoyed' by developed countries. Consequently, political tensions among and inside countries are unavoidable, and situations will develop in the periphery that 'will have' to be dealt with by ideological persuasion, by local political co-operation and, whenever necessary, by force.

As a consequence, the central objective of American foreign military policy is to develop weapons of mass destruction and highly sophisticated conventional weapons. Furthermore, they aim through international agreements to forbid other states (especially in the periphery) to develop similar capabilities. As a complement to this policy, a network of military agreements and bases abroad are maintained as indispensable. This is for quick action and supply, without having to ask for local permission to engage in deployments in each emergency. This network also has a persuasive effect on local governments about the ultimate risk of developing policies hostile to American interests.

In this highly complex foreign policy (due to the extreme diversity of American interests in all countries that have themselves divergent and conflicting local or regional interests) the US strives to create informal global political, economic and military governance by the hegemonic structures of power, which are controlled by developed countries. This global governance is exercised preferably through international organisations of several kinds such as the United Nations Security Council, the IMF, NATO, OAS, OECD, NPT, MTCR, AIEA, World Bank, and so on. It is a network (Anglo-Saxon style) of bilateral, regional and multilateral agreements and arrangements 'imposed' on nominally independent countries that 'transform' themselves into 'rogue' states whenever they defy American supremacy and will.

US policy towards Latin America is radically different according to the geographical areas it applies to: Central America (and Caribbean) or South America properly, where Mercosul lies. The Central American (and Caribbean) region is absolutely vital for the defence of American territory and of the maritime channels between the East and West Coast and between the Gulf and the North of South America. Venezuela is the largest individual supplier of oil to the US, in amounts larger than the exports of all Persian Gulf states combined. From Colombia comes the frightening flow of illicit drugs, generated by the uneradicable demand of American consumers.

South America, especially the area South of Colombia and Venezuela, has a different and a lower degree of priority in the context of American foreign policy and strategy as a whole. This may be a positive fact for Mercosul political aspirations. However, the same principles of general American strategy apply to this region, with the aggravation that the US is trying to incorporate legally the whole region into the American economy. This attempt is through the negotiations of an FTAA and dollarisation policy, to maintain demilitarised the states of the region, while at the same time stationing American troops and matériel in some areas of the region.

In other regions of the world beyond the Western Hemisphere, American foreign policy initiatives have to confront the interests of the EU, China and Russia. Furthermore, the US cannot credibly affirm that they are genuinely a 'European' and much less an 'Asian' or 'African' country. In the case of South America, the situation is just the opposite. All other strategic players are more distant geographically from the region than the US, and tend to consider and accept South America as a natural area of influence of the US. South America is also under the 'psychological area of influence' of the US, to the extent that its traditional elites, in an attitude that reveals a mixture of opportunism, fear, submission and admiration, accept the American 'right' to world and regional hegemony.

EUROPEAN UNION FOREIGN POLICY

The paramount (even if never explicit) foreign policy priority of the EU is to recover the pre-eminent role enjoyed by Western European countries in world affairs, lost to the US (and Russia) as a result of the two Great Wars. To achieve this goal it is essential to recover military control over all European territory. This objective requires extremely complex and delicate manoeuvres due to the presence and growing reassertion of NATO power, to the influence of Atlanticist (Americanising) circles that exist in each European country (especially in the United Kingdom), and to the interest of Eastern European countries in the American presence to counterbalance traditional German and Russian dispute for influence in the region.

The tendency and policy of the EU bureaucracy and of the member governments is to incorporate gradually all other European countries into the Union system. Nowadays, the system includes the monetary union, vast social and economic regulation, political structures, and common defence and foreign policies.

In the foreign policy of the EU, different levels of priority can be observed. The geographical areas of interest for the EU, besides the US, may be classified according to concentric circles of importance: Eastern Europe and Russia, Mediterranean countries, former African colonies, the Middle East, and only then, South America and Asia. This situation, combined with the acceptance by Europe of the 'natural' American influence over South America, gives a very low priority to Mercosul in the context of real, not rhetorical, European political strategy.

During the long period from the Second World War to the Treaty of Maastricht and the fall of the Berlin Wall, Europe (Continental) concentrated efforts in its economic recovery, accepting less and less American political leadership. During this period, Europe accepted South America as a natural area of political influence of the US. With time, Europe started rebuilding the close links that existed in the past with South America, especially economic ones, through direct investments. Nevertheless, they carefully avoided contesting American political initiatives in the continent. However, from the beginning of the Cuban embargo and the aggravation of Central American conflicts, Europe started disagreeing discreetly with American policies, hegemony and title to exclusiveness in the region.

It is true that European and American economic interests are generally similar, especially when it comes to relations between the centre and the periphery. They both wish to maintain South American economies open to foreign trade and investments, but at the same time, Europe, in its increasing assertion of an autonomous foreign policy, tries to 'exploit' Latin American resentments and desire for greater autonomy. The admission of Portugal and Spain into the EU created an interesting 'window of opportunity' and an instrument for greater European political activity. This has been carefully disguised under the economic negotiations between Mercosul and EU and the Ibero-American periodical summit meetings.

Portugal and Spain, as semi-peripheral developing countries in Europe, have great interest in strengthening their negotiating position inside the EU. Therefore, they present themselves to their European partners as a 'bridge' between Europe and Latin America. At the same time, to their ex-colonies in Latin America, they strive to appear as a 'door' for Latin American investments [*sic*] in Europe, and as the 'champions' of South American demands for the opening of European agricultural markets.

As one of its necessary objectives, Europe wants to promote multipolarity of the international system. This actually means to achieve an equivalent *status* for Europe in relation to the US in the world scene and in the 'administration' of the global system. This objective is behind the EU's somewhat reluctant acceptance to engage in negotiations of a free trade area agreement with Mercosul, which would, in principle, include agricultural goods. The objective would require loosening the grip of American hegemony (including in the Americas), and the economic objective of keeping the extremely profitable Latin American markets open and 'friendly' for its products and investments, as well as to defuse opposition towards the Common Agricultural Policy.

However, the EU, like all other major players of the WTO, knows at heart that a free trade area agreement of this nature is a legal and political impossibility. For this reason, they do not attach exaggerated importance to this deliberately protracted negotiation exercise. The EU cannot open their agricultural markets through a free trade agreement with Mercosul without negotiating agricultural issues with the US. Furthermore, they cannot celebrate a free trade agreement with Mercosul without including agricultural products, due to the requirements of coverage of products established by the WTO. Therefore, Mercosul insistence on the negotiation of a free trade agreement with the inclusion of agricultural products tends to harm the political climate between the two areas. As a consequence, the possibilities of political and technological co-operation between Mercosul and the EU (which have a long-range importance for the creation of a multipolar world system), is an objective of much greater relevance to Mercosul and Brazil, rather than the eventual and improbable world trade liberalisation in agricultural products.

CHINESE AND JAPANESE FOREIGN POLICY

The main long-term objective of Chinese foreign policy strategy is to consolidate its position as a Great Power in a multipolar world system in which Europe and the US will necessarily participate, but will not be hegemonic, especially in Asia. The reincorporation of Taiwan into the Chinese territory is the most important specific short-term objective of the PRC. All other objectives are subordinated to this short-term goal, and in light of it, all political (and economic) manoeuvres should be analysed.

On the other hand, the objective of all American strategic movements is to prevent the emergence of independent, potentially hostile and highly competitive actors in Asia (China plus Japan), in Europe (EU plus Russia) and in the Americas (Argentina plus Brazil). The divisive manoeuvres of

American foreign policy *lato sensu* are permanent. They have the support of co-opted elites in each one of those areas, who are fascinated by the idealised world-wide struggle of liberalism against authoritarianism; or frightened by the prospect of a defeat after a 'clash' of Eastern versus Western civilisations; or linked by a myriad of economic interests to American businesses.

China recognises the sensitive nature of this American strategic objective, and acts carefully to attain step by step its own objectives: the reunification of the mainland (Hong Kong, Macao and Taiwan); settling frontier disputes to the North with Russia; stimulating the withdrawal of American troops from the Asia mainland; and gradually approaching Japan. Simultaneously, China has developed a diversified economic policy to consolidate material progress and to increase economic ties and prestige with the Chinese diaspora in South East Asia. China also seeks to establish links with American and European business, in order to make difficult the articulation of hostile alliances of Western interests against its long-range objectives.

On its side, Japan's main objective is to recover full autonomy and the status of political Great Power that it has enjoyed in the past. This status was lost with the defeat and humiliation at the end of the Second World War, symbolised by the American-written constitution, the 'castration' of military power, the loss of divine identity of the Emperor and the establishment of American military bases in Japanese territory.

American military bases are the most visible proof of the less than full sovereignty of Japan. The patient effort to end the American military presence in Japan and the half-willing acceptance of the role of the Western ally in Asia to be able to recover military independence and to gain a seat in the Security Council of the UN are long-range goals carefully pursued by the Japanese elite. Furthermore, in order to attain nuclear capability, it is essential for Japanese political objectives and for the exercise of regional influence. Japan already has the technology, the plutonium and the financial resources necessary to build nuclear weapons and carrier missiles.

The structural problem of Japanese society is the scarcity of natural resources, which were, are and will be essential for industrial (and military) activities. The indices of the Japanese consumption of imported strategic inputs contribute to the explanation of the direction of historical Japanese expansion to get access to the natural resources and markets of the Asian mainland. Therefore, a long-term close economic relationship with China is a natural objective, short of military conquest and occupation, which would be impossible and unthinkable today. The political alliance between China and Japan would have to overcome the rivalries and grievances of the past, but should not be considered a complete impossibility. In fact, the extraordinary levels of trade and investment already attained contribute to this aim. The articulation of a Sino-Japanese bloc, even if informal, to face the West in the strategic games of the future multipolar world, is a long-term possibility that haunts strategists in Washington.

Due to these political, geographical and cultural reasons China and Japan tend to view South America and Mercosul as distant and exotic regions, very much under the influence of the US (and Europe). However, in spite of this and due to their permanent interest in multipolarity and their recognition of the importance of Mercosul (especially of Brazil) industrial and technological development, they would have (as they had in the past) great interest in consistent, concrete and permanent programmes of scientific and technological co-operation, especially in those more restricted and zealously guarded fields.

A NOTE ON INDIA

The position of India is extremely delicate in the Asian geopolitical scenario and power game, pressed by China to the North, and by the irremovable rivalry with Pakistan to the West. The serene consideration of the potentialities of its large territory and population, a desire for an autonomous place in the world system, and historical links, would probably make it move politically towards a closer alliance with Russia as well as a building of links with South Africa. In spite of difficulty in visualising the possibility, there may be an interesting long-range strategic opportunity for Brazil to work towards the articulation of concrete co-operation programmes of technological and political nature among Mercosul/South Africa/India. This initiative might effectively complement Mercosul political movements towards the North of South America. This will be a much more arduous political articulation than it may first appear, because it will face, if it develops seriously and successfully beyond the inoffensive level of rhetoric, the strong resistance of the US. Furthermore, it will also develop resistance in the circles under its traditional influence in that sub-region.

A NOTE ON RUSSIAN FOREIGN POLICY

Russian foreign policy will concentrate its attentions and concerns in the next decades in its 'near abroad', in dealing with extremely complex separatist movements inside the Russian Federation, and in its relations with

Europe and Asia. The present situation of domestic economic inarticulation and retrogression makes it difficult to imagine a more active Russian
foreign policy in other regions of the world, including South America. This
is especially true after the loss of prestige and image of Russia during the
1990s. However, the emergence of a strong political domestic centralisation
movement, the reaffirmation of national self-esteem and a stronger (auto-
cratic?) government in Russia, which is a hypothesis that should not be
easily discarded, would have very profound consequences for the world
political scene. It would certainly contribute to multipolarity and to the
opening of a wider manoeuvring space for the greater peripheral states and
organisations such as Mercosul.

A NOTE ON THE ARAB WORLD

It was the permanent Arab–Israel–US confrontation in the Middle East
that led to the oil price hikes in 1969 and 1973, and had the unforeseen consequence of imploding the economic and political articulation of peripheral countries (in the 77-Group in the UN and in the Non-aligned
Movement) towards a more democratic organisation of the world political
and economic system. The oil crises divided the Third World into oil
exporting (and suddenly rich countries) and oil importing (and suddenly
ruined countries), and had a profound impact on the Non-aligned
Movement. The transfer of the enormous financial windfall from the Arab
states to Western banks brought about the petrodollars recycling effort, the
sudden disequilibrium of the foreign sectors of oil importing countries, the
recklessly induced indebtedness of many countries, the adoption of fluctu-
ating interest rates in loan contracts, and the consequent foreign debt crises
that resulted from the US policy of suddenly raising interest rates to strato-
spheric heights.

There are many factors that have made it extremely difficult for the Arab
world to articulate a common and consistent strategy in the political world
system, except in occasional manifestations of 'oil price politics'. They
include: the fundamental reactionary nature of oil monarchies, their links
with the US and Europe; the irresolvable nature of the Israeli situation; the
fundamentalist movements created or at least carefully nourished by the
US as part of its anti-Russian strategy in Afghanistan; the internal rift
between fundamentalist Islam and modern Islam; and the central role of
the US in the region. However, the Arab world and fundamentalism fulfil
an important role as a 'bogeyman' in the ideological effort of the US administration to justify the huge American military budget.

A NOTE ON SOUTH AFRICA

South African foreign policy still suffers from the psychologically inherited consequences of the Apartheid white regime, and the supposed need to present the new black African regime as reliable, and the 'new' South Africa as a 'normal', well-behaved progressive country, friendly to the economic and political Great Powers. This psychological attitude, the scarcity of personnel, and the complexities of the political situation in Sub-Saharan Africa, and in some of South Africa's neighbouring countries, make it difficult for South African foreign policy to articulate a strategy beyond relations with the Great Powers. Furthermore, it is hard to build concrete co-operation programmes in the political and economic fields with other states and organisations of the periphery, such as Mercosul. South Africa has an inherent internal instability, which is aggravated by the audacious application of conservative economic policies in a country with the characteristics of income concentration and growing political frustration. This may reserve some surprises for the future orientation of South African domestic and foreign policy.

A NOTE ON MEXICAN FOREIGN POLICY

Mexico's foreign policy has a special importance for the political role of Mercosul in South America, in Latin America, and in the world. Therefore, it deserves at least a short comment. Mexican radical change of foreign policy contributed to the political inarticulation of Third World countries in multilateral and regional economic negotiations. Furthermore, this radical change also had important political consequences and strongly affected Latin America' s attitude towards the US policy in the continent.

Mexican demand for free trade negotiations with the US and Canada (without asking for preferential treatment), its acceptance of America's position in regard to intellectual property rights, and of American proposals in the Uruguay Round negotiations, gave special support for internal neoliberal pressures in Latin American countries asking for change in traditional foreign economic policies. Furthermore, it gave support for the renunciation of its demands for preferential and non-reciprocal treatment in negotiations with developed countries.

After its admission into NAFTA, Mexico started an aggressive campaign to convince Latin American governments of its unchanged Latin American nature, and of its special condition as a 'door to Latin American investments [*sic*] in and exports to' the US market. The Mexican negotiations of free trade, or preferential bilateral agreements with certain Latin American countries (such as Colombia and Venezuela) to form the G-3, and the Mexico-Uruguay agreement, were part of a strategy to preserve the trade preferences Mexico enjoyed in ALADI. In addition, they helped mollify opposition to Mexico's radical change of foreign policy, and even to open the way to future FTAA negotiations.

The example of Mexico was important for the decision of other Latin American governments when accepting the American proposal for negotiations towards the constitution of a Free Trade Area of the Americas (FTAA). However, Mexico' s special geographical position, and the access (legal or illegal) of its population to the US labour market, with the consequent immigrant remittances, are not valid for other Latin American countries. Therefore, they delude themselves when they think that if they agree to participate in a FTAA, they will reap the same 'benefits' as Mexico supposedly does.

MERCOSUL

For South America, a region that has twice as much territory and a larger population than the US, in order to be able effectively to defend its long-run interests in an unstable, violent and arbitrary world, it is imperative to work consistently for the emergence of a multipolar world system. Within this system, South America should aim to constitute one of the poles, rather than just a sub-region of any other political or economic pole.

The patient, persistent and gradual building of the political union of South America, and a firm and serene rejection of policies that submit the region to the strategic interests of the US, must constitute the centre of this strategy. To achieve this objective, Mercosul is an essential instrument. This is to the extent that Brazil and Argentina, if they keep isolated and, worse, contradictory foreign policies, will not be able to play an effective international role. They will tend to compete wastefully for influence. Furthermore, obviously without close co-operation between Brazil and Argentina, Mercosul political co-ordinated action, and even more South America political common action, would be a total impossibility.

Mercosul means Brazil and Argentina.[1] This in the same way that the EU means Germany and France, and NAFTA means the US and Canada. When thinking about Mercosul, we have to realise that Argentina and Brazil must actively build a reasonable identity of world view, a common comprehension of the possibilities of action, a close co-operation, and a system that promotes a 'perception' of equilibrium of costs and benefits between them. These factors are essential to articulate an affirmative and positive international political role for Mercosul (and for themselves).

If these efforts are not undertaken daily, Mercosul may become, at most, a political instrument for the 'adaptation' and submission of foreign policies of its member countries to American hegemonic interests in the world. It would never become an instrument for the construction of South America political union and of a multipolar economic, political and military world system, which should be legitimate goals for South American societies.

The Mercosul Mechanism for Political Consultation and Co-ordination (MPCC) has given great emphasis to the implementation of the so-called 'democratic clause' which led to the adoption of the Ushuaia Protocol between the Mercosul countries plus Bolivia and Chile. Another focus of Mercosul MPCC has been the continuation of efforts to disarm the Armed Forces of the region, not only in the area of nuclear, biological and chemical weapons, but also in the area of land mines and conventional weapons. The Declaration of Ushuaia, mentioning in its preamble the Tlatelolco Treaty, the Mendoza Declaration on Chemical and Biological Weapons, established Mercosul, Bolivia and Chile as a Peace Zone, free from weapons of mass destruction (without, however, mentioning the passage or stationing of these weapons in ships of third countries). There are no permanent co-ordination mechanisms besides the realisation of high level political meetings on the occasion of Mercosul meetings.

It is possible to conclude that the political co-ordination efforts of Mercosul countries have been more successful in relation to two topics of special interest to the United States policy for the region: first, the disarmament of the area, and second, the maintenance of formal democratic regimes, transparent and open to external political and economic influence. The democratic compromise or 'democratic clause' is a deviation from the traditional non-intervention in internal affairs principle and may, in the future, pose very delicate questions when it comes to its implementation. The political co-ordination among Mercosul countries was much less effective in relation to the general initiatives of the foreign policies of the two main member countries, and the day-to-day activities in negotiations in all political international fora of the UN system and of the OAS system or the Rio Group.

In spite of the efforts to co-ordinate the political initiatives of Mercosul members (the so-called 'Mercosul Politico'), and due in part to the non-existence of common permanent institutions to co-ordinate this military/political role, what actually happened in the recent past was not a jointly planned political action of Mercosul. Rather, it was predominantly

a series of initiatives mainly conducted by Argentina in a bold and flamboy-
ant fashion, received critically by Brazil many times. However, some of
those initiatives were tolerated, or later accepted, and they were even followed in a discrete, traditional and responsible way. This process could
give, to an outside observer, the illusion of the existence of a co-ordinated
and planned joint Mercosul political action since 1990.

The period from 1990 to 1999 is an exceptional historical period. This
is because of a similar interpretation of the world, of acceptance by one
partner of some of the political initiatives of the other partner, and of a perception of long-run interest and equilibrium in Brazil–Argentina economic
relations. It does not mean that the emphasis, the enthusiasm, and the
tactics of foreign policy were equal in the two countries. It also does not
mean that there were not moments of disagreement, dissatisfaction and
irritation.

The political view that became hegemonic in Brazil and Argentina from
1989 to 1999 was a consequence of the sudden and bloodless victory of the
US over the Soviet Union, which supposedly would inaugurate a New
World Order. This New Order would be peaceful, with the end of all conflicts, whether global (East vs. West; North vs. South) or regional (Central
America, Angola), because at the bottom of all conflicts was the communist
influence. However, there was a residue of conflict and the possibility that
certain countries, or groups inside countries, would not accept the New
Order and would thus jeopardise it. As a consequence, all efforts at the
multilateral, regional and national levels should be made to disarm the
world, especially in 'less responsible' developing countries, and to avoid
proliferation of weapons of mass destruction. Confrontation among countries should be replaced by co-operation and by the diplomatic practice,
which some analysts call the 'new geometry of power'. Old stereotypes and
ideas, such as ex-colonies versus ex-metropolises, developed versus developing and North versus South, should disappear from the political and
ideological arena. In this 'new geometry' diplomacy, countries should
search for alliances beyond and regardless of their common identities,
developed or developing, rich or poor, belonging to the same region or not,
etc. In the internal political sphere, liberal Western democracy had proved
to be more efficient as a political and social system than socialism and
authoritarianism. Therefore, all countries, for a matter of logical behaviour,
should adopt Western model democratic regimes, with free periodic elections, Western legal systems, separation of powers, democratic civilian
leaders, and effective human rights legislation and policies.

The economic view of the world was very similar in the two countries.
Neoliberal capitalism with the end of the Soviet Union and its conversion

to capitalism, proved to be technologically and economically more efficient than socialism, or even than any other form of capitalism. However, neoliberal capitalism, in order to bear all its fruits, should thrive in a friendly atmosphere in each country and among all countries. Governments should adopt classical economic policies, whose successful historical application had been interrupted by the accidents of Communism, Nazism, colonialism and extensive state intervention, based on Keynesianism. There should be true belief in free competition in free markets, and therefore downsizing of the state should be quick, irreversible and total. Deregulation of all markets – labour, capital and technology – should be complete and no areas should remain 'reserved' or out of limits for private companies. No discrimination among companies due to size or nationality should be accepted, and therefore no antitrust legislation and no limits to their action should remain. Barriers to the free flow of goods and capital among all countries should be removed for the greater efficiency and well-being of the world globalised economy, which would equally benefit all countries.

According to this view, military regimes had been strictly military (non-civilian) and responsible for economic stagnation, inflation, corruption, regulation and bureaucracy, business discrimination, voluntary development programmes, capital flight, authoritarianism, human rights violations and confrontation with the Great Powers. Therefore, for political, economic and strategic reasons, Armed Forces should be reduced in size, placed under civilian control, demystified in the eyes of public opinion and reduced to internal security activities such as police and drug trafficking control. In South America, these measures would prevent a regional arms race and competition (Brazil–Argentina), military adventurism (Malvinas), risk of conflict (Argentina–Chile–Peru), as well as promote democracy, reduce antagonism and suspicion of the Great Powers, and therefore win their respect and friendly co-operation. Foreign policies based on 'peripheral realism' and the twin theory of 'scarcity of power' would avoid confrontation with powerful countries and the inevitable and terrible resulting damages.

Argentina's elites, for several historical reasons, were very much convinced of the above sketched interpretation of the world and of their own societal possibilities. They considered that the *status* of Argentina as an advanced nation in the 1910s and 1920s was lost by the mistaken policies of a succession of governments that tried to abandon the traditional agro-exporting natural advantages and artificially industrialise the country. Antagonism with the US was seen as a constant, self-defeating permanent feature of Argentina's foreign policy, at least since the refusal to accept the free trade area proposal presented by the US in 1899. Later, this confrontational attitude turned against Britain with fateful consequences.

Military regimes had been very closed and violent in repression, resulting in an estimated 30,000 deaths and disappearances. Finally, they looked at neighbouring Brazil as an example of success in co-operating with the US, and with the result of being able to overcome Argentina economically, and in political influence in the region such as in Paraguay, Uruguay and Bolivia.

Therefore, Argentina's foreign policy in the Carlos Menem presidency was very much the result of four traumatic experiences:

1. the defeat in the Malvinas War and its economic consequences;

2. the brutality and inefficiency of previous military regimes;

3. the experience of almost hyperinflation and the failure of heterodox economic stabilisation plans; and

4. the perception of decadence in prosperity and relative loss of historical prestige and power even in Latin America.

The Menem government strategy was to change, radically and abruptly, Argentina's economic and foreign policy, and to wholeheartedly align the country with the US and with the European Powers in order to demonstrate:

1. the credibility and reliability of the Argentine government's policies;

2. the peaceful, harmless and predictable nature of Argentina's foreign policy;

3. the irrevocable acceptance by Argentina of orthodox economic policies as symbolised by the legal adoption of the peso–dollar parity.

With this radical realignment of internal and external policies, the short- and medium-term objectives of the Argentinean government were:

1. the re-establishment of diplomatic relations with the EU countries and especially with the United Kingdom;

2. the suspension of the EU economic embargo;

3. the diplomatic and peaceful recognition of Argentina's sovereignty over the Malvinas;

4. the participation as a full member in exclusively Western institutions, such as NATO and OECD;

5. the *status* of main partner of the US in the execution of its Latin American policy; and finally

6. the right to recover its 'lost' and 'rightful position' in the civilised and developed world.

The two central simultaneous objectives of Carlos Menem's foreign policy seemed to be the peaceful recognition of sovereignty over the Malvinas, or at least to reach some form of joint British–Argentine sovereignty over the Isles. Furthermore, it aimed to obtain economic and financial support for the programme of modernisation and normalisation, actually 'transformation towards the past', and 'modern' reinsertion of the Argentine economy in the world. To achieve these objectives it was considered necessary to, first of all, transform Argentina into a 'normal' (underdeveloped, post-colonial) country: peaceful, unarmed, friendly to foreigners, militarily co-operative, submissive and respectful of the Great Powers' natural superiority and ascendancy.

In order to attain these central objectives, Argentina considered that it had to disarm. Therefore, it was necessary to convince the Brazilian government and its Armed Forces of the sincerity of this new strategy and foreign policy. The military question with Brazil and Chile was central. Argentina's new civilian government had to reassure the Argentine military of the absence of threat from Brazil (and from Chile) and therefore of the absence of risk in the policy of reducing the size of the Armed Forces. Voluntary disarmament was a supposed condition to persuade the US and the United Kingdom that the risk of Argentina's military revanchism and authoritarianism had disappeared, and that it was economically profitable and politically feasible to support Argentina's economic programme. Disarmament was presented as a 'reasonable' policy for Brazil as well, because after Argentina's disarmament (conventional and non-conventional), there would be no threat in the region. Argentina would have no weapons, other countries in the region were small and peaceful and the US was a distant and non-aggressive country and, besides, it was militarily invincible.

The normalisation of political relations with Chile was reached with the successful negotiation from 1990 to 1999 of 24 border disputes, the Beagle arbitration, the signing of the Peace and Friendship Treaty and the celebration of agreements for the exploitation of natural resources in the Andean border region. In relation to Brazil, besides the specific military issue, the situation was more complex. The question was how to align, radically, Argentina's foreign (and military) policy with the US without raising

Brazilian suspicions, and simultaneously keeping the Brazilian markets open for Argentinean products, a situation obtained with the signature of the Asunción Treaty. These double, and seemingly contradictory, objectives were possible to attain due to the basic similarity of world views entertained by the ruling elites of the two countries. This was despite occasional disagreements over specific issues, and due to the Brazilian strong desire to preserve Mercosul and the trade partnership with Argentina.

A list of public declarations and official initiatives illustrates the character of Argentina's foreign policy during the Carlos Menem presidency, in its extreme effort to win the acceptance of the Great Powers:

- 1990: only Latin American country to participate with troops and battleships in the Gulf War;
- 1991: voluntary dismantling of the Condor II missile project;
- 1991: presentation of candidacy to join NAFTA;
- 1991: transfer to civilian control of space activities (CONAE);
- 1991: strident exit from the Non-aligned Movement;
- 1991: approximation towards Israel, first country to be visited by Menem in the Middle East;
- 1992: formal request for admission into OECD;
- 1992: abstention in UN General Assembly voting of resolution condemning American embargo to Cuba;
- 1993: adhesion to the Missile Technology Control Regime (MTCR);
- 1994: adhesion to the Non-proliferation Treaty (NPT);
- 1994: proposal for the creation of a United Nations white-helmet force;
- 1994: support to US intervention in Haiti;
- 1997: active antiterrorist initiatives, including the organisation of the II Hemispheric Conference on Terrorism;
- 1997: admission by the US into the category of special extra-NATO ally;
- 1997: new formal request for admission into OECD;
- 1998: 'charm offensive' to gain support of Malvinas' residents for Argentine claims;

- 1999: formal request for admission into NATO;

- 1999: support to the American plan of sending troops to Colombia to control the civil war;

- 1999: full support to NATO's unilateral action in Kosovo;

- 1999: defence of transfer of legal intervention right from the United Nations to NATO;

- 1999: official request for American support for the dollarisation of the Argentine economy;

- support to US resolutions in the UN regarding human rights in Cuba;

- public definition of United States/Argentina relations as 'carnal relations';

- exit from the developing countries group and admission into the Western Group in the Disarmament Conference;

- support to American military strategy to fight drug production in Colombia;

- support of American proposals in FTAA negotiations;

- militant criticism of the Cuban regime;

- declaration that Argentina was more a European than a Latin American country;

- active participation in United Nations peace-keeping operations;

- candidacy to APEC;

- voluntary acceptance of limits to the emission of pollutant gases in the context of the Kyoto Protocol.

Due to specific historical reasons, Brazil was much more reluctant to adopt a 'new' foreign policy that would radically change its traditional positions. Brazilian economic development was a success story during a long period, transforming the Brazilian economy into one of the largest industrial economies in the world. Brazil's political relations with the Great Powers had been a mix of co-operation, demand, confrontation and accommodation since at least 1930. This mixing pot of relations led to important results, such as the negotiation of Brazilian entry in the Second World War and the attraction of foreign investments during the Kubitschek period.

Military regimes in Brazil were less corrupt, more efficient and much less violent than in Argentina, and in Brazilian historical experience there had been nothing similar to the Malvinas episode. In the end, the number of neighbouring countries, the extension of frontiers, the traditional campaign to internationalise the Amazon region, the historical rivalry, and the memory of resentments between the Republican regimes in Spanish America and the Brazilian Empire were all factors that prevented the full impact of the 'co-operative security' policies championed by Argentina, with strong US support, on the role of Armed Forces in Brazil.

During the 1990s, Brazil's foreign policy shared the same objective with Argentina's strategy. The aim was to present Brazil as a 'mainstream' country, a normal country, no longer developing and confrontational, but only an 'unjust' country. Brazil was a nation willing to recognise its 'sins' and guilt, and was ready to repent for its previous economic behaviour, and for some political deviations of conduct. None, however, were remotely similar to the 'disrespect' shown by Argentina in the Malvinas episode. Brazilian foreign policy aligned itself with the supposed demands of the economic stabilisation plan, trying to help in all possible ways its implementation. In this manner, Brazil assumed some political initiatives in the hope of obtaining the support and appreciation of the economic (and political) Great Powers. The 'new' political foreign policy put special emphasis onto the so-called new global issues to which the US attributed special importance. These were issues such as human rights, environment, terrorism and drugs and the promotion of democracy, regardless of the traditional principle of non-interference, which was a historic pillar of Brazilian foreign policy. Brazilian new foreign policy presented itself as one based on 'high moral ground' principles, unselfish, generous and peaceful, ready to anticipate (economic and political) concessions without reciprocity for the 'superior interests of mankind'.

Some of the Brazilian foreign policy initiatives were justified by the two principles of political support for the economic reform, and the stabilisation programme and 'high moral principles':

- 1994: enthusiastic initial acceptance of the Free Trade Area of the Americas (FTAA);

- 1994: acceptance of the developed countries' proposals for the treatment of intellectual property, investments and services in the Uruguay Round;

- adhesion to the Missile Technology Control Regime (MTCR);

- adhesion to the Non-proliferation Treaty (NPT);

- condemnation of Indian nuclear explosions;

- final support to NATO actions in Kosovo;

- reduction of Armed Forces through the reduction of military budgets;

- decision to create a Defence Ministry under civilian control;

- renouncing the demand for non-reciprocal preferential treatment in economic negotiations;

- 'civilianisation' of the Brazilian Space Agency.

However, several Brazilian initiatives were not in line with US interests and positions, such as:

- 2000: support to Fujimori right for re-election against foreign interference in Peru;

- 2000: refusal to give active support to the Colombia Plan;

- 2000: organisation of the South American Presidential Summit;

- 2000: refusal to accept American military bases in Brazil;

- strong support for the creation of the International Criminal Court;

- refusal to accept voluntary targets for gas emissions in the context of the Kyoto Protocol;

- the 'building blocs' and 'global undertaking' negotiating proposals in the FTAA process;

- initial condemnation of NATO action in Kosovo;

- continuity of the space programme;

- continuity of the nuclear submarine programme;

- candidacy to a permanent seat in the UN Security Council;

- proposals for the disarmament of nuclear nations in the UN disarmament conference;

- refusal of American proposals regarding the inclusion of social and environmental clauses in trade agreements; and

- opposition to the Helms–Burton Act.

Besides discomfort in Brazil with several of the most sudden, publicised and 'mediatic' Argentinean foreign policy initiatives, Argentine delegations have actively aligned themselves with the American or developed countries' positions in negotiations in different fora. One special case of opposition of views was regarding the Brazilian candidacy to the UN Security Council that was publicly rejected by the Menem government. This orientation of Argentina's foreign policy created an increasing malaise in the most diverse sectors of the Brazilian administration and, together with a bureaucratic treatment of diplomatic activity and trade frictions, it limited co-operation and resurrected old resentments and stereotypes.

The articulation of an effective non-aligned Mercosul political role will be facilitated by the frustrated expectations in relation to the evolution of the economic, political and military regional and world environment since 1989. The implementation of neoliberal economic policies in the developing peripheral countries was afflicted by a sequence of crises in the so-called 'emerging markets'. In some cases this resulted in serious economic retrogression, or at least stagnation, aggravation of poverty, economic denationalisation, increased corruption and greater external vulnerability. The economic and social promises of the apologists of globalisation and of neoliberal policies failed, and nowadays, criticism of globalisation asymmetries, technological divide, extreme volatility of capital flows, continuous protectionism and internal subsidies of developed countries are common everywhere. This is true even in the public reports of conservative international financial agencies and in the speeches of political leaders, even of those leaders that continue to support and to implement neoliberal policies.

These crises and their consequences both directly and indirectly affected Brazil and Argentina. In spite of all efforts made to implement the recommended policies, imposed or supported by the IMF and the US, the economic and social situation in both countries is extremely serious, and the effects of domestic crisis in each country impacted on Mercosul performance and image. Mercosul is now strongly criticised in Brazil and Argentina, and considered by some analysts and politicians as having reached a deadlock situation and being a flawed or insufficient scheme in urgent need of reform. From the *status* of a beyond criticism, successful project, Mercosul became a sort of obstacle to the execution of some national economic policies, especially in the face of latent external crisis and the eventual need to control imports. On the other hand, political and military alignment and careful non-confrontation with the Great Powers did not bring the expected economic benefits; nor did it reduce the arbitrary exercise of power, conflicts and the stockpiling of weapons by powerful countries or did it give more voice and influence in world affairs to 'co-operative' peripheral countries. Concentration of power and arbitrary use of force are now the two central characteristics of the world scene, and the disarmament of Southern Cone countries did not reduce the risk of conflict in South America. On the contrary, it facilitated, and was followed by, growing American military interference in the region.

As a reminder of the extent to which many of the expectations and hopes enjoyed at the beginning of the 1990s have not materialised (to the increasing disappointment of Brazilian and Argentinean elites), a short list of events follows:

- 1997: US trade sanctions against Argentine exports;

- 1997: American sale of military planes to Chile;

- persistent UK refusal to negotiate the issue of sovereignty over the Malvinas Islands;

- American pressure to get GATT-plus concessions in economic negotiations;

- NATO and OECD countries' refusal to accept Argentina as a full member;

- United States' refusal to support the Argentine dollarisation proposal;

- consistent refusal of the main financial centre and governments, specially the United States, to impose legal control over volatile international capital flows;

- refusal of nuclear nations to fulfil their commitments to disarm according to article 6 of NPT;

- increase of emission of pollutant gases by developed countries in disrespect of targets accepted in international agreements;

- insistence of developed countries that developing countries accept voluntary gas emission reduction targets in contradiction to the Kyoto protocol;

- increased American political intervention in South America, as happened in the elections in Peru;

- failure of the economic strategy based on the dollar–peso parity;

- loss of international competitiveness due to the so-called foreign exchange anchor;

- increased frictions in Mercosul, due to accelerated tariff reduction, unco-ordinated exchange rate policies and absence of compensatory policies;

- increased protectionist unilateral measures in the United States, such as in the case of Brazilian steel;

- American refusal to supply weapons to Argentina;

- APEC refusal of Argentina's request for admission;

- United States' insistent demand for trade opening measures in Mercosul, in spite of trade deficits in member countries and their need to achieve trade superavits;

- increased unemployment and social unrest in the region; and

- modest growth rates.

SUGGESTIONS

There are therefore reasonable grounds to justify a careful revaluation of Argentinean and Brazilian foreign policies, and to devise strategies to build mechanisms for a common Mercosul foreign policy. A *sine qua non* condition for the effectiveness of such a policy is to redefine a common view of the world and of the role of South America within this world.

Brazil, Argentina and Mercosul have to face the fact that the world system is more conflictive, highly competitive and violent in nature, with a strong and growing concentration and crystallisation of power, than of a peaceful, co-operative and benign system, moving towards some ideal of *pax perpetua*. There is no real evidence for widely believed and trumpeted myths such as 'trading nations', 'end of frontiers', 'science and technology brings peace', etc. The reconstruction of the old empires are in full course, and their strategic planners and ideologues have already reserved a role of 'modern colony' for South American countries: disarmed, dependent, currency-less, and administered by native technocratic proconsuls.

However, Brazil, Argentina, Mercosul and South America have specific diverse historic, cultural and economic natures. These natures are different from the countries that are participating in the mega-blocs, in the process of formations such as NAFTA, the EU and (perhaps) the Chinese 'area of co-operation'. South America, Mercosul, and even Brazil by itself, have such an economic, territorial and demographic dimension, that they cannot be incorporated with reasonably equal rights into any of those mega-blocs, including into a future FTAA.

One of the first issues that has to be dealt with then, is the nature of the participation of Mercosul and South America in the evolution of the political and economic world system towards a multipolar and conflicting configuration. Obviously, if one insists in not admitting this process of evolutionary multipolarity, or insists in considering that American hegemony will be a permanent feature of the world system (which is a hypothesis rather different from recognising the pre-eminent status of the US for a long time in this system), or that there is no such a thing as the exercise of 'joint hegemony' by the central countries, the question of Mercosul strategy would not have to be considered. In this idealistic vision of the world, Brazil, Argentina and Mercosul should just follow and adapt themselves to the 'natural' and 'beneficial' movements of a political system, supposedly without severe asymmetries. Alternatively, they should resign themselves to the inevitable role of simple followers of the *hegemon*, or actually be 'absorbed' by it.

However, a multipolar world system is not wishful thinking, but a real process in course of formation, and it is in itself a better political configuration for Brazil, for Mercosul and for South America than a unipolar system. Countries that are underdeveloped, that need capital, that are relatively weak economically, politically and militarily, and at the same time have to overcome extreme social disparities, strong social tensions and external vulnerability, will profit from a greater equilibrium and dispersion of power at the world level. They will benefit from this power equilibrium and dispersion because of the greater possibilities of multiple alliances to defend themselves from arbitrary violence, political and economic pressures, to attract capital in better conditions and to develop scientific and technological programmes. Finally, for a country with the dimensions of Brazil, participating in a multipolar system as a subordinate part of a bloc, is a political and economic situation even worse than to be a lonely country (which does not mean to be an autarchic, isolated or rogue country) in a unipolar system.

A second but simultaneous question is to develop a gradual strategy to transform Mercosul from a neoliberal, 'open integration' scheme, into an economic development regional scheme. This development scheme should have, first of all, compensation mechanisms and compensatory policies to anticipate and reduce frictions among participants over time, and to permit the recovery of the co-operative spirit necessary for the success of a process of real integration. Without reducing trade tensions (and consequent political frictions) it will be difficult, if not impossible, to advance in the design of common commercial, industrial, science and technology policies, and even more of a common foreign policy.

In tackling the issue of rebuilding Mercosul and working politically towards a multipolar system, there is an urgent need to develop a 'new thinking' in the field of agricultural production and trade. Brazil, Argentina and Mercosul have been insisting that their first priority of foreign trade policy is the reduction of, and eventual elimination of, agricultural protectionism in the EU. This position has been reiterated in the WTO negotiations and in the conversations on the free trade agreement between the EU and Mercosul. Argentina and Brazil participate actively in the Cairns Group articulated by Australia, Canada and New Zealand, which is viewed by Europe as an auxiliary instrument of the US diplomatic strategy against the European Common Agricultural Policy.

However, in spite of all the 'common sense' and diplomatic efforts already spent on this issue, it is necessary to consider the following aspects of the agricultural trade question:

1. the EU long-run strategy is not to organise a neoliberal economic group in a neoliberal, peaceful, cosmopolitan world but, rather, a political Union, with common state institutions, common Armed Forces and a single currency in a multipolar (many times violent) world. It cannot, therefore, disorganise or fragilise the agricultural sector of the European economy and become completely dependent on world trade and American food supplies;

2. the inclusion of certain Eastern European countries in the EU would necessarily reinforce the Common Agricultural Policy, those countries being as they are, traditional or potential agricultural exporters to Western European countries;

3. if the EU 'liberalises' its agricultural sector, the great beneficiaries would possibly be the US and Canada, which are more 'efficient' suppliers, and not Argentina and Brazil;

4. the 'food deficit' is so huge in Brazil that any reasonable and urgent policy to overcome this deficit would make Mercosul in itself a 'complete' market for all present and future possible agricultural production of Brazil and Argentina;

5. the insistence in agricultural trade liberalisation is a source of a permanent disagreement between Mercosul and the EU, and harms the articulation of concrete co-operation programmes in strategic fields with the EU.

Developing autonomous science and technological capabilities is an essential condition, even to become just a minor participant in the world system, be it unipolar or multipolar. The most profitable markets are those built in a monopolistic way, through the temporary exploitation of innovations, allowed by intellectual property rights legislation. The high profitability of these markets permits the recovery of capital invested in R&D and production facilities, and heavy investment in marketing and sales activities. On the other hand, in the field of known technologies of production, the R&D effort is essential to reorganise production and to reduce costs.

Countries that are not able to develop scientific and technological capability at least to follow and to imitate (not to lead) this accelerated process, cannot be industrially competitive in the world market and, even in the field of agricultural production and exports, will face increased competition. Furthermore, the military (and therefore) political effects of science and technology are essential to build not aggressive military capability, but dissuasive (and indispensable) military capability. Mercosul and South America assemble all the conditions required to develop important common programmes in science and technology in all fields. In the present stage of economic evolution, all economic activities are being reorganised by microelectronics, information and communications technology and by biotechnology and genetic engineering in the basic fields of agriculture and health. These should be the fields in which common efforts should be concentrated (and resources spent).

Mercosul (and Argentina and Brazil) face three short-term challenges in the process of articulating an autonomous political role in the multipolar world system in gestation:

1. How to resist absorption in the American economy and political bloc, which is quickly advancing through the disguised way of FTAA negotiations and gradual dollarisation.

2. How to face the possible foreign military intervention in Colombia and eventually in the whole Amazon region.

3. How to recover political control over their domestic and foreign economic policies now, under very extensive control of the IMF (and of WTO). It would be possible to develop suggestions to face these three challenges, but the dimension of this paper and the nature of these issues do not recommend to present them at the moment. However, these are 'the' very short-term questions for Mercosul (and for Brazil).

This redefinition of world view and the careful design of a concrete, articulated, set of foreign policy initiatives for Mercosul would demand permanent joint co-ordination mechanisms between the organisations in Brazil and Argentina that are responsible for the formulation and execution of foreign and military policy.[2] Periodical meetings of presidents, important as they are, cannot and should not substitute the difficult task of a permanent and detailed study of world and regional scenarios to develop common strategic perceptions and organise initiatives in the four strategic areas for Mercosul political role.

There are vital long-run strategic questions for Mercosul international role, and they may be classified as political, military, technological and economical:

1. In the economic area, the central issues are the reduction of external vulnerability and of social domestic disparities and the recovery of autonomous capacity to formulate and execute policies. Without reducing external vulnerability in the financial field and in the 'real economy' field (such as in the question of energy) it will be extremely difficult to develop an active and important international role for Mercosul. Social disparities cannot be reduced by palliative, even if generously assisted, programmes, and they have to be solved through employment and productivity raising programmes and great social investments in sanitation and public health care. The submission of economic policies to close control by the IMF, when they are not formulated by the Fund, creates a situation of reduced sovereignty that, properly speaking, 'spills over' the political field.

2. In the technological field, the urgent pooling of resources and efforts in the two strategic fields of information (and communications) technology and biotechnology (and genetic engineering) is essential, even just to keep the capacity to compete in the world economy and political/military system. The removal of economic bottlenecks should be the focus of science and technology common Mercosul programmes.

3. In the military field, the two basic issues are the development of autonomous defence capacity in the conventional field and in the highly advanced technology fields, and the serene refusal to any attempt to establish foreign military bases in South American territory. The success in dealing with these two issues will be essential for the defence of Mercosul interests abroad, and of the full exercise of sovereignty at home in a future world of great instability and arbitrariness and intervention.

In the political field *stricto sensu*, the vital question is the membership in, and the competence of the United Nations Security Council. One may reasonably expect that the UN system is not going to be discarded or thoroughly remodelled along democratic lines. This is due to the privileged participation of the Great Powers in the Security Council that do not have the remotest intention to relinquish this privilege. Space will be made to accommodate the second and third economic world powers. Currently they are Germany and Japan, and there is already a world-wide consensus on the desirability of their admission as full permanent members, with veto power, in the Council. However, the mechanics of the process to reform the Council would make it possible and necessary to include India, the second most populated country of the world, and countries 'representing' Africa, Islam and Latin America.

The competence of the Council will be gradually and informally expanded to include topics of great interest for Brazil and Mercosul, such as environment, drugs, terrorism, political regimes, poverty, etc. The Council will become the centre of the global government. The reform of the Council would be a unique opportunity to consolidate the political role of Mercosul and to permit an effective defence of its interests. Brazil and Argentina may, and should, promote their candidacy for membership in the Council, and should co-ordinate their policies actively to this end. Mercosul capacity and power and influence to act in all future international issues will depend on having, or not having, the status of a full permanent member of the Security Council of the United Nations. This status will immediately confer the possibility of becoming a member of the G-7 (G-8) and other international central co-ordination mechanisms of the world system. However, it will not be vice versa, that is, becoming a member of the G-7 does not bring the sure consequence of gaining a full permanent seat in the Security Council.

NOTES

1. An effective co-ordination of Brazilian and Argentinean foreign policies would certainly be able to obtain Uruguayan and Paraguayan support due to the nature of their relations with the two main partners of Mercosul, and it would be necessary due to their fragile position in face of 'tempting' (even if small) concessions of the Great Powers (especially the US) directly or through third countries to fracture eventual common positions of Mercosul. For this reason, Uruguay and Paraguay foreign policies will not be dealt with in this text.

2. To build a common view of the world and common policies and political initiatives, Brazil and Argentina would have to develop pragmatic and effective co-ordination mechanisms:
   (a) to promote the immediate renegotiation of Mercosul mechanisms to increase flexibility and

establish compensatory and industrial reorganisation funds with adequate and permanent resources proportional to the increase of interzonal trade;

(b) to organise common R&D programmes in selected fields adequately funded with proper and permanent resources;

(c) to organise frequent reserved informal meetings of political advisers of the Foreign Office, the Defence Ministry and the Economy Ministry at several levels of responsibility;

(d) to organise joint programmes for permanent training of diplomatic and military officers at several career levels;

(e) to develop joint studies on specific international issues;

(f) to avoid dispersion of diplomatic efforts and define priority countries (neither regions nor continents) to concentrate scarce diplomatic resources and to establish strategic operative alliances;

(g) to develop a common commercial policy effort to remove obstacles to industrial exports of Mercosul in third countries;

(h) to co-ordinate initiatives in the existing political fora such as the OAS, Rio Group, Ibero American Conference, Defence Ministers Conferences, etc. to assure a common negotiating front.

SEVEN

Globalisation, Argentina and Mercosul*

ALDO FERRER

In Argentina, positive signals of economic growth and price stability, together with an increase in unemployment, poverty and social exclusion, currently coexist. Mercosul, in turn, is confronting increasing difficulties and uncertainties. There is a connecting link that explains those conflicting tendencies, namely, the quality of responses to the challenges and opportunities of globalisation.

Previous studies have developed this conceptualisation. They point to the fact that the existence of a global order confronts every country with challenges. The answer to those challenges will determine its development path.[1] The economic history and the analysis of the current situation of each country are examinable through the 'good' or 'bad' quality of the responses to globalisation. It requires taking into account the complex network of historical, economical, social and political circumstances, which will finally delineate each country's path, and its insertion in the world-wide order. This viewpoint can also be applied to the analysis of a regional integration process, such as Mercosul.

If Argentina and Mercosul now have a poor performance, it is due – from such a perspective – to the result of very unfortunate responses to the challenges of globalisation. In Argentina, the problem is not new,[2] like indeed in the rest of Latin America.[3] Today, mistakes are at a higher cost than in the past because of the overwhelming sphere of globalisation. Allow me here a brief personal reference. At the beginning of the 1980s, in the threshold of the debt crisis, I published a book entitled *Vivir con lo nuestro*.[4] It suggested that it was essential to put the house in order, balance the international payments and, on those bases, negotiate with creditors. The external liabilities could then be honoured without resigning the fundamental interests of the country. The contrast of that proposal with the hegemonic

thought, namely, the 'fundamentalist vision' of globalisation,[5] still rever-
berates. In almost all the public presentations of my views, in conferences
or meetings, someone always asks about *Vivir con lo nuestro*, about its feasibility in a global world. This possibly displays the underlying suspicion
that the direction taken, in the antipodes of that recommendation, has not
given good results in the end.

Before making a brief analysis of Argentina's behaviour with reference
to globalisation, and the Mercosul situation, it is necessary to identify
certain relevant elements of the global order for this analysis.

GLOBALISATION

International capital movements

International capital movements in the second half of the twentieth century
have grown much more than real variables of the world economy, such as
production, employment, investment and trade. For instance, international
net loans stood for 8 per cent of international trade in 1964; at present, it
represents more than 100 per cent.

The great majority of funds are concentrated in speculative operations
that arbitrate interest and exchange rates and stock price variations.
Deregulation of financial transactions and the transformation of markets
prompted by the informatics revolution, have created a mega-market on a
world-wide scale. This market operates, taking into account the local time
differences of the principal markets, practically 24 hours a day, seven days
a week.

The increase of financial currents is not reflected in an increase of real
productive and social capital accumulation in the world economy. The
investment rate is maintained in the order of 20 per cent to 25 per cent. The
international financial market is mostly a self-contained system of assets
and liabilities transactions. Its influence on the real process of capital accumulation is mostly due to its effects on customer behaviour (the wealth
effect), rates of interest and governments' macro-economic policies.

The increase of private direct investment has also been substantial. At
present, 60,000 trans-national corporations have 500,000 foreign subsidiaries. The subsidiaries' assets amount to more than US$4 trillion. Their
participation in the world product and capital accumulation is less than 10
per cent.[6]

In summary, on a world-wide average, domestic savings finance more
than 90 per cent of real capital formation. The same proportion is valid in

Argentina and Latin America. The challenge of investment policy is thus to conciliate financial globalisation and private direct investment with rules that contribute to encourage domestic savings (from enterprises, the public sector and individuals), which is the dominant source of investment financing.

New production patterns

The growth of international trade, financial flows, private direct investment and, especially, of the diffusion of information, data and image processing at a planetary scale have generated a new productive framework, strongly influenced by the global scene.[7]

These facts display the impact of micro-electronics and their multiple applications on consumer behaviour and the organisation of production and markets. Furthermore, they show this impact on the development of new capital goods and products of massive use. In turn, biotechnology and new materials have multiplied and diversified the supply of goods and services.

A remarkable result of the new technologies is the flexibility of the production organisation, due to the incorporation of multipurpose equipment (capable of producing efficiently short production series) and the workforce versatility. In multiple activities, economies of scale have disappeared. Therefore, a new frontier is open to medium and small enterprises that operate at the technological frontier, with high efficiency and competitiveness. These productive units have at their disposal the same informatics and equipment sophistication as the great corporations. In turn, the relationship between personnel and managers of those enterprises is generally more prone to assimilate industrial relations arising from new technologies. The creation of networks, hives and industrial districts of medium and small industries, and between them and great conglomerates, has strengthened the access to markets and financing. These were traditionally a blockage in the development of production units of a relatively small size. These accumulative processes within the productive structure are the principal component of what is actually referred to as the 'new economy', and a source of the productivity, incomes and investment growth.

In this way, capital, technological, organisational and market accumulation, which have been operating since the diffusion of the industrial revolution in the nineteenth century, acquire nowadays, a renewed importance.[8] The accumulation process not only takes place at company level, but also in the associative networks among companies of different size, in the industrial districts, in the hives of enterprises and in other ways of cross-company relations. This involves simultaneous subcontracting, outsourcing and other linking processes, where the aggregate value engages the participation of different companies. In new relations with suppliers and clients, demands and inventory rationalisation arise, which contribute to increasing the efficiency and competitiveness of the companies.

Many of these changes are usually related to the so-called 'knowledge society', in which the intangible assets (research and development, patents, licences, training, etc.) acquire relevant importance. The telematics, that is the convergence between informatics and telecommunication, is closely associated to this new economy, *based* on knowledge.

Endogenous dimension and global scene

These transformations take place in a context where the opening to the global order and domestic formation of technological capacities converge. Success is related to the ability of each society to incorporate globalisation signals, in order to impulse the endogenous process of capital accumulation and wealth creation. Solving the strains between the world context and the internal environment is, in the end, the key for development.

The problem is not solved by focusing only on the global market. Exports represent about 20 per cent of world-wide production, which means, on average, that domestic markets absorb 80 per cent of world output. In Argentina, Brazil and other Latin American countries, the percentage is even higher. On the other hand, the percentage of the internationalised production, which can be measured by the intra-trade of trans-national companies, represents less than 10 per cent of world output.

Domestic markets are therefore essential for demand and employment (on average about eight out of every ten workers are occupied in production for the internal demand). The new production patterns require an integrated approach for access to the domestic as well as the international market. Resources should be organised along lines able to satisfy the requirements of an open economy, but integrated in the accumulative endogenous synergy of organisation investment, knowledge, and institutional and social improvement.

Notoriously, globalisation increases the importance of the endogenous dynamic of economic and social development. The historical experience reveals that the success of countries reflects their capacity to participate intensely in trans-national transactions, grounded on the domestic accumulative processes. On this aspect, very little new exists nowadays.

Technical change strengthens the endogenous contents of development. The relative weight loss of primary products in world-wide output and demand reduces the importance of the international division of labour.

This is based on the exchange of peripheral countries' primary products for central countries' manufactured products. In the old peripheral productive structure, it was possible to incorporate technology in the primary activity and to participate in some way in the expansive currents of the world economy. This possibility has disappeared. The only means of dynamic insertion in the global order now is by way of 'intra-industrial' specialisation, which requires the existence of a complex productive structure. This cannot be imported 'turnkey'. It requires, on the contrary, the accumulative processes mentioned above. In the contemporaneous global order, the endogenous dimension of development is more important than in any other moment of the past.

Public policies

The significance of domestic market and savings, and of the endogenous dimension of development, reveals how groundless are the *assumptions* of the 'fundamentalist vision' of globalisation. Indeed, it is not true that most transactions take place in the world market, that production is mostly trans-nationalised, that capital accumulation is nowadays essentially decided by trans-national actors; nor that, consequently, the frontiers and capacity of each country to decide its own destiny have disappeared. The relevance of public policies has not vanished either.

In fact, nowadays, the quality of the response to globalisation depends largely on the efficiency of public policies and on their capacity to organise available resources, in order to join, in an equitable symmetric, non-subordinated way, the world order. An example is the experience of medium and small companies in advanced economies. Their development resulted from the coexistence of the initiative of private actors and technological, organisational, financing and trade promotion public policies. To this end, states able to mobilise resources with sufficient autonomy were required.

ARGENTINA

An apparent paradox

Once again, during the 1990s, the Argentine economy was the stage of paradoxical events. The period registered a yearly GNP growth rate close to 5 per cent and a cumulative product per capita of about 30 per cent. This was an outstanding performance, taking into account the extended previous standstill. At the same time, the high inflation installed since the end of the

1940s, and the hyperinflation in 1989/90, were replaced by price stability. Growth registered two interruptions during 1995 and 1998/9. In both cases, it seemed an inevitable consequence of the international financial turmoil.

Other significant events were the expansion of the agricultural, energy and mining natural resources frontiers, and the improvements arising from the privatisation of public services (telecommunications, electric power energy, gas, highways, etc.), the commercial networks managed by great operators, and the banking services. Foreign subsidiaries in the manufacturing sector as well as some conglomerates of domestic capital have induced a profound transformation in the production of basic supplies (aluminium, steel, petrochemicals, oil refineries), food, automobiles, and different products of massive consumption. In these branches, production concentration in few companies and an increase in investment, technology and productivity took place.

These facts are closely related to changes in the world scene and to the policies of President Menem's government. With respect to the former, it is worth remembering the change of direction of the transfer of resources to Latin America. During the 'lost decade' of the 1980s, there was a net transference of resources *from* the region to the rest of the world of US$220 billion. Since 1991, a considerable increase of private direct investment and financial flows has taken place, generating a positive net transfer of US$170 billion. This enabled the financing of the Latin American countries' current accounts deficit, and an increase of the international reserves of the monetary authorities.

Regarding the policy changes in Argentina, since the beginning of his administration, President Menem launched a strategy of privatisation, market deregulation and incentives to private direct investment and external financing. Convertibility at a fixed exchange rate at the beginning of 1991 consolidated the new strategy within a price stability context.

A series of circumstances became very favourable for the evolution of the model. The net transference of resources (capital flows minus interest and profits remittances) turned from negative into positive: from minus US$35 billion in the 1980s, to more than US$55 billion between 1992 and 1999. At the same time, price stability had a positive effect on public opinion, internal demand and the tax revenue. Fiscal resources also increased by US$20 billion due to the sale of public enterprises. All these enabled the expansion of public expenditure, private demand, production and income. However, a social uneasiness, and the perception of uncertainty about the future, accompanied this growth, stability and transformation scenario. Let us investigate some causes of this paradox.

Unemployment and poverty have reached the highest recorded levels. Average salaries in manufacturing activities have practically frozen in the 1990s, and have decreased for the major part of the workforce. Wealth and income distribution has worsened in the last years. Argentina is reaching juxtaposition with those countries with the worst record of income inequality.

The advances in some sectors have been accompanied by a contraction in regional economies and in a myriad of small and medium enterprises. Structural changes registered during the last years tend to create a dual economic system and labour market. In one segment, highly productive and growing activities prevail. In the other, low capital, technology and production levels per worker prevail.

The first segment generates about one-third of the GNP and approximately 20 per cent of total employment. It includes capital intensive manufacturing, privatised public services (particularly those with rapid technological change, like telecommunications), large commercialisation networks, companies in the new natural resources frontier, the most efficient agricultural enterprises, and services where informatics technology has penetrated. These activities have increased the proportion of imported supplies, disorganising previous links with internal production of goods and services (including the science and technology domestic system) and, as a whole (excluding primary product exports), they register a large deficit in their foreign currency transactions. These activities are characterised by a low capacity to generate employment and salaries substantially higher than the average for the labour force. Non-tradable goods and services, such as public utilities, register additional benefits due to the improvement of their relative prices.

The other segment generates about two-thirds of the GNP and approximately 80 per cent employment. These comprise the universe of small and medium companies, the major part of the regional productions and the post-privatisation national, provincial and municipal public service sector. In these areas, informal employment and a low level of productivity and salaries prevail. These activities produce, almost exclusively, for the internal market and their inputs are essentially supplied by domestic goods and services. The links of these traditional sectors with the modern area of the economy have been weakened since the middle of the 1970s, especially during the 1990s. The inferior growth rate of these activities has been worsened, in the case of traded goods, by the opening of the internal market and the movement of relative prices. They suffer the effect of a fixed exchange rate and the increase of internal costs that cannot be transferred to sale prices. These circumstances have provoked the bankruptcy and disappearance of numerous companies, particularly in metal mechanics, textile and clothing. Others, like those operating in the retail trade, could not survive the competition of the supermarket networks.

This duality of the productive system and the labour market coincides with the loss of competitiveness and the increased external debt. As we shall see later, Argentina has the highest debt ratio in Latin America (after Nicaragua). Debt services generate a growing demand for foreign currency, and those of the public sector represent increasing parts of the consolidated public expenditure. The loss of competitiveness is reflected in the persistent deficit of the trade balance.

The Argentine economy is subordinated to an enormous and growing deficit in its international payments. To the debt, and the operational foreign currency deficit of trans-national enterprises, one must add the loss of competitiveness produced by the deterioration of the productive structure and peso overvaluation. Hence, Argentine exports are largely dependent on commodities and fuels. Thus, there is an increasing gap in the technological content of foreign trade. While exports suffer the relative weakness of international demand and price instability of primary products, imports increase due to the overvaluation of the peso, and the increasing imported input coefficients of the leading economic activities.

In 1999, GNP declined 3.5 per cent, but the trade balance registered a deficit of about US$5 billion. In the new context, the traditional mechanism to re-establish the balance of payments equilibrium, that is, generating a commercial superavit by a contraction of domestic production, has been weakened. As a result of this sum of events, the need of external financing keeps increasing. At present, it reaches US$15 billion, equivalent to 4 per cent of GNP.

The conditions that were initially so favourable to the model have changed. No public assets are left for sale, the fiscal situation worsens by the stagnation of tax revenue and the growing burden of the debt services, the behaviour of international interest rates is uncertain, and price stability has exhausted its positive effect on internal demand.

Responses to globalisation

As in many other countries, today in Argentina reforms oriented to open the economy, privatise public services, eliminate regulations and transmit friendly signals to the markets prevail. These reforms were intended to produce a more efficient use of available resources, promote competitiveness, and increase production and employment. Thus, a better functioning of markets would allow an equilibrated and dynamic relationship with the rest of the world. However, as we have already seen, the results were not those promised. In fact, the new strategy incurred three fatal mistakes: an excessive debt; an indiscriminate inflow of private direct investments; and the renunciation to the management of economic policy. Let us briefly examine these three points.

External debt

The *coup d'état* in 1976 coincided with the rapid growth of international capital movements and the globalisation of financial markets. Since then, the external debt has continuously grown. In the early 1970s Argentina's foreign debt was negligible. At present it reaches US$145 billion. In the 1990s, it increased 150 per cent. In relation to export values, Argentina shows the worst debt indicator in Latin America (except Nicaragua): 5.3 times against 2.2 of the regional average. Interest on the external debt represents more than 40 per cent of export values in comparison with 17 per cent for Latin America as a whole.

The effect of the external debt on public finance is also notorious. Services of the public external debt actually represent 20 per cent of the consolidated public expenditure, a proportion four times higher than at the beginning of the 1990s.

Private direct investment

During the 1990s, there was an inflow of US$50 billion. About 80 per cent of those investments were devoted to the purchase of existing assets corresponding to privatised public utilities, and private industrial firms and commercial networks. At present, the presence of affiliates of foreign companies in the Argentine economy is probably the largest in the world. The infrastructure, the largest industrial firms, the banking system, the commercial networks, and the informatics and communication services, belong largely to non-residents. The relationship between profits remittance and exports is more than 10 per cent, while in the rest of Latin America it is around 6 per cent.

Affiliates produce mostly for the internal market, but they import supplies and capital goods, and pay royalties and dividends to their parent companies. The operational foreign currency deficit of foreign subsidiaries represents about one-third of the balance of payments deficit in the current account.

Exchange regime

The establishment of a currency board regime since 1991 was initially due to the imperious necessity of eradicating hyperinflation. The initial parity was overvalued by approximately 30 per cent. Until the convergence of internal and international prices was reached, the gap amounted to around 50 per cent. Since the beginning (as had already happened with the financial reform in 1977), the international competitiveness of the Argentine production of traded goods and services deteriorated. The opening of the domestic market to imports, together with an overvalued exchange rate, constituted an explosive combination.

Long-term high inflation and eventually hyperinflation destroyed the national currency. By 1990, the dollar largely fulfilled the roles of mean exchange and reserve value. Convertibility, in turn, has led to a chronic overvaluation and reinforced dollarisation of the Argentine economy. The dollar circulates as a mean of domestic payment, in parity with the peso. About two-thirds of the financial liabilities and assets are denominated in dollars. In such conditions, the monetary supply is determined by the evolution of the Central Bank reserves, the rate of interest reflects the 'country risk' and the fiscal deficit is limited by the access to international credit.

The consequences

These fatal responses to the challenges and opportunities of globalisation are functional to sectorial interests associated with financial speculation, the appropriation of undervalued public assets and the corruption of decision-makers on issues of vital interest to the country.

Be that as it may, the social and economic consequences were very unfortunate and a lethal blow to the self-determination of Argentina. They installed subordination to external forces without precedent. Let us examine some of the main issues.

Economic policy

The continuous and increasing need of external financing has reduced economic policy to the administration of the debt. Its main objective is to influence the market's expectations. This domestic perception of economic policy is reinforced by the creditors' conditionalities, orchestrated by the Bretton Woods institutions. The evolution of economic activities is essentially determined by exogenous factors, in the first place, by the response of international financing markets and, to a lesser degree, by the evolution of exported *commodities* prices.

The economic policy does not have the instruments to manage the economy. The currency board, which was successful in eliminating hyperinflation, implies, in fact, a situation very close to full dollarisation. The slightest suspicion about the permanence of the peso parity is confronted with the contraction of economic activity and the deterioration of social conditions.

Economic policy is limited to transmitting friendly signals to the international financial markets intended to reduce their perception of the country's risk. Thus, supposedly, rates of interest would decrease, investment would increase, and investment and employment would grow. However, that is mostly wishful thinking, which is rarely confirmed by reality.

The economic policy of Argentina is nowadays residual and it moves within narrow operating margins. Hence, it is to a large extent impotent to mobilise domestic resources and tackle the grave problems of the regional economies, small and medium companies, and the social situation. It is also impotent to face the turmoil of the international financing markets. During the so-called 'tequila effect' in 1995, and in 1997/8 owing to the Russia insolvency and the crisis in several Asian countries, the only feasible answer was recession, unemployment, and the aggravation of the social situation. Changes in the international rates of interest or the modification of the country's risk qualification, introduces an unstable element in the budget and in the international payments, unmanageable with available instruments, namely, without an exchange, fiscal or monetary policy. The same happens with the modification of the dollar and euro parity, which affects the competitive capacity of the country in different markets. The peg to the dollar impedes the rate of exchange from compensating those variations among the main currencies.

A remarkable fact of Argentina's situation is that privatised public services (electricity, water, gas, telephones, highways) have tariffs adjusted by the inflation of the United States. In the last four years, consumer prices in the US increased by 9 per cent, while in Argentina they have not changed. Therefore, whether domestic prices increase or decrease, tariffs go up. This behaviour of one segment of the economy, essential for the overall price level, together with the enormous and uncertain incidence of the debt service, determine that salaries become the only adjustment variable to sustain convertibility and the peso parity, one to one, with the dollar. In this way, Argentina is probably at present the only country in the world in which the reduction of nominal salaries becomes an instrument of economic policy.

The productive structure
Reforms inspired in the Washington Consensus, together with the external debt, the indiscriminate inflow of private direct investments and the currency board regime, produced a drastic change in the rules of the game. The state has not remained aloof on these events. On the contrary, its strategy encouraged capital and wealth concentration and punished the regional productions

and those enterprises that could not (or did not have the necessary time to) accommodate to the new context. Changes in demand composition, because of income concentration and the opening of the domestic market, direct a great part of expenditure to sectors favoured by the strategy adopted. The result is the duality that characterises the economy and the labour market.

The inflow of private direct investments consisted mainly of the purchase of public utilities, private companies, assets and trade networks already existent in Argentina. One of the consequences of these events has been the sharp reduction of personnel and the increase of productivity. Frequently, the leading economic activities have closer links with parent companies and foreign suppliers than with the domestic economy. For many firms, Argentina is at present a market intended to sell imported goods and services or, if they are produced locally, with an increasing participation of imported inputs. The problem lies in the fact that this process does not simultaneously promote exports and competitiveness.

In developed countries and the most successful emerging economies, hives and industrial districts are found that display the integration of the economy. In Argentina, instead, we find a degradation of the productive structure and the fracture of links among their principal agents. Internal links have disappeared and new bonds with the external context have emerged. Thus, globalisation does not promote synergic relations between the world market and the domestic reality. On the contrary, it encourages inarticulation and fracture of the economic system.

These responses to globalisation frustrate the development of medium and small companies, even those intensive in the use of technology. Thus, productive units disappear from the scenery; units that, given the predominant technological changes, could have a wide horizon for development in the domestic and the international markets. Therefore, opportunities of the so-called 'knowledge society' are reduced to concentrated sectors. It is not sufficient to have access to informatics and the Internet, if the rules of the game are hostile to the growth of existing and new domestic productive units.

This context explains the poor effect of current policies to promote the development of small and medium companies and the regional economies. One of the reasons is the limited amount of resources destined to that purpose, owing to the continuous necessity to restrain expenditure, to increase the tax burden and to transmit friendly signals to the international financial markets.

Science and technology
The above-mentioned trends have weakened the links between the production of goods and services and the domestic system of science and technol-

ogy. The increase in the imported content of capital accumulation has reduced the demand for locally produced technology, machinery and equipment.

Hence, problems in the scientific-technological system depend not only on the limited resources, but understandably otherwise, given the budget restrictions. The neoliberal policies have weakened the links between production and the science and technology system in a decisive way.[9] Those facts are reflected, for instance, in the reduction of the domestic production of capital goods, the dismantling of research and development departments in numerous enterprises, and the substitution of technology and domestic innovation for imported equipment and 'turnkey' processes.

Saving and investment

Until the debt crisis of the 1980s, the investment rate in Argentina was around 22 per cent. Internal saving financed practically the totality of capital accumulation. The external debt and the indiscriminate opening to private direct investment have changed this situation. In the 1990s, the external debt increased by US$85 billion, and there was an inflow of private direct investments of US$50 billion. That is, an aggregate inflow of foreign capital totalling US$135 billion. Only at the end of the decade did the investment rate recover levels of about 22 per cent. Now, however, the domestic saving finances only 80 per cent of capital accumulation. CEPAL has observed that in several Latin American countries the increase of foreign capital is accompanied by a decrease of local savings. In Argentina, the rate of domestic savings/GNP is 30 per cent lower than it was prior to the debt crisis.

Hence, capital accumulation has deteriorated. Besides, the transference of the most dynamic and profitable sectors of the economy to foreign subsidiaries implies that the allocation of resources reflects the priorities of the parent companies, rather than the objectives of Argentina. Fundamentally, the accumulation process is exogenously determined.

System organisation

In summary, the poor responses of Argentina to globalisation entail that the economy be organised according to trans-national axes: financial markets criteria, subsidiaries policies and Bretton Woods institutions conditionalities. The country has lost a great part of its capacity to conduct its policy and to organise its resources.

In all probability, the worst is not the existence of very real restrictions, but the acceptance by influential economic and public opinion sectors of the inevitability of those facts and their irreversibility. It is a 'fundamentalist vision of globalisation', according to which this may not be the best world, but it is the only one possible.

This scenery is incompatible with sustainable development, social progress and the establishment of a two-way symmetric relationship with the global order. Therefore, the country is dragged out of control by a flow of events. We shall see their effects on Mercosul in the following pages. These problems go beyond the economic sphere and engage the exercise of democracy and sovereignty in Argentina. Let us briefly refer to this point.

Democracy and sovereignty

The increasing restrictions to the management of economic policy and the predominance of the fundamentalist vision of globalisation modify both the rules of the democratic system and the exercise of sovereignty.

Sovereignty, namely, the capacity of the country to decide its own destiny in the global order, requires the existence of social and political actors with the necessary decision-making power to draw relations with the rest of the world. That is, to organise markets and resources according to criteria that, taking into account available means and actual restrictions, pursue the development of a national project.

Democracy, according to the fundamental principles established by the great political thinkers of the seventeenth and eighteenth centuries, John Locke and Charles Montesquieu, and incorporated in the Argentine constitutional order, imply that power lies in the people. In turn, division among the executive, legislative and judicial branches of government imposes the necessary equilibrium to avoid the installation of a despotic authority. Within this framework, people choose their rulers to promote common interests.

These requirements for the existence of a democracy and sovereignty have been altered now in Argentina. As we have already seen, the economy is organised around a trans-national axis, instead of rules aimed to sketch her own destiny in the global order. To influence the perception of markets beyond its consequences, on economic, social development and macro-economic equilibrium, is the dominant objective of the economic policy.

Consider the concept 'governability of democracy'. It consists of a behaviour of the government, compatible with market criteria. If the first differs from the latter, democracy is 'ungovernable'. This approach violates the principles of democracy. In conclusion, in the new stage, power does not lie within the people. Periodical elections to choose the representatives of the people's will, is to a great extent, a symbolic act *vis-à-vis* markets, which emit their votes every day and decide which direction to follow. To make democracy governable, the executive, legislative and judicial branches of government must satisfy market criteria.

These transformations also alter the theory of conflict. Namely, the resolution of a disagreement between parties requires each one to define its interests. These interests will then be defended by their representatives. This does not apply in the present situation because one of the parties negotiates with the criteria of the other party and, very often, it is represented by people associated with the interests of the counterpart. These facts contribute to explain the deterioration in the credibility of political leaders and of the democratic system as the natural space to defend the identity and own destiny in the global order.

MERCOSUL

Relations between Argentina and Brazil

Now, let us apply this analysis to the context of Mercosul and the relations between Argentina and Brazil, which constitute the nucleus of the regional scheme. The Foz de Iguazú Act, signed by the presidents of Argentina and Brazil on 30 November 1985, is the starting point of the recent convergence of both countries. In a few years, miscommunication and reciprocal suspicion inherited from the colonial past, different development styles and the hegemonic pretensions following the independence were overcome.

Several events helped to transform the context and intensify the bilateral relations in such a brief period of time. Among them were the return to democracy and the empathy of the new political leaders, the opening of the economy and the reciprocal guarantees regarding the peaceful objectives of the nuclear programmes of both countries.

The new framework liberated the centripetal forces among countries that share a geographical space. Neighbourhood generates potential forces of convergence due to different factors, such as lower cost of transport, reciprocal knowledge and cultural affinities.

Centripetal forces of geography are reinforced by the technological and industrial development level. Let us remember the experiences of the EU, the relations between the US and Canada, and the dynamism of the Pacific Asian Basin interchanges. On the contrary, the regional integration programmes between underdeveloped economies produce poor results, as shown in Latin America, or even more, in Africa.

In the case of Argentina and Brazil, the fact that the Rio-Sao Paulo–Córdoba-Rosario-Buenos Aires axis constitutes the most developed region of South America, is an important element to explain the expansion of bilateral trade. Complementary natural resources have also contributed in the same way.

After the Foz de Iguazú Act, the Argentine-Brazilian Act (July 1986) and the Integration, Co-operation and Development Treaty (November 1988) were both signed. In July 1989, Presidents Menem and Collor established a strategy radically different from that accorded by the previous presidents and founders of the process: Alfonsin and Sarney. To this crucial issue we shall return later on. Finally, with the incorporation of Paraguay and Uruguay in March 1991, the Asunción Treaty, constitutive of the Common Market of the South (Mercosul), was signed.

Integration requisites

Although the historical restrictions for the Argentine–Brazilian convergence were removed, other events, essential for the success of integration between countries that share a common geographical space, have not yet been resolved, in particular, the following.

Member states self-determination

An integration strategy imposes great challenges for the national policies of each party. A sufficient degree of control on the strategic macro-economic variables (balance of payments, budget and money supply) is required. Otherwise (i.e. severe external debt and vulnerability *vis-á-vis* speculative financial flows), the economic policy is subject to uncontrollable factors that will inevitably affect the relations of the participating countries.

Common policies are essential integration tools. Critical areas, such as science and technology, leading industries and infrastructure, require joint strategies for the development and reasonable distribution of costs and benefits.

Common actions on those fronts and the harmonisation of macro-economic measures are possible if the parties keep control of their respective economic policies. Otherwise, it is impossible to harmonise the macro-economic strategies and sectorial common policies are difficult to implement.

Social development

Social development is another determining factor for integration. Fairness in income distribution, employment, cohesion among social sectors, among other factors, contribute to the convergence of nations that share a geographical space. On the contrary, countries with a strong inequality in the distribution of income, a high unemployment level and indigence, and deep and historical fractures in the social order cohesion suffer internal strains that will inevitably affect the integration process. When negative contexts of such a nature prevail, the common market shrinks, possibilities of interchange diminish, and the integration itself can be used as a scapegoat for evils that have other origins.

National strategy convergence

For integration to achieve a fair distribution of its costs and benefits and the development of all participating countries, it is necessary that national policies converge in a growth strategy. This is required for an intra-industrial division of labour, which is indispensable for the simultaneous transformation and development of partner countries. On the contrary, if national policies have different objectives (i.e. only one of the partners privileges industrialisation), the benefits are unfairly distributed, which provokes strains within the system. If this happens, a 'central peripheral relation' is established in the regional division of labour, which is fatal for the future of integration.

World views affinities

The decision to integrate a pluri-national space is intended to widen the common market, increase available resources and strengthen the negotiating capacity *vis-á-vis* the rest of the world. This implies that member countries share a vision of the global scene and a common project for their international insertion. Integration means much more than trade promotion through the liberalisation of reciprocal changes. Above all, integration is a political project based on a shared vision of the world. If the parties have different ideas on these issues, they will adopt different positions in their relations with the rest of the world. Sooner or later, these divergences will surface and the integration frontiers be narrowed.

The years between the Foz de Iguazú Act and the late 1990s constituted the 'period of grace' of the Argentine–Brazilian relationship. It was then when the impact of the above-mentioned favourable factors for the convergence of both countries was operational. At present, the consequences of the 'original sins' are emerging; those related to external vulnerability, social dissatisfaction, asymmetries in the national development strategies and the ideological crisis of globalisation.

It is in these critical issues where the actual problems of the Argentina and Brazil relationship lie. They are restraining the centripetal force of geography and narrowing the bilateral integration and the Mercosul frontiers. Let us briefly investigate each one of them.

The four original sins

Dependence

Argentina and Brazil suffer a serious external vulnerability. This is a historical characteristic of the underdevelopment of these countries, which has been aggravated in the last few years.

The situation in Brazil is less critical, albeit serious as well. The external debt increased more than 100 per cent during the 1990s. The external debt/export relationship is the worst in Latin America, after Argentina and Nicaragua. The external debt, loss of competitiveness, and the trade balance deficit, all converge in a deficit of the current account, which in 1998 represented 60 per cent of exports. The accrued interest plus profit remittances represented 44 per cent of exports in 1999.

In January 1999, the exchange policy collapsed in the course of a few months, owing to a speculative attack: two-thirds of international reserves were lost. After devaluation, the external situation started to recover. However, in Brazil the continuous need of external financing is also a main determinant of economic policy.

Brazil's flexibility of the exchange policy allows a certain level of autonomy in the management of macro-economic policy, non-existent in Argentina owing to the convertibility regime. Anyway, a central variable of the bilateral relation, the peso–real parity, is determined by exogenous factors. In such conditions, co-ordination of macro-economic policies is only an impractical wish. Integration policies are therefore the residual element in a framework exogenously determined by the extreme external vulnerability of both countries.

Financial globalisation influences the policy of all countries, but only in those indebted and vulnerable (such as Argentina and Brazil) does it provoke such a restriction on the management of economic policy.

The problem is aggravated, probably much more in Argentina than in Brazil, by the predominant 'fundamentalist view' of globalisation. According to this vision, the actual is the only world possible. Therefore, only policies that adapt the criteria prevailing in the world power centres and financial markets are realistic and viable. This vision has an amazing capacity of survival even after the greatest catastrophes provoked by neoliberal policies.

Poverty and social exclusion

Argentina and Brazil face serious social problems. Brazil, according to President Cardoso, 'is not an underdeveloped country, it is an unfair country'. Brazil is certainly one of the nations with the greatest inequality in the distribution of income and wealth. Conspicuous consumption coexists with indigence and poverty, prevailing in the majority of the population in the vast national territory. In spite of its considerable development during the twentieth century, Brazil was not able to overcome the inheritance of the slavery regime and its colonial past.

The evolution was different in Argentina. Immigration of European origin from the second half of the nineteenth century transformed the demographic composition, and practically the whole population was integrated into the market economy. The abundance of fertile lands in the Pampas region enabled a high productive agriculture system, which sustained the considerable development of the country until the 1920s.

In spite of a significant income and wealth concentration, economic growth and a successful public education policy, it conformed to an integrated social system. The industrial development following the crisis of the 1930s intensified those characteristics of the Argentine society.

The situation changed drastically during the last quarter of the century. The economic standstill, external vulnerability, hyperinflation registered in various periods and neoliberal policies, increased the income and wealth concentration. Nowadays Argentina suffers indexes of unemployment and poverty unknown during its whole historical trajectory. Insecurity, corruption and social strains reflect the consequences of these tendencies.

The social situation prevailing in Argentina and Brazil is an obstacle to integration. It affects the development of both countries and reduces the common market dimension. Also, the bilateral problems in the trade field are used to explain the problems, which convey more complex internal reasons: for instance, the treatment given by Argentina to the devaluation of the real at the beginning of 1999. Although exports to Brazil represent only 3 per cent of the Argentine GNP, the idea that all problems in the country were due to the 'Brazil dependence' was disseminated.

Fear of contamination and danger that the convertibility regime could collapse deepened the adjustment in Argentina and its consequences on the economy and society. However, the problem was not provoked by the Brazilian situation, it was due in the first place, to the external vulnerability of Argentina.

The social problems of both countries constitute one of the 'original sins' of the integration process, which has tended to be aggravated during the last years.

National strategy asymmetries

The third 'original sin' of the bilateral relationship is the asymmetry of the national development strategies. In the long term, Argentina's strategy has been more erratic. Brazil has maintained, in spite of all domestic contingencies

and changes in the international context, a policy oriented towards industrialisation and promotion of technical changes. This policy has not been sufficient to defeat, definitively, the underdevelopment and dependence, or to
resolve serious social problems. However, Brazil has created a considerable
industrial system and a scientific-technological base to sustain it. The development of the domestic market and the leading role of the Brazilian business-
men are a traditional characteristic of the Brazilian situation.

In opposition, Argentina has led an erratic strategy and development
path since the crisis of the 1930s. Starting with the military dictatorship
installed in 1976, an extraordinary policy of dismounting the industrial
apparatus, destruction of the scientific-technological bases and the external
indebtedness started, whose consequences still prevail and have not yet been
overcome. Argentina suffers the absence of a critical mass of leading entrepreneurs with the willingness to accumulate power in the national scene and
to project themselves to the international market. The associative and subordinate behaviour towards trans-national finances and organisations has
not enabled a consolidation of a nucleus of local entrepreneurs and finan-
ciers, powerful enough to make feasible an 'Argentine capitalism'.[10]

The government of President Menem consolidated the subordination
to exogenous factors through a successful stabilisation policy and the
foreignisation of the principal nucleus of the Argentine economy. The
asymmetry of the national development strategies is reflected in the modification of the relative weight of the two economies. Until 1950, the
Argentine GNP was higher than the Brazilian one: at present, it represents
only one-third. The different population growth rate has been an influence, but the main reason lies in the prolonged stagnation of the Argentine
economy since the second half of the 1970s. As we have already seen, the
1990s recovery was due to the exceptional conditions of external financing
and the initial impulse of price stability.

The asymmetry of the national development strategies is reflected in the
bilateral division of labour. In Argentine exports and in Brazil's manufac-
tures, commodities prevail, revealing the creation of a 'centre periphery'
regime. This narrows the integration frontier. The only model that makes
integration and development of each party compatible in the long term is
'intra-industrial specialisation'. The integration strategy of Menem and
Collor's governments validated the current predominant style of the bilateral relationship.

International insertion divergences
The agreements of Presidents Alfonsin and Sarney show that their
governments shared a common project of insertion in the world-wide

order, and an interpretation of globalisation. Foundational documents and declarations reveal that the two governments were certainly worried about the dimension of their internal problems, and what they considered necessary to modify their relations with the rest of the world in order to solve them. Debt, external vulnerability and creditors' conditionalities were problems in which a co-ordinated approach would strengthen the negotiating force of both countries. They did not pretend to be isolated or ignore the existing restrictions, but they did intend to defend, together, the interest of each party. They aimed, in conclusion, to define an adjustment and development strategy alternative to the *Washington Consensus.*[11] This implied not only the co-ordination of the foreign policy, but, at the same time, a style of division of labour within the common space. Hence, the *intra-industrial integration* strategy of leading sectors, in which the protocol referred to capital goods, was the most relevant.

The strategy was drastically modified by Presidents Menem and Collor. Since the Buenos Aires Act (July 1989), the *intra-industrial* sectorial integration was substituted by linear and automatic reduction of imports tariffs. The market then assumed the command of the process, and policy practically disappeared from the scene.

Argentina also adopted revealing decisions in which her strategic option was not the integration with Brazil, but the unconditional alignment with the US. (Thus, the dollarisation proposal and the relationship with NATO.) In turn, Brazil took diplomatic initiatives, such as negotiations with Mexico, which also revealed the loss of the strategic significance of the relations with Argentina.

In different stages of the Menem government, from the official sphere and influential private groups, accusations were made about the 'Brazil dependence' and promoted the strengthening of the unconditional alignment with the US, including the preference of the American free trade zone in opposition to Mercosul. Within this context, the relationship with Brazil was maintained only by the centripetal forces of geography, and the private interests related to bilateral interchange expansion. Political initiative disappeared, and the Argentina and Brazil relationship was reduced to the insufficient formal reiteration of integration objectives.

The situation changed with the triumph of the Alianza. In its electoral campaign, the coalition recovered the strategic meaning of the relationship with Brazil, and the foundational principles of convergence. However, the new position of the President de la Rua government has to face the problems inherited and the 'original sins' of the process.

Current problems

The notable expansion of the reciprocal trade since 1985 shows the influence of the favourable factors of the 'period of grace', mentioned at the beginning of this chapter. The increase of total imports of Argentina and Brazil, sustained by the abundance of international financing, has also contributed.[12]

Once the external vulnerability fell again in a critical phase and economies entered into a recession, the Argentine–Brazilian trade diminished. In fact, in 1998 and 1999, the tendency installed since 1985 was interrupted.

The devaluation of the real in January 1999, drastically modified the exchange parity between both currencies. This is not new.[13] The volatility of parity is the consequence of one of the 'original sins': external vulnerability of both countries. It is now particularly serious because of the current economic situation in Argentina.

Given the Argentine exchange regime, although a certain revaluation of the real is expected in the short term, a loss of competitiveness of Argentina is feasible, with its consequences in the bilateral trade balance. In this scene, problems arise one after the other: footwear, textiles, milk products, rice, chickens, pork, paper, steel, etc. Only the administered trade areas, such as automobile and fuels, remain practically outside the consequences of the exchange turmoil.

The difficulty of solving these problems is not due to the lack of common institutions, like the Commission of the EU. During the 'period of grace' direct negotiations between the governments were sufficient and successful in the treatment of the questions discussed. The real problems lie in the 'original sins'.

All comparisons of the Mercosul experience with the EU are of limited value, among other reasons, because none of the four 'original sins' of the Argentina and Brazil relationship existed during the French–German convergence and the signature of the Rome Treaty in 1957. Attitudes of public and private actors of Argentina and Brazil towards integration reveal the complexity of the situation.[14] Recent events have weakened the strategic priority that the bilateral relation had for the two countries in the foundational times.

The 'period of grace' of the Argentina and Brazil convergence is exhausted. Advances achieved in the bilateral trade and closer relations of public and private actors will probably be maintained. After all, the gravitation of the centripetal forces of geography is there. However, the concretion of the original project seems, at the moment, a distant possibility.

The four 'original sins' now present challenges that can no longer be ignored. We should ask ourselves if two vulnerable countries, with enormous social problems, different development strategies and remarkable asymmetries in their international insertion, could achieve objectives as those stated in the Foz de Iguazú Act and in the Argentine–Brazilian agreements previous to the Asunción Treaty. The answer is no, unless the 'original sins' are tackled. It would be necessary to remove the external vulnerability and to recover enough operational freedom in the execution of national policies, in order to install an effective convergence of the macro-economic strategies. This is a precondition difficult to achieve in the near future. A sensible improvement of the social situation is also difficult to attain.

However, the problems arising from asymmetries of the development and international insertion strategies could be solved, if the foundational spirit of Argentina and Brazil convergence is recovered.

In summary, the bilateral relation and its future depend on the removal of the political and ideological barriers. This is a necessary condition to work jointly in the resolution of the external vulnerability and the social situation, i.e. of the underdevelopment and dependence of these two countries.

The new stage

The relaunching agenda of the foundational project of the Argentine–Brazilian convergence includes the following priorities.

Ideological crisis solution

It is necessary to recover a realistic vision of the development process, which is necessarily endogenous and open to the world. The fundamentalist vision of globalisation should be rejected. It is necessary to recognise the coexistence of a global dimension with the decisive weight of internal resources and markets, and that development has always been and still is a process of political construction, social cohesion and aptitude to decide their own destiny in the global order. It is in these inspiring ideas where the revival of the Argentina and Brazil convergence lies.

Recognition and understanding of each country's problems

Precisely due to the existence of the 'original sins', Argentina and Brazil convergence is facing complex problems. Argentina should recognise that the devaluation of the real in January 1999 was not an autonomous decision of the Brazilian economic policy. On the other hand, Brazil must understand that Argentina will remain, for an undetermined period, crucified to convertibility. With her hyperinflationary experience, the country is ter-rified of descending from the cross, to face what lies below, in the real world of flexible variables, including the peso parity. While Argentina does not resolve her exchange dilemma (which is an unsolvable obstacle for macro-economic effective co-ordination), *ad hoc* mechanisms, compensatory of brusque changes in the peso–real parity, should be found.

In these as in other issues, it is essential to defend the strategic objective with a frank and comprehensible discussion of the problems that each country is facing.

Harmonisation of the regulatory framework

The Programme of Activities for year 2000, approved in December 1995, included joint actions, within Mercosul, in issues like the custom code, competence defence, services trade, antidumping standards, trade barriers, mutual recognition of national standards in health matters, purchase regimes of the governments and social security, regulation and supervision of the financial sector. In all these issues, a strong political support would enable harmonisation of the regulatory framework of integration.

Emphasis on the sectorial agreements and the common policies in strategic areas

It is necessary to recover the decisive importance that sectorial agreements had in the foundational project of the Argentine–Brazilian convergence. In the main economic areas, it is possible to establish agreements that will promote trade and investments within a model of *intra-industrial* division of labour. The automobile agreement is an example in this subject.

In science and technology, the possibilities of association are numerous. For instance, in the nuclear sector, it is possible to create a common strat-egy for the development of the nuclear energy applications, as electricity production, food preservation, medical uses and training of human resources. In this field, the Atomic Energy Commission of Argentina has proposed the creation of an *Argentine Brazilian Agency on Nuclear Energy Applications*, to programme the common development. In other areas, like biotechnology and informatics, the possibilities of association are also numerous.

As in the origins of the Argentine–Brazilian convergence, the initiative depends, in the first place, on the political leadership. If the ideological crisis can be unravelled, and development and international insertion strat-egies converge, better conditions to remove the external vulnerability and to resolve the great social problems of both countries would be created.

The future of Mercosul and the development of Paraguay and Uruguay, as well as the widening of the common market with the incorporation of Bolivia and Chile, depend on the Argentinean and Brazilian capacity to remove the 'original sins' that hinder their bilateral relations.

NOTES

*This chapter was translated by Mrs Alicia Semino and revised by the author.

1. Ferrer, A. *Historia de la Globalización*, Fondo de Cultura Económica, Buenos Aires, 1996.
2. Ferrer, A. *El Capitalismo Argentino*, Fondo de Cultura Económica, Buenos Aires, 1998.
3. Ferrer, A. *De Cristóbal Colón a Internet: América Latina y la Globalización*, Fondo de Cultura Económica, Buenos Aires, 1999.
4. Ferrer, A. *Living Within Our Means, Third World Foundation*, Westview Press, Boulder, CO, *Vivir con lo nuestro*, El Cid Editor, Buenos Aires, 1985.
5. Ferrer, A. *Hechos y Ficciones de la Globalización*, Fondo de Cultura Económica, Buenos Aires, 1977.
6. UNCTAD World Investment Report, Ginebra, 1999.
7. Kosakoff, B. and López, A. *Los cambios tecnológicos y organizacionales en las pequeñas empresas. Repensando el estilo de desarrollo argentino*, Revista de la Escuela de Economía y Negocios, Universidad Nacional de San Martín, April 2000.
8. OECD *Technology and the Economy: The Key Relationships*, Paris, 1992.
9. Ferrer, A. *Ciencia, Tecnología y Desarrollo, Archivos del Presente*. Buenos Aires, enero-febrero-marzo, 2000.
10. Ferrer, A. *La relación Argentina-Brasil y la Construcción del Mercosur*, in Hechos y Ficciones, 1977.
11. Ferrer, A. *Entre el Consenso de Washington y la Integración Sostenible*, in Hechos y Ficciones, 1977.
12. Markwald, R. *Mercosur: Aspectos Comerciales de la Crisis Actual*, in SID Sociedad Internacional para el Desarrollo, Ediciones Trilce, Montevideo, 2000.
13. Ferrer, A. *Ajuste, Crecimiento e Integración. Revista Comercio Exterior*, México D.F., Febrero, 1991.
14. Lavagna, R. *Mercosur: zona de libre comercio o área de decisión brasileña*, in SID.

EIGHT

───◄○►───

Mercosul: An Interpretation of the Past and a View to the Future

CARLOS PÉREZ LLANA

A look at Mercosul necessarily involves making distinctions and comparisons. Analysing this sub-regional integration scheme necessitates the discussion of a series of subjects with pertinent historical references. Based on this criterion, the present chapter has adopted an analytical structure, arbitrarily subdivided into decades. It attempts to tie together three agendas (the international, the regional, and the specific Mercosul agendas), by placing emphasis on Argentina and Brazil. All references to the 1980s point to the results of the agreements formed by Presidents Alfonsin and Sarney.

THE WORLD OF THE 1980s

When in the mid-1980s the Presidents of Argentina and Brazil signed the agreements that provided the foundations of Mercosul, the international agenda was marked by the developments and changes taking place in the former Soviet Union. The figure of Gorbachev met with greater external than internal support. This paradox can be easily explained: the population of the USSR did not hold much hope insofar as Gorbachev was forever vacillating between continuity and breakdown, while the rest of the world was urgently looking for a way to break the *status quo* that accompanied the Cold War.

In those years, it was possible to speculate on the emerging structure of world power, and on some of the ideas intended to give it content. When President Reagan advocated space defence, his advisers were right to compel Moscow to accept its defeat. Without technological capacities, with falling oil prices and with an ideocratic system populated by non-believers, the result was obvious. At the same time, the Reagan and Thatcher duo incarnating neo-conservative ideas waged war against the economic paradigm that had become prevalent since the post-war period. This ideological body was urgently looking for a way to discredit not only the role of the state in the economic order, but also its role as the guarantor of welfare.

In the meantime, a genuine technological revolution was taking shape in the field of communications. It erupted in the 1990s, transforming power relations on a world-wide level. For European corporations and companies governed by state socialism, this involved both changes and adaptations. Business enterprise was possible on the Old Continent, but proved unattainable for the communist bloc steered by Moscow.

In the same decade, China was confronted with a process of economic reforms inspired by a strategically correct analysis. The Asian situation proved challenging due to the successful economic performance of the region's 'Tigers'. The only viable solution for Peking consisted of preserving its political regime while changing its economic system. In the 1970s China had learned several lessons: capital was landing in Taiwan, in the islands and neighbouring territories where the Chinese diaspora played a relevant role. In the meantime, continental China was running the risk of being left behind. China also knew how to predict the consequences of Brezhnevian *status quo* in the USSR. Finally, the military failure that intended to 'teach Vietnam a lesson', brought to light the weakness of a military structure plagued by its ageing systems and doctrines.

Europe opted for doubling the stakes of integration in order to recover from one of its many 'Europessimist' cycles. The 'common act' paved the way for ambitious projects, and especially for common currency. The search for greater integration became relevant and a number of the adjustments made by Old Continent economies, were presented as the price of building a common future. The renewed hope in integration was durably undermined when the communist system collapsed. In reality, history remains to be written, but it is nevertheless possible to speculate.

Europe believed that Gorbachev was going to succeed. Circles prone to reason in terms of strategy were predominantly in favour of the social democratic project that he inspired. Looking beyond the actual intentions of the Soviet leader, Europe came out of this scenario strengthened. It succeeded in averting the disappearance of a leading strategic actor whose vacancy would have weakened its relative position. The ensuing disintegration left it highly exposed to the predominant role of the US. Gorbachev's references to a 'common house of Europe' were highly appealing to its interests, consistently directed at wielding influence in the East without having to pay the price for the collapse of the communist system.

This interpretation explains the consternation of many European leaders when they realised that it was impossible to influence the events affecting general European interests and the integration timetable drawn up in the mid-1980s. They were not, as was presumed at the time, excessively attached to history or incomprehensibly afraid of returning to the past. On the contrary, their way of thinking was realistic. However, in many cases, actual events surpassed expectations, for instance, when it did not seem possible that Gorbachev would accept the reunification of Germany. It was decreed that, in the name of realism, history should not be precipitated in order to avoid reverting to the Kremlin. Unquestionably dependent on the Cold War, the political structure of the European system was doomed and its institutions were clamouring for reform.

As was to be hoped for, soon after Central Europe realised the significance and the direction of the changes taking place in the USSR and Germany, the reformist sectors were supplanted by partisans of revolutionary change. The ex-Czechoslovakia came to symbolise this new cleavage. The reformists were excluded in the 1960s, after the defeat of the Prague Spring stood in opposition to the emerging power of sectors committed to Havel, formed after the Helsinki Conference (1975). The new Central Europe rapidly became aware of its need for security and prosperity. This meant striving for admission into NATO and the European Union (EU).

Soon after the initiation of the post-communist transition, applications for admission into NATO and the EU became the symbols and the expression of divergent national projects, which, in this respect, remained closely related. The process was characterised by efforts to form a national identity following the destruction of the state and the decomposition of communist ideology, including endeavours to become part of supranational and multilateral organisations; and adherence to the vision of an effortless and immediate conversion to democracy and to market economy.

When the decade came to a close, replying to Central Europe's requests for admission with vague promises made no sense. The demand for entry into the Union was relentless while, in certain cases, existing doubts consolidated the trends in favour of a greater US presence in Europe. Paradoxically, when conditions were ripe for Europe to accept new members, it was NATO that benefited from expansion.

In conclusion, the world at the end of the 1980s withdrew into itself, accompanied by a real geopolitical cataclysm resulting from the disappearance of the Eastern bloc. Political and ideological structures, as well as the international architecture that emerged in the light of the two world wars, were obliterated.

LATIN AMERICA IN THE 1980s

The political agenda of Latin America more or less revolved around the so-called 'economic reforms'. The Washington Consensus transformed into a programme of recommendations requiring nearly blind acceptance. Formulated in line with neo-conservatism, predominant concepts contaminated the political language borrowed from the Anglo-Saxon world. Governments, international organisms, 'specialised press', think tanks, companies and, more generally, the markets, promoted a strategy of which the premises were essentially economic.

Beyond this 'imposed agenda', two specific factors had an impact on Latin America's 'own' programme. From the economic point of view, the explosion of external debt, with an epicentre in Mexico, revealed heavy structural heritage. From the political point of view, the transition towards democracy marked the advent of a new cycle that followed the long darkness of military dictatorships. In this sense, the political flip side of the 'lost decade' denoting economic hardship is evident: the region returned to democracy.

This return to democracy did not simply result in a new cycle. Support for democracy came from sectors which, in the 1960s and 1970s, were known for questioning the so-called formalist vision of democracy. Following a long and sad apprenticeship under dictatorships, many former detractors came to defend the system. It is therefore possible to say that considerable progress was made in terms of the region's democratic culture.

In those years, the East/West conflict was highly present in Central America. This was due to political experiences in Nicaragua and El Salvador, and the importance of certain ideas prevalent in the White House – particularly in the first Reagan administration, which was influenced by the concepts of the so-called 'Santa Fe Group'. In the remainder of Latin American countries, the thawing of East/West relations eased numerous ideological items on the external agenda.

THE SOUTH CONE IN THE 1980s

After Argentina and Brazil returned to democracy, the external agenda was a rare reflection of internal changes due to the predominant concepts within the Alfonsin/Sarney governments. In the following decades marked by a debilitating geopolitical rivalry, the two governments founded a new agenda of co-operation. Globalisation in those years was not yet alluded to, although both countries were manifestly striving to maximise their resources in order to improve the quality of their international insertion.

Argentina's external policy had to shut out the more recent past weighed down by issues relating to the Chile conflict and the Falklands War. The weight of the foreign debt, the external consequences of trying military juntas, and the search for options in favour of autonomy, were relevant and highly present in the electoral campaign of 1983.

At the same time, Argentina and Brazil agreed on the necessity of separating the Central American conflict from the overwhelming East/West logic. This concern was not simply rhetorical. Both countries had suffered the consequences of Cold War logic, which was not alien to the political instability experienced for decades. In this context, the 'chemistry' established between the governments of Alfonsin and Sarney explained the break in the previous logic. For years, a certain part of the academic and political elite, in particular Argentina's radical party and the Brazilian PMBD, deepened their relations to the point of sharing a common vision of internal and external problems. The concepts of striving for greater autonomy, modernising productive capacity and consolidating the internal market, counting on human resources for technological development, and promoting the sub-regional market in view of opening up to the world, formed the ideological core for both governments.

Given that the democratic experience had to be strengthened under complex conditions involving directing efforts at long-standing expectations, replacing confrontation by co-operation resulted in modifying the constitutive elements of the regional diplomatic agenda. Both old and new concepts were added. Boosting growth through sectoral programmes constituted the crux of the new policy. The mitigated experience of the regional integration process and basic literature criticising the classical approaches to integration, generated confidence in these programmes, which embodied both countries' hope for change, in terms of production and trade. Regarding security, the most noteworthy aspect of the new agenda concerned the elimination of all hypotheses of war, which were replaced by a new policy paradigmatically symbolised by nuclear co-operation.

THE WORLD IN THE 1990s

The beginning of the decade was marked by post-Cold War. The collapse of the Berlin Wall was, in reality, the consequence of a crisis made evident by Gorbachev. Although the Soviet Union disappeared soon after, it is important to remember that this incident represents the downfall of one of the leading totalitarian regimes known to mankind.

In spite of the lack of open archives and the fact that 'memoirs' written by the protagonists are laden with subjectivity, it is safe to speculate that Gorbachev had a 'master plan' intended to transform communism into social democracy. Gorbachev believed that the Soviet system could tolerate a revolution. He also seemed to believe that internal conflicts, i.e. the question of nationalities, could be resolved through a nearly Leninist voluntarism, capable of waking the allegedly dormant energy of a society waiting for the party to separate from the state, and for transparency to pave the way for collective awareness. In terms of external policy, the die was cast in the mid-1980s: withdrawing from Afghanistan, abandoning the communist countries of Central Europe to their own fate, strongly advocating Europe ('the common house of Europe' in the words of Gorbachev) and putting an end to the armament race, which was inspired by new generation arms and in which Moscow was not in a position to participate (space defence, etc.).

On this point, we should not forget that certain distinguished representatives of the Russian armed forces had been aware that the USSR was lagging behind as of 1983. This was due to the growing breach between the USSR and the United States, which formed with respect to the information revolution. 'Brezhnevian immobilism' explains why nothing changed until Gorbachev came to power. His government assumed authority with a globally devalued power, having to accept to return to the negotiating table in matters of security, following the ill-timed withdrawal of the man who embodied Soviet diplomacy, i.e. Chancellor Gromyko.

This new reality meant the end of an era, the Cold War, and practically the end of the twentieth century, a 'short' century marked by two wars and by violent ideological confrontations.

The bipolar system, the existence of which required major detail, was destroyed and all hope for multipolarity remained frustrated. This was due to the advent of new static relations of power, graphically defined by the French Minister of External Relations (Hubert Védrine, 'Les cartes de la France') as revolving around the presence of a single hyper-power.

The Gulf War is a mandatory point of reference when we try to conceptualise the international situation after the end of the Cold War. For certain observers, the Gulf War betrayed the high degree of unipolarity governing world politics. According to other analysts, the Gulf War was an exception. From a decade's perspective, we can say that the 'new' and the 'old' had converged in this conflict. The Security Council endorsed the operation with the support of the USSR and the passiveness of China. Both attitudes can be explained by the Soviet efforts to reform and the Chinese necessity to return to the international scene after the Tiananmenn incident. These 'new' factors are difficult to identify with the Cold War. On the other hand, the 'old' arguments, based on anti-totalitarianism, did not change. Other 'old' factors included the embargo policy and the idea of defending Kuwait, a country that combined oil interests with the preservation of an ally regime in an area historically defined by Washington as strategically important. 'New' elements included the arms used, the policy of 'strategic control' applied before, during and after the war, and the application of the so-called 'duty to interfere' (Resolution 688 of the Security Council).

The cohabitation of 'old' and 'new', as it occurred in the Gulf, paved the way for President Bush's 'new order', insofar as it called on more idealistic, rather than realistic, content. Clinton's first actions and words as President were later turned in the same direction. This was also true for the internationalist democrats, renamed 'pragmatic Wilsonians', who emphasised compromise in favour of democracy and the role of the United Nations. As we all know, the failure of the Somalia mission and the electoral results in the half-period of his first mandate prompted President Clinton to introduce changes in his foreign policy, which veered to more unilateral solutions. This change of direction became evident in the Balkans. In Bosnia and in Kosovo, the American presence emerged as a reply to the European demand for US involvement.

Regarding this last point, it is important to point out the degree of correlation between US intervention in ex-Yugoslavia and the expansion of NATO, driven not only by the US, but also by the majority of European countries – including those of Central Europe. In many aspects, this policy, reflected in the 'new strategic concept', collided with the authority of the Security Council. For certain observers, it constituted the resurgence of the Cold War spirit and facilitated the creation of grey areas, i.e. regions without coverage (e.g. Ukraine).

In the 1990s, Europe was forced to redefine its policy as a direct result of the end of the Cold War. In concrete terms, priority shifted from integration to expansion. Understandably, Central European countries defined their external priorities based on acceptance in the EU (economic security) and NATO (military security). The estrangement of the USSR prompted them to look for a new mode of external relations, which required European backing, in order to join the ranks of democracies. At the same time, Europe implemented its single currency, the euro, making similar headway in terms of external policy and security (CSFP) and in some of the leading multilateral negotiations, including international trade.

While the US gained the status of a 'hyper-power', and Europe embarked on a complex process of re-adaptation, a series of events in Asia forced us to redefine our perceptions of a region that is far from homogeneous.

Until the crisis that started in Thailand, most analysts (including Krugman) considered that area as an example worthy of being followed.

The impact of demographic and geographic elements kept this great geo-political and geo-economic bubble afloat. The 1997 crisis imposed a differ-ent interpretation. The institutional weakness in many Asian countries became evident, and perhaps most emblematically in Indonesia. What had been defined as a miracle was, from then on, considered from another angle, as was the case with South Korea. Simultaneously, the real political and eco-nomic importance of religion remained manifest.

LATIN AMERICA IN THE 1990s

In this decade, the Latin American policy of international insertion was greatly modified. The change was not about adapting to the new interna-tional agenda of post-Cold War, although some of it occurred on a smaller scale, especially in the paradigmatic case of Cuba. In reality, changes in the external agenda can be explained by the region's search for congruence between a liberal economic model and external policy. The pre-eminence of a market-friendly policy, the declining prevalence of politics over the economy, the devaluation of utopias, the decomposition of concepts including autonomy, and, more generally, the precedence of an analysis associated with the 'Washington Consensus' constituted the most notable points of reference.

In the new agenda, economy was not simply ranked. The bilateral/uni-lateral dimension also underwent transformation. 'Summit diplomacy', the appeal of an organisation such as the WTO, the power and influence evinced by the FTAA, the growing leadership of the ONGs and the active presence of 'new' factors in the 'positive' and 'negative' agendas formed new diplomatic challenges in a context of weak critical capacities. Latin America's wealth of literature was no longer consulted, and new conditions of sub-regional integration lead to a casuistry that helped destroy the stra-tegic ideas that had been important since the 1950s.

MERCOSUL IN THE 1990s

The Alfonsin/Sarney agreements in the 1980s were inspired by politics. In the 1990s, on the other hand, Mercosul was given over to market forces, meaning that its members no longer applied their constituent strategic cri-teria.

Insofar as the international, regional and sub-regional context was peaceful, trade suddenly grew in leaps and bounds. Nobody was interested

in reintroducing state objectivisation. It was assumed that everything was
going to be easy. In the first half of the 1990s, this nearly idyllic context benefited from an additional advantage in terms of Mercosul consolidation: the
scarce importance assigned to the region by the US. In the first Clinton
administration, preoccupations in Washington revolved around redefining
external policy, relations with Russia and the Middle East and, more generally, commercial diplomacy, which, under the leadership of Mr Kantor,
concentrated on the WTO. Latin America was included in this last agenda,
but its importance was subordinated to Mexico's entry into NAFTA.
Mercosul had no relevance, which turned out to its advantage. Omitted
from the list of strategic US priorities, the South Cone was able to make
progress escaping the vigilance of an influential player. As early as President
Clinton's second mandate, Washington modified its approach and started
to show interest.

However, a series of events that took place eroded optimism. The international monetary crisis, aggravated in Russia and later in Brazil, brought
an end to all optimism. In the meantime, political interpretations regarding
the nature and functioning of the international system began to differ
depending on the country, but more particularly in Argentina and Brazil.
The definition of relations of power, the significance attributed by each
actor to globalisation and, more particularly, the nature of relations developed bilaterally and multilaterally with Washington (state to state,
Mercosul and FTAA) formed a watershed.

The growing incongruence within Mercosul was accompanied by
President Menem's unpopular declarations in Brazil, an impetuous dispute
regarding a hypothetical entry into the Security Council. This conflicted
with visions of the 'Colombian question' and, finally, the definition of
Argentina as an extra-NATO ally.

Following the 'easy' phase, divergent interpretations, different styles
and sensitivities, absence of strategy, abandonment of sectoral politics and
a low level of institutionalism in a context of growing conflicts (which presidential diplomacy was supposed to resolve) all combine to explain
'Mercopessimism', which began to be felt as of 1998. Many observers had
predicted the scenario: with Mercosul given over to spontaneity, a multi-
tude of demands and the absence of sectoral policy were bound to affect
sub-regional dynamics. Overdue solutions were also the product of asyn-
chronous electoral periods in each country.

In addition to all these events, the devaluation of the Brazilian currency
foreshadowed the end of the spontaneous phase. Sectors less favourable to
Mercosul seized the opportunity to question the benefits of a strategic decision based on Argentinean interests. Pessimistic observers, mainly concen-

trated in Buenos Aires, did not realise that Brazil was compelled to devalue its currency. Nobody thought of a 'competitive devaluation'.

A LOOK TO THE FUTURE

In view of the current situation of Mercosul, only a strategic approach can restore energy to this undertaking. Otherwise, it may be infected with the virus of irrelevance that affected Latin American efforts of integration.

The key to success implies restructuring politics. Counting on taxes for salvation does not make any sense considering that this choice is not capable of creating new dynamics. Developing the co-ordination of macro-economic politics is of most relevance to the economy. It is also the principal responsibility of the state.

Looking ahead into the future, we must preach the primacy of politics. In this sense, the best that we can do consists of identifying the options of international insertion available to our countries, in light of the leading international trends. In this order of things, a precise interpretation of the international agenda and of existing relations of power proves indispensable. As for globalisation, the first thought that comes to mind when thinking in terms of world-wide relations is obvious. Globalisation equals the loss of sovereignty. External policy, which transcribes both internal necessities and external possibilities into a realistic code, cannot ignore the importance of restrictions without falling into resignation (a conclusion usually arrived at by hyperrealists).

Without Mercosul, South American countries lose the only multiplier of power that is determined by geography: critical mass. In today's world, it may be said that the following actors share a dimension between the state and strategy: NAFTA, Europe, China and India. Russia represents an unknown element, doubtlessly due to the success of President Putin's project, which defined the reconstitution of the state/territory relations as a priority. There also remains a lingering doubt pointed out by Hélène Carrere d'Encaussé in 'La Russie Inachevée': the consequences of a significant drop in the population mass. Although Japan does not constitute a forum in itself, it is nevertheless a natural candidate for an Asian leader, thanks to its powerful economy of regional magnitude. However, following the crisis that crippled the area as of 1997, and due to the behaviour of the Japanese economy in the past few years, it would be exaggerated to promote the leadership of an insular country. The same analysis also applies to the future of ASEAN. There are other less influential entities and Mercosul is most prominent among them.

Absorbed by problems, South America sometimes fails to notice that, among the alliances formed by 'average' countries, it has the best profile and the highest appeal. This perception is justified by the weight of the markets, the investments made in South American countries, and the political instability that hinders other candidates from forming an integrated forum.

When looking for other reasons explaining South America's advantages as a sub-regional entity, there are three basic points:

1. South America advocates a multipolar system and its inherent benefits cannot ignore the difference between an FTAA with Mercosul and an FTAA without Mercosul. Nobody can fail to notice that in this case the sub-region is helping define global criteria of power.

2. Developed countries, particularly in Europe, represent increasingly ageing societies. More and more young people are looking for ways to find new geographic solutions to an anti-fiscal rebellion. In order to maintain the implemented structures of welfare, capital in those countries will have to find productivity outside their borders. Taking into account the demand which is bound to fall, the apparent over-investment observed in many sectors and the ongoing race for profitability, these countries will be forced to look for solutions outside their Union. This is despite the new borders formed by Central Europe.

3. Finally, speculating on 'predominant' trends, only a few languages on a global scale will achieve the required dimension of a 'lingua franca'. Those languages include English, Mandarin, Arabic and Castilian. Combined with Portuguese, French and Italian, Castilian will be without a doubt the Latin world's point of reference. In addition, the Castilian language has the enormous advantage of growing within the NAFTA-associated sphere of influence occupied by English. This represents another reason why Mercosul should include Mexico, especially in the politico-cultural dimension.

These arguments follow the earlier defined direction: Mercosul will have to be multidimensional and enlarged, or it will cease to be. In concrete terms, it means that politics will once again have to stand at the centre of construction strategy. Member states will be required to make the most of this process and integrate Chile and Bolivia within a short period of time. The European experience is paradigmatic. The EU came into being by promoting cycles characterised, at times, by enlargement, and at other times, by integration.

MERCOSUL AND THE RECENT DEVELOPMENTS IN THE INTERNATIONAL SYSTEM

Returning to the original outline and the content of the agendas involved in the process of sub-regional integration, it is necessary to point to certain open questions concerning the new foreign policy of the US, and the priorities of Europe.

The new American policy

It is premature to formulate, in reference to the foreign policy of the Bush administration, definitive analytical judgements on the subjects under discussion. They are generally associated with questions concerning the influence of persons involved in the 'first' Bush administration; the emerging differences with the Clinton administration, the coherence between distinct sectors of bureaucracy (Vice Presidency, the State Department, the Defence Department, the Security Council); the emphasis on unilateralism, the re-definition of alliances, etc.

It is manifest that the attitude and the path adopted by the people involved in international diplomacy, as well as the definition of foreign policy, as formulated from the electoral campaign to date, are linked to a world vision closely associated with international security criteria. The repeated references to 'national interests', the return to the subject of contention, the search for new enemies and the revision of foreign policy elements associated with the use of military force constitute the relevant indications.

In relation to this renovated vision of security, we should not be surprised by the emergence of strategy in direct contrast to the policy advocated by President Clinton. For example, Russia does not play a relevant role in the Republican vision and China is perceived as the 'next problem'. Economic diplomacy, one of the core elements of the former policy, has not yet been put to the foreground while the so-called 'global questions' are absent. Matters related to the war/peace chapter of the international agenda, including the case of regional conflicts in the Middle East and the Balkans, are seen as part of a policy, with lesser emphasis on direct involvement in the Palestinian/Israeli tragedy and with greater interest in Iraq. In the meantime, the ex-Yugoslavia's problem is being delegated to the Europeans, although the exacerbation of conflicts such as those in Macedonia shows that the Americans will not be easy in spite of the presence of NATO.

Attention is concentrated in the nucleus of international security: new threats and the redefinition of strategic policy. The catalogue of threats includes the previous definitions of the 'rogue states', subsequently referred to as 'worrying states'. Many observers add to this list new elements, including China and Russia. However, officially these countries are not categorically conceptualised in the same terms. In addition, notorious contradictions come to light, including the recent identification of terrorism by the Director of the CIA as the major threat to US security. This was in fact a line launched by the Clinton administration (especially in cases of Sudan, Afghanistan and Yemen), evading the issue of 'rogue states'.

As for strategic policy statements, the core programme of the Bush administration consists in the set-up of the NMD anti-missile system. This programme has its roots in the Reagan and Clinton administrations. In December 1992, Clinton had decided to cut resources although he did not cancel the programme, redirecting it later toward a tactical anti-missile system. In September 1997, Washington and Moscow launched – at the US initiative – negotiations on the ABM Treaty (1972). In the second half-year of 2000, Clinton decided to postpone the decision to deploy the anti-missile protection system intended to shield the US territory.

The new government is decidedly in favour of the project and everything leans to the criteria finally being imposed. In fact, in spite of the manifest opposition of the Russian government, certain analysts do not exclude the possibility of Russian and American negotiations establishing mutual concessions. These concessions comprise reform of the ABM Treaty and a dialogue through which Moscow could satisfy some of its strategic interests. (This includes the ambition to maintain its place in major negotiations, obtaining favourable results in the START III negotiations, ensuring that the US accept to reduce their offensive nuclear weapons arsenal, and dismantle, with US assistance, the nuclear arsenals of the Soviet era.) The pragmatism of many new Russian leaders may lead them to adopt a more staunch position at the negotiating table. Russia is interested in establishing a balance between what should be the withdrawal of a missile interception system and the possibility, implicit in the NMD, of supporting it until a later phase involving a greater traditional strategic dimension in agreement with regional objectives. The scenario involving militarisation and anti-satellite arms would open the door to a new arms race that Moscow would almost certainly lose.

In support of NMD, Great Britain will back the US, and Berlin is thought to adopt the same stance. In the German case, the subject at hand evokes the political fracture that took place in the 1980s, when Chancellor Kohl supported NATO's decision to set up Cruise and Pershing missiles in order to offset the threat of Soviet SS-20s. At the time, the ruling social democracy opposed withdrawal at a high cost, in light of the fact that some sectors supported the Christian-Democratic government, which paradoxically counted on the backing of the Socialist Mitterrand. The Australian government (with Australia belonging to the core base of NMD) indicated that a military base could be used on its territory for the NMD project. France currently appears to be less inclined, but could very well dodge the opinion of its European partners. Four dimensions must be reviewed in order to understand the development of the events related to the space defence programme. These four areas consist of the threats, technological viability, the impact on the overall strategic balance, and the intra-NATO dynamics.

To conclude the discussion on continuity and change in US foreign policy, allusions to the content of certain regional policies do not seem relevant. From the beginning of his term, President Clinton placed a strong diplomatic emphasis on Asia, and more particularly on China, which was at the time defined as a strategic partner. This decision was inspired by disproportionate optimism in regard to this region.

Asian policy suffered the consequences of the economic crisis that started in Thailand in 1997, although this later transformed into a political situation. From that time on, the US was forced to apply 'case by case' policy (for example, with respect to Indonesia, Thailand, South Korea, etc.). In those years, Taiwan lost its relevance for Washington, while the most innovative aspect in matters of security consisted of the intention to apply the non-proliferation programme to North Korea.

Assigning priority to strategic analysis, the new administration is redefining its goals, thus explaining changes in the approach to China, the backing of Taiwan, and the more reserved dialogue with North Korea. In this region, the missile shield represents very concrete results: setting up such a system in Taiwan makes the 'strong arm' attitude of China less credible. Farther away, India is an example of continuity in American strategic interpretation, the reason for which the initial assessment of the Clinton administration is not subject to revision. In a few words, the 'Pacific Basin' project, motivating for Clinton and laden with economic expectations, is sure to be revised in light of newly defined priorities.

For the Republicans, China appears as a strategic threat with economic opportunities. For this reason, Washington's approach has changed, although its relevance is maintained. It suffices to say that 100,000 soldiers are stationed in Asia to guarantee security in a region that does not have a collective system.

In regard to Europe, attention drifts to the fact that many suggest the problem of a renewed division between Atlanticism and Europeism.

However, when subjected to greater scrutiny, this interpretation proves to be highly inconsistent. No one in Europe today can seriously consider a fracture of this type. There is talk, however, of intense strategic complementarity. Both parties are definitively asking questions; Europe will have to take advantage of the unavoidable and invaluable dynamism of the euro. It will have to ensure the compatibility of the two major projects based on its ambition for greater depth and outreach, and define its political geography tracing the new frontiers that are likely to arise. Finally, the Old Continent will be forced to show that 'he who wills the end wills the means', assigning economic resources to foreign policy and joint security objectives. Nuances and questions are obviously abundant; should the European border end in Russia or include Turkey? Is the Union simply an economic alliance or does it represent a vaster project which must be necessarily crowned by a constitution? In the meantime, on a more realistic level, the US is interested in preserving NATO, and other subjects are in the position to optimise hope. As a superpower, the US has a multidimensional and global outreach. Due to this privilege, going beyond the sensitivities of various other players, the anti-Atlanticist opinions that form in certain sectors of the government thrive with difficulty. We should not forget that the ex-President Bush had revised certain foreign policy premises of the Reagan administration, particularly those referred to as anti-European. Paradoxically, they were permeating US leadership with a strong Atlantic vocation. We should also keep in mind that while some European leaders showed ambivalence at the fall of the Berlin Wall, President Bush senior had strongly supported the reunification of Germany, orchestrated by the former Chancellor Kohl.

Closing the chapter on regional policy from the US perspective, we move to the Latin American aspect. During the electoral campaign of 2000, it was clear that Latin American problems met with greater responsiveness from the Republican platform than from the Democratic camp. Under President Clinton, Latin America was included in the commercial (Mexico's inclusion in NAFTA, FTAA) and the 'negative' (drug trafficking, migration) agendas, bearing residual manifestations of the Cold War (Cuba). Today, indications allow us to infer a convergence of geo-political and geo-economic interests that will result in the acceleration of the FTAA project. This is reality, but dates and terms must still be discussed. While in Europe it is realistic to say that NMD is a decision of the past, our region must assume that the FTAA project cannot be avoided. This is why it is necessary, from the Mercosul perspective, to rapidly establish the best possible conditions for negotiation.

European priorities

In the present overview, we can say that the founding phase of the EU, expressed by the ambition for greater depth, ended in the creation of the euro. Today, a new Europe is rising to cohabit with its goals of a wider outreach.

At the summit in Nice, in December 2000, it was evident that German prerogatives gravitate around 'Eurocentral priority', forcing certain countries to redefine their external solutions, restricted due to the conditions imposed by the logic of unity.

Extension through post-Cold War Eastern Europe, or in other words Europe with a reunified Germany, leaves open questions concerning the definition of the EU's priorities in terms of foreign policy. The old architecture of concentric sub-regions (Central Europe, the Mediterranean, Northern Africa, etc.) requires a new plan and this will have an impact on Latin America and Mercosul.

Although no one is seriously questioning the outward push, there are different interpretations of what can be done with the remaining diplomatic options. This dimension includes negotiations between Europe and Mercosul, as well as Chile, which, inspired by Mexico, is searching for bilateral formalisation.

Historical periods are prescriptive. The future of European agreements with Mercosul, the preparations of which are well on the way, depends on reinforced engineering that will have to incorporate the renewed pro-FTAA vocation of the Bush administration. In addition it must include the favourable attitude of many Latin American countries and the Caribbean, as well as the needs and objective interests of each Mercosul member. If the pro-Eastern feeling in Europe bears nearly exclusive results, and if South America's agricultural interests are not reached in international trade negotiations, this Atlantic triangle, originally conceived as the ideal model for the international integration of Mercosul, will lose its viability.

NINE

Brazil in a Globalising World

AMAURY DE SOUZA

INTRODUCTION

Emerging market economies such as Brazil and Argentina face difficult times in today's globalising world. A combination of adverse circumstances in the world economy is likely to affect their potential for growth negatively in the near future. Oil prices have tripled since 1998; interest rates have been on the rise since 1999; investors have taken a flight to quality, and global economic growth is expected to slow. Furthermore, recent developments in security and global affairs do not bode well for international relations. This is especially true with the decision by the United States (US) to unilaterally repeal the Kyoto convention on global climate change and the international nuclear arms control regime, in order to have it replaced by a global missile defence.

Uncertainty regarding the evolution of the world economy has affected trade arrangements everywhere. Since the World Trade Organisation's (WTO) global trade round collapsed in Seattle, there has been a world-wide race to negotiate bilateral or regional free trade agreements. The US has concluded a free trade agreement with Jordan and plans similar deals with Singapore and Chile in addition to the proposed Free Trade Area of the Americas (FTAA). The European Union (EU) has negotiated bilateral agreements with Mexico and South Africa, and there are plans to incorporate Eastern European countries, as well as to form a free trade area with Mercosul. In Asia, Singapore's bilateral deal with New Zealand has been followed by ASEAN's ambitious design for a free trade area with China, Japan and South Korea. Such arrangements have become particularly attractive in relation to trade blocs, which now conduct over 40 per cent of global trade. Membership in sub-regional organisations, such as Mercosul, is increasingly viewed as a way to gain preferential access to markets, lest multilateral talks continue to limp along.

The proliferation of free trade agreements should encourage Brazil and Argentina to adopt a more aggressive stance towards sub-regional integration, and use it to expand their participation in world trade. This will not be a trivial pursuit. In the past two years, pessimism has enveloped the prospects for Mercosul and sub-regional integration. Since Brazil's sudden devaluation of the currency in January 1999, Mercosul has been overwhelmed with squabbling. Chile's recent decision to negotiate a bilateral free trade agreement with the US did nothing to dispel fears that Mercosul may come to a halt and open the way for the eventual domination of trade arrangements in the hemisphere by the FTAA. The main Mercosul trade partners have traversed much less of the distance to sub-regional integration than is generally acknowledged. The fear of losing autonomy in domestic policy-making, the power of entrenched interests and bureaucratic inertia, have together stalled progress toward deeper integration. The consensus finally collapsed in the wake of Brazil's devaluation crisis, and it never recovered.

The best-case scenario for Brazil is to successfully 'relaunch' Mercosul by setting up effective macro-economic co-ordination mechanisms, and taking more decisive steps toward deepening the customs union. A renewed Mercosul can greatly expand the power of the participating nations in the more exacting FTAA negotiations. It would also be in a more favourable position to pursue a trade agreement with the EU in addition to gradually broadening the number of countries under Mercosul preferences in South America, thus moving towards a regional free trade area. As Chile's decision intimates, the worst-case scenario for Brazil is to see Argentina and other trade partners scurry to enter bilateral trade agreements with the US, with Mercosul drifting to the point of irrelevance. In any event, it is to Brazil's advantage to forgo its defensive role as a veto player, and take instead the lead in the negotiation process.

It is argued here that, from Brazil's point of view, such a move entails sharp dilemmas. The first problem is whether deeper economic integration may exact a loss of sovereignty. The other, is the extent to which the opportunities offered by world markets contribute to accelerate domestic economic development. As Rodrik[1] points out, the results of trade negotiations – bilateral, sub-regional, regional, or multilateral – should not be judged by whether the volume of trade is augmented, or market access overseas is increased. Rather, they should be judged by whether it 'contributes to the construction of a high-quality institutional environment at home (that can) spur unexpected levels of entrepreneurial dynamism and economic

growth'. The focus of these notes is on recent developments that may constrain Brazil's leadership role, or conversely, provide the momentum for
furthering Brazil's interests in its multiple agendas.

BRAZIL IN THE INTERNATIONAL SYSTEM

Much of the writing on Brazil emphasises its projection of itself as a
regional power. Although Brazil faces no single overarching threat to its
existence as a sovereign state, the aspiration to leadership in past decades
has been accompanied by an acute sensibility to American unilateralism. In
the context of Huntington's post-Cold War unimultipolar system,[2] unilateral action by the single superpower is restrained to a certain extent by its
need to act in consultation with several major and secondary regional
powers. Brazil's preference for multilateral forums and institutionalised
codes of conduct reflect the desire to limit the manoeuvring room enjoyed
by the hegemon and other major powers. Simultaneously, it reflects the
need to enhance the soft power of its international credibility.[3]
Huntington's metaphor also accounts for the often difficult relations that
regional powers, such as Brazil, maintain with secondary powers in their
sphere of influence, such as Argentina. From this point of view, Mercosul
represents both a means to dilute traditional rivalries between the two
nations and replace it with co-operation, as well as a means to boost Brazil's
leverage in international negotiations.

A different issue of sovereignty is raised in the discussion about Brazil's
insertion into the international economy. The vision of globalisation as 'the
nemesis of national government',[4] as Wolf aptly dubbed the notion that
national sovereignty stands to lose by the increasing autonomy of market
forces, has inspired the section of opinion in Brazil that opposes an increasing exposure to world markets. Rather than evidence of Brazil's increasing
competitiveness, the long-running trade rows with Canada over aircraft
subsidies, and with the US over drug patents, are seen as an omen of what
is in store for Brazil in the FTAA. Scepticism reached a new pitch after
Canada temporarily banned Brazilian beef imports for fear of infection by
'mad cow' disease. The effects went beyond Brazil's threat to resort to retal-
iatory measures if Canada did not withdraw the ban. Many Brazilian critics
of trade integration felt vindicated when President Fernando Henrique
Cardoso spoke of a trade war, and warned that the dispute might jeopardise
the FTAA negotiations.

More realistically, elites in government have long recognised the importance of an expanding web of international commitments to safeguard and

advance Brazil's national interests. Adherence to the principles of multilateralism is the central vision guiding Brazil's foreign policy. On the issues of trade, commitment to the WTO agreements and the multilateral trading system constitute the basic normative framework for Brazil's insertion into the global economy and the defence of its interests as a global trader. International rules established in multilateral forums, while constraining the range of policy choices that states can pursue, also reinforce their sovereignty by preventing stronger states from unilaterally imposing their will.

Mercosul is, in many ways, the crowning achievement of this strategic vision. The decision to share collective decision-making derived from the recognition that there may be no effective exercise of sovereignty in a globalised system, where the capacity of national states to shape events alone is diminishing. When Mercosul was founded, strategic and political goals played as large a role as possible to attract investment and improve market access conditions. 'While the latter have been damaged by the devaluation in Brazil', remarked Roett, 'the former remains an integral component of the association.'[5]

Major challenges confronted Mercosul at a relatively early phase of its development. Its engagement in an overly ambitious agenda of trade negotiations on a regional (South America), hemispheric (FTAA) and transatlantic scale (EU) was partly motivated by exogenous circumstances. The commitment to create the FTAA and a free trade zone with the EU derived originally from Mercosul's reactive response to external initiatives. However, it also represented a response to the failure of multilateral organisations to attend to sub-regional needs. Brazil actively supports a new round of multilateral trade negotiations to correct trade distortions stemming from the Uruguay Round agreements, and to promote agricultural trade reform. Brazil has also been using the WTO more aggressively in order to remove barriers to its exports. However, the rise of protectionism in rich countries and the Seattle fiasco required both a change of posture, and a more serious consideration of regional integration arrangements.

Although Brazil continues to value global multilateralism, the turn to regionalism as the organising principle for multilateral action is consequential for the long-term prospects of Mercosul. The agenda for the negotiation of the FTAA, by the year 2005, includes WTO plus commitments that go far beyond border barriers, and trade in goods issues that had hitherto been the staple of Mercosul evolution. The US's attraction to the FTAA was based on the possibility of reaching agreement on issues and commitments not covered by multilateral rules: for example, protection of intellectual property rights, treatment of foreign direct investment, competition

policy, trade in services, domestic regulations and government procurement, and labour and environmental standards.[6] Thanks to its diversified
economy, Brazil stood to gain the most from a preferential access to the US
market. Other trade-offs, however, appeared to be rather less attractive.
The potential for trade diversion might weaken Brazil's valued position as
a global trader and increase its dependence on the US market for exports.
In addition to that, the US was unwilling to reduce trade-distorting agricultural subsidies, or restrict trade dispute mechanisms that are often used
to sideline foreign competition, rather than to ensure fair trade, such as
antidumping actions, countervailing duty investigations, and cumbersome
rules of origin. Another issue of contention was Brazil's fierce resistance to
lower domestic trade barriers beyond the commitments made at WTO.

   In this context, a free trade agreement with the EU offered Brazil a
chance to retain as much autonomy as possible in the negotiation of a hemispheric free trade zone. For one thing, there are more similarities between
the EU and Mercosul than between NAFTA and Mercosul. Like the EU,
Mercosul has common political and foreign policy goals and, regardless of
how remote the prospect appears to be today, there is at least an expectation that the sub-regional association will move towards supranationalism
and a common market in the long run. To an extent, such differences
mirror the divergent paths followed by the US and the EU. Daalder[7] has
persuasively argued that the two sides look at the world in increasingly
different ways. The US is more concerned with security threats in Asia and
the consolidation of democracy and free markets in the Americas, whereas
the EU is more concerned with the 'new agenda' of issues like environmental degradation, world poverty, and the digital divide resulting from globalisation. Likewise, the US appears to be more inclined to resort to unilateral
actions and the projection of military power, while the EU relies on multilateral forums and international rules to settle problems. Notwithstanding
such differences, the economic trade-offs involved in the negotiation of a
preferential agreement with the EU seem to be less favourable to Brazil and
to Mercosul, than hemispheric integration might offer.

   International constraints are only part of the dilemmas faced by Brazil
and Mercosul. The sub-regional economies remain volatile with mounting
trade deficits and a dependence on foreign capital. Faltering rates of growth
and social unrest have given a sense of urgency to the matter. Hence the
need to step up the pace of reform to deal with these challenges, especially
those reforms that are intended to lower the domestic costs of production
and increase competitiveness at home and in global markets. However, frustration with the pace of sub-regional integration has led many to believe
that progress will not be made without the towering threat of integration

with a more competitive economy. Between 1991 and 1995, Mercosul progressed rapidly from a free trade area to a customs union, with a common external tariff. In the post-devaluation atmosphere, the conception of Mercosul as an inner core of countries that would move toward deeper integration seemed to command less consensus than it did in the past. The recent decision by Argentina to break, unilaterally, the common external tariff, raising import tariffs on consumer goods and eliminating duties on capital goods imports, has dealt a blow to expectations that Mercosul might remain a cohesive body in trade negotiations. Actually, Argentina's finance minister Domingo Cavallo, announced that Mercosul would be better off by reverting to a free trade zone, rather than seeking to consolidate itself as a customs union.

The issue at hand is how to achieve fast economic growth in the short run. However, behind these events lies the broader issue of the future of Mercosul. The possibility that Argentina may thwart Mercosul's bargaining strategy by unilaterally seeking a trade deal with the US over a deeper integration in Mercosul, has sobered up its trade partners. It may be up to Brazil to lead a change of strategy, quickening the pace toward a deepening of the trade bloc based on similar WTO-plus commitments. A difficult road lies ahead, but the determination to traverse it would reassure its partners that Mercosul has a future.

BRAZIL, ARGENTINA AND MERCOSUL

Brazil's currency devaluation and the adoption of a free floating exchange rate in mid-January 1999, forced Mercosul to face its hardest test ever. Trade within the bloc dropped about 30 per cent and the region slipped into recession, halting an intra-bloc trade growth trend that had grossed US$22 billion in 1998, up from US$4 billion in 1990. After having accumulated a trade surplus of over US$5 billion with Brazil in the preceding four years, Argentina saw trade revenues evaporate. She reacted by imposing curbs on cheaper imports from Brazil and demanding that safeguards be set to compensate for losses caused by the change of the exchange rate system by its trade partner. Brazil reacted to what was interpreted as Argentine protectionism, stating that safeguards were incompatible with the terms of the Treaty of Asunción. The mounting tension was partly defused through skilled presidential diplomacy and voluntary arrangements negotiated directly by businessmen on each side of the border. However, the two countries have been locked in endless trade disputes over issues such as autos and textiles ever since. The election of new presidents in the participating countries who are supportive of Mercosul – Fernando de la Rúa, in Argentina, Jorge Batlle, in Uruguay, and Ricardo Lagos, in Chile – provided much-needed breathing space to consolidate the progress achieved thus far. However, the strength of commitments to Mercosul remains a matter of grave concern.

The crisis was not only an issue of different exchange rate regimes, even though that was the primary trigger. In 1994, Brazil installed the Real plan, a pegged-currency regime that brought annual inflation down from over 2,600 per cent in 1994 to about 6 per cent today. Under such a regime, the price of successful stabilisation is the risk of a balance of payments crisis. Ideally, such crises are avoided in floating and currency board regimes, because market mechanisms should automatically adjust exchange rate and monetary policies. In the former, monetary policy is set by the central bank and the exchange rate is allowed to float. In the latter, a currency board fixes the exchange rate and monetary policy automatically adjusts. If the current account deficit increases suddenly, money supply tightens to cool the economy and moves the system back towards equilibrium.

Under the Real plan, the central bank set both exchange rate and monetary policies, keeping an appreciated currency in order to lower domestic prices through cheaper imports. An undesirable upshot of the overvalued currency was Brazil's poor export performance from 1995 onwards. As long as high interest rates attracted sufficient capital to finance investments and the current account deficit, inflation was kept under control and the economy went through a booming period. However, the moment the confidence of foreign investors in the economic fundamentals dissipated, devaluation was the only way for the country to avoid bankruptcy. After Brazil's abrupt devaluation of the Real, the economy was expected to be in the clutches of a serious recession. Rather than contract, however, Brazil's GDP registered a minuscule, but positive, 0.5 per cent annual growth in 1999, and inflation remained comfortably within the central bank's 6–8 per cent target range. Moreover, the economy grew past 4 per cent in 2000, before expectations of sustained growth were again dashed by the energy crisis of 2001.

Furthermore, as the exchange rate was allowed to float, interest rates were no longer required to prop up the balance of payments and economic policy was 'set free from the imperative of acting in a procyclical manner'.[8] Argentina, however, is still struggling to pull out of recession. To restore investor confidence and attract needed capital inflows to resume growth, the Argentine government was compelled to act precisely in a procyclical fashion, cutting the fiscal deficit and deepening the recession. Although Argentina has already regained its trade surplus with Brazil (thanks in no small measure to trade restrictions negotiated by Brazilian companies with their Argentine counterparts with prodding by Brazil's government), charges of using currency devaluation to gain unfair trade advantage continue to poison bilateral relations.

The sense of vulnerability engendered by the crisis brought to light serious flaws in the operation of Mercosul, as well as the divergent ways in which the economies of the main trade partners have evolved since 1995. It is true that tariff barriers have been largely eliminated within the bloc. Non-tariff barriers, however, have thrived along with bureaucratic inefficiency, and many exceptions to the common external tariff still exist. Mercosul trade partners have also failed to establish shared guidelines on anti-dumping actions and to liberalise services and government procurement. To be sure, significant advances have recently been made with respect to macro-economic policy co-ordination. In April 2000, the presidents of member countries sought to 'relaunch' the Mercosul by grafting macro-economic guidelines onto the regional trade agreement. The goal was to reduce economic volatility by promoting an enforceable code of macro-economic conduct with common targets for inflation and public debt. To this end, the members have moved to harmonise economic statistics, and to set up a system to monitor each member's progress toward meeting their targets. Other developments, however, have the potential to thwart the consolidation of Mercosul as a customs union.

Mercosul and the transformation of Brazil's economy

The evolution of Mercosul can be viewed in three distinct phases. The first phase covers the years 1990 to 1995 and was characterised by a commitment to trade liberalisation. The Collor government's unilateral decision to open the Brazilian economy to international competition set the stage for the adoption of a tariff reduction timetable in Mercosul. Consequently, intra-bloc trade surged and, in 1995, the trade partners decided to move towards a customs union, implementing a common external tariff.

The Collor government's decision set in motion a radical process of industrial re-structuring. However, no industrial policies were put in place to ease the transition, and thus, domestic industry was left to fend for itself. Between 1990 and 1994, according to Motta Veiga,[9] 'trade liberalisation was practically the only major industrial policy initiative in Brazil'. Industry's initial reaction involved a major effort to streamline productive and organisational structures via rationalisation and extensive cost reduction. Investment in the expansion of industrial capacity came later. Although numerous national firms disappeared under the onslaught of foreign competition, many others were able to thrive once trade barriers, which kept the more efficient competitors at bay, were lifted.

Contrary to expectations, trade liberalisation did not de-industrialise Brazil. Actually, the opposite is closer to reality – to the extent that increased competition spurred rapid productivity growth and a swift restructuring and upgrading of the industrial structure. However, successful industrial restructuring was not accompanied by a surge in foreign trade, which was required to finance technology and capital goods imports necessary to sustain the modernisation drive. Brazilian industrial goods lost market share in most export markets while traditional commodities increased in importance. In fact, trade liberalisation made inward-oriented strategies more attractive to business. To survive in an open economy, firms engaged in a type of 'trench war' to defend their share of the domestic market, rather than seek new market niches abroad. The sheer size of the domestic market and the increased levels of consumption stimulated by an appreciated currency also made Brazil more attractive to multinational firms seeking to substitute imports. The domestic market was the main reason for the increase in direct foreign investment from US$77.9 billion in 1995 to US$116.9 billion in 1999.[10]

Brazil also failed to eliminate policies with a significant anti-trade bias. Although the Cardoso administration succeeded in modernising the economy through market deregulation and the privatisation of state assets, fiscal and tax reforms were only partly implemented. It also failed to remove a host of factors that are usually referred to as the 'Brazil cost'. This terminology stresses the negative impact on the economy's aggregate efficiency stemming from logistic factors, production chain bottlenecks and inadequate supply of physical infrastructure factors such as energy, transportation and telecommunications. Tax-induced distortions on economic activities also hamper Brazilian exports. Federal and state value-added taxes, which are applied on an origin basis with multiple rates, penalise business inputs. As argued elsewhere, the Cardoso administration's efforts to balance the budget were light on expenditure cuts and heavy on tax hikes[11] (Souza, 1999). The overall tax burden currently reaches over 31 per cent of GDP. Faced with ballooning deficits and unable to cut constitutionally embedded spending such as intergovernmental transfers, the federal government created new taxes it did not have to share with other tiers of government. Such taxes hamper competitiveness because they tend to apply in cascade or are levied on payrolls. 'Trade policy', Mendonça de Barros summed up, 'has been subordinated to the interests of fiscal policy.'[12]

Insufficient levels of investment are another major hindrance to building economies of scale that would allow industry to simultaneously satisfy domestic and foreign demand for goods and services. Between 1994 and 1998, industrial investment increased significantly, but it remained below the average rates of the 1970s and 1980s.[13] Government deficits and the need to service a large public debt are the main reasons why national savings and investment rates remain low. Up to 1999, congressional resistance to slash Brazil's massive deficit spending forced the government to keep high interest rates in order to attract much needed capital from abroad. The cost of money made the economy stall in 1996 and 1997 and brought it to a halt in 1998 in the aftermath of the Russian debacle. Fiscal and current account deficits are still high and interest payments on the public debt continue to crowd out private investment. A study conducted by the McKinsey Global Institute in 1998, indicated that the gap in investment rates between South Korea and Brazil in the past 15 years was largely derived from Brazil's lower public sector savings (51 per cent); higher prices of capital goods due to import tariffs (20 per cent); higher cost of financial intermediation (17 per cent), and lower private savings rate and net capital inflows (12 per cent).[14]

The second phase in the evolution of Mercosul began in 1994, with the successful implementation of the Real plan. In 1995, Brazil had its first trade deficit in over a decade. As the currency appreciated and foreign imports flooded the market, protectionism became the rallying cry of industry. To prevent further deterioration of the balance of trade, the Cardoso administration sought to restrain the flow of imports by raising tariffs while it tried to expand exports through subsidies, the elimination of the value-added tax levied on exports, and export loan guarantees. A telling sign of the new protectionism was Brazil's adoption of a new automotive regime in mid-1995, which sharply hiked the same import tariffs that had just been reduced in anticipation of Mercosul's common external tariff.

From 1996 onwards, the processes of trade liberalisation and subregional integration became gradually unglued and the original goal of 'open regionalism' that would turn Mercosul into a building block of free world trade faded away. As intra-bloc trade surged, Brazilian industry became more attracted to Mercosul's enlarged consumer market than in trade with third-world countries. 'Exports to the countries of Mercosul (and ALADI)', Motta Veiga remarked, 'performed an important counter-cyclical function in sectors affected by the considerable growth of imports in the domestic market, as in the case of machinery and machine equipment.'[15] Mercosul was also instrumental in attracting sizeable foreign direct investment flows to Brazil. Access to the domestic market, as well as to other Mercosul markets, loomed large in decisions to invest in the

country. At the same time, the country backed off from sub-regional initiatives that might have required an additional lowering of barriers to trade or
reduce its policy-making autonomy. Rather than creating a permanent
dispute settlement mechanism, Brazil insisted on a case-by-case approach
to intra-bloc trade disputes, curbing progress toward the consolidation of
Mercosul as a customs union. Moreover, Brazil did not shy away from
negotiating a bilateral trade agreement with Mexico, to lower tariffs for the
automotive industry, in order to halt the deterioration of the trade balance.

The near collapse of Mercosul after Brazil let the currency float in early
1999 opens a third phase in the evolution of the trade bloc. Brazil's speedy
economic recovery in the aftermath of the devaluation crisis was stimulated
by the Cardoso administration's commitment to fiscal discipline in line with
the 1998 IMF agreement. The country has managed to secure a primary
fiscal surplus in excess of 3.1 per cent of GDP since 1999, opening the way
for a substantial reduction of the benchmark interest rate and, hopefully,
for a sustained path of growth.

Today Mercosul is at the crossroads. The brush with disaster in 1999
and more robust economic fundamentals, encouraged Brazil and Argentina
to 'relaunch' Mercosul and revive the agenda to deepen the sub-regional
association. There are signs that the consensus regarding the trade bloc
may have worn down. 'From the strategic viewpoint of strengthening our
bargaining position *vis-à-vis* the FTAA in 2005, Mercosul is dead', stated
former Secretary of Economic Policy Mendonça de Barros.[16] There are also
reasons for cautious optimism. One reason is the extraordinary growth in
intra-regional trade since Mercosul was founded. Another reason is the
trade partners' common interest in strengthening Mercosul as a core strategy to deal with hemispheric integration along the lines set by the FTAA
proposal.[17] A cohesive bloc is also a prerequisite to engage the EU in the
negotiation of a transatlantic free trade agreement. A stronger Mercosul
may also become a platform for enhancing the participation of the trade
partners in world trade. However, the key to progress is a shared vision of
sub-regional integration. 'What is at stake is not what Mercosul is', suggested De la Balze 'but what Mercosul might be.'[18]

The initiative to 'relaunch' Mercosul

Many of the reasons why Brazil and Argentina pursued regional integration in the Southern Cone have gone astray over the years. Originally, the
creation of a trade bloc related to a broader aspiration to enter the global
economic market. Mercosul was expected to be a building block for international integration, providing a learning ground for economies that

remained closed for too long a time. Trade diversion was expected, rather than trade creation, while intra-bloc trade relations fostered the economies of scale and a more efficient allocation of resources that domestic producers needed in order to compete outside the region. However, the promise of an 'open regionalism' remained somewhat unfulfilled. To a large extent, Brazil went on exporting manufactured goods to Mercosul and other neighbouring countries while its trade with the US and the EU remained limited and poorly diversified. In turn, Brazil became the destination of over a third of Argentina's trade, increasing her dependence, as well as Uruguay's and Paraguay's dependence, on Mercosul's largest market. Competitiveness and productivity gains were mediocre because investment in industrial production was targeted to the region rather than to the global market. In this sense, protectionism and a sharp rise in trade disputes were predictable outcomes of Brazil's currency devaluation.

The devaluation crisis apparently strengthened the trade partners' resolve to preserve Mercosul. Recognition of its importance was buttressed by the quickening pace of the FTAA and the EU trade negotiations. To 'relaunch' Mercosul, however, a series of initiatives are required to complete the trade bloc's transition to a customs union. The top priorities are the co-ordination of macro-economic policies to avoid new exchange rate shocks and the creation of more adequate conflict resolution mechanisms to handle trade disputes. In late 1999, the Montevideo meeting of Mercosul presidents approved a set of initiatives designed to consolidate economic stability and avoid abrupt policy changes within the trade bloc. The most important initiative is the decision to limit public spending and to establish common standards for fiscal responsibility. National statistics will be harmonised to allow for meaningful comparisons of economic outcomes and each country's effort to maintain economic stability will be closely monitored by the trade partners. Such measures are expected to lay the foundations for what president Cardoso called 'a mini-Maastricht', after the treaty that led to the creation of the euro. Needless to say, the eventual adoption of a single currency for Mercosul remains a highly controversial issue given Argentina's currency convertibility scheme. However, the simple mention of it indicated the depth of transformation required to put the Mercosul back on track.

Some sources of friction within Mercosul have been removed. Brazil's commitment to fiscal discipline apparently persuaded Argentina to drop antidumping charges against Brazilian firms who gained a significant cost advantage out of devaluation. The agreement regarding the automobile industry, stipulating that cars made in Argentina should have a certain proportion of locally manufactured parts, opened the way for industry-level negotiations to be ratified, a posteriori, by governments. Other issues seem to be less tractable, such as the adoption of common competition and fair trade practices policies. Lowering import duties to homogenise tariffs between Mercosul and the rest of the world is another hurdle. However, the bone of contention is the creation of a supranational tribunal to serve as Mercosul's permanent arbitration mechanism. Brazil has fiercely resisted the loss of autonomy it entails while Argentina seems to be equally determined to move beyond the existing *ad hoc* arrangement provided by the Brasilia protocol.

A primary focus on the region, and the relocation of some components of national sovereignty to supranational entities, run against the grain of Brazil's traditional foreign policy orientations. Regionalism, as Soares de Lima pointed out, 'is a second-best strategy for Brazil regarding the institutionalisation of multilateral arenas and rules'.[19] In 1999, about 22 per cent of Brazilian exports went to the US, 14 per cent to the Mercosul members, 10 per cent to other countries in the hemisphere, 29 per cent to the EU, and 25 per cent to the rest of the world.[20] Being a global trader and a recipient of world-wide investments, Brazil prefers multilateralism to regionalism. Mercosul is the exception, not least because it represents a power resource to be used in the bargaining table against stronger contenders. It is probably inevitable that continental size nations, dubbed 'monster countries' by George Kennan, will always be engaged in dual-track international negotiations, balancing the imperatives of international integration against the imperatives of national autonomy. In the ensuing two-level game of international negotiation, the risk is that Brazil's and Argentina's commitment to the future of Mercosul become the main casualty.

Dan Rodrik's provocative notion of a 'political trilemma of the world economy'[21] may help to flesh out the implications for Brazil of deepening Mercosul or letting it languish in waiting while pursuing its own national interests. Rodrik's point of departure is the well-known economic impossibility of simultaneously choosing monetary autonomy, a fixed exchange rate and capital mobility. In the political realm, a similar 'trilemma' is set around three nodes: international economic integration (requires that national jurisdictions do not interfere with economic transactions); the nation state (whose sovereignty gives rise to a wide array of transaction costs); and mass politics (i.e. the extent to which political institutions are responsive to mobilised groups).

A country can opt to have, at most, two of the three elements. 'If we want true economic integration', Rodrik suggested, 'we have to go either with the nation-state, in which case the domain of national politics will have to be significantly restricted, or else with mass politics, in which case we will have to give up the nation-state in favour of global federalism.' To opt for national sovereignty while markets become international, requires that a country puts on a 'Golden Straitjacket' – that it abides by the rules of the international marketplace, implementing tight fiscal and monetary policies and market-oriented reforms in order to attract trade and capital. The price of wearing the 'Golden Straitjacket' to the concert of nations is that 'the ability of mobilised popular groups to access and influence national economic policy-making has to be restricted', regardless of the party that happens to be in power.[22]

The alternative to what Rodrik dubbed the 'Argentinization of politics' is global federalism – a perfectly integrated world economy in which national jurisdictions do not entail additional transaction costs. Regional common markets are the closest we are likely to get to global federalism in the foreseeable future. As in the EU, national governments need not disappear, 'but their power would be severely circumscribed by supranational legislative, executive, and judicial authorities' and mass politics would simply shift to the federal level.[23] The price of joining a federation is of course the loss of a significant measure of national policy-making autonomy.

Rodrik's ideal world integration landscape is nowhere to be seen, but it serves to map the range of alternatives open to Brazil in Mercosul. From the point of view of international economic integration, a sub-regional trade bloc is compatible with multilateralism as long as it seeks to foster internal competitiveness as a means to increase trade with the rest of the world. In this sense, domestic reforms are the key adjunct to intergovernmental policies designed to exploit economies of scale and gains from productive specialisation. The issue is that 'Brazil's bargaining power will become increasingly dependent on its acceptance of the concept of qualified sovereignty with respect to Mercosul.'[24]

MERCOSUL, SOUTH AMERICA, FTAA AND THE EUROPEAN UNION

Of the various parts of Brazil's many-pronged agenda, Mercosul is the indisputable priority. Furthermore, the resolution of the issues that currently confront the sub-regional association is a prerequisite for entering negotiations leading to the creation of the FTAA and the establishment of a trade agreement with the EU. Araújo Jr correctly remarked that 'the future of Mercosul hinges more on the consistency of its internal policies than on external challenges'.[25]

Mercosul

Deepening and broadening are the central dimensions of choice for Mercosul. Focusing on these dimensions, De la Balze[26] sketched out three suggestive scenarios for the negotiation of Mercosul's future. The first is the consolidation of a 'genuine customs union' involving a greater opening toward the world economy and the creation of supranational institutions, such as a permanent tribunal, a macro-economic co-ordinating commission, and a permanent commission for international negotiations. Deeper integration of the trade partners would form a 'critical mass' able to negotiate access to other markets under more favourable conditions than each country would have if they were to act in isolation.

From the viewpoint of losing autonomy over decisions that affect the national interest, this scenario appears to be the least appealing for Brazil, although it does maximise the country's clout at the FTAA's bargaining table. However, there is a risk. A genuine customs union must see globalisation as an opportunity for integration into the world economy. However, if protectionism and the desire to substitute imports on a regional scale prevail, Mercosul may find itself transmuted into a 'closed and introspect regional bloc', frustrating the trade partners' aspiration to become increasingly integrated in the world economy.

The second scenario envisages the transformation of Mercosul into a 'full-fledged free trade area' along the lines of NAFTA. The common external tariff would be abolished and the trade partners would regain a considerable measure of autonomy in the management of their respective trade policies. Participating countries would be free to unilaterally reduce protection levels, as well as to enter bilateral free trade agreements with other countries and regions, as Mexico did recently. This feature should practically eliminate the risk of a closed regional bloc; but it would also leave each member to fend off by itself in hemispheric negotiations.

The third and least desirable scenario is what De la Balze calls the 'imperfect integration scenario'.[27] It is essentially a return to the situation that existed before Brazil's currency devaluation, '*a sui generis* combination between an "incomplete free trade area" and an "incomplete customs union", with a low degree of institutionalisation and a *de facto* pre-eminence of Brazil in the management of the region'. De la Balze believes that Brazil stands to profit more from the last scenario. In the absence of compensatory mechanisms that exist in genuine customs unions or in fully fledged free trade areas, the largest partner can attract the lion's share of investment flows. This scenario also dovetails with Brazil's aspiration of regional leadership without a loss of national autonomy. To keep its decisional power intact, Brazil chose, thus far, to keep Mercosul at a minimal level of institutionalisation, operating on the basis of intergovernmental, rather than supranational, mechanisms. 'The Mercosul style has been one of informality and consensus,' remarked Roett (1999b), 'with no central secretariat that has the power to enforce decisions, and practically no con-flict-solving mechanisms.'[28] In the long run, this may leave the sub-regional association in a weaker bargaining position and lower its credibility to enter agreements. Institutionally fragile arrangements may also encourage Brazil's partners to act unilaterally. Argentina's search for a special trade relationship with the US and Chile's reluctance to commit itself to full membership, exemplify the difficulties arising from Mercosul's ambiguity regarding its own future.

The free trade area of South America

Broadening Mercosul poses similar dilemmas. As described by Rios,[29] in the late 1990s Brazil's optimal strategy to implement its foreign trade agenda appeared to be a concentric pattern of trade liberalisation, with the consolidation of Mercosul standing at the centre. The next step would be to consolidate a South American Free Trade Area (SAFTA) while striving to advance agricultural trade liberalisation in a new WTO round of nego-tiations. Only afterwards would Mercosul implement the FTAA and the free trade agreement with the EU.

Seeking to forge a new diplomatic role in the region, Brazil also intro-duced a geo-political distinction between South America and Latin America (which also takes in Mexico, Central America and parts of the Caribbean). This occurred during the first Summit of South American presidents, convened in 2000, to move toward a potential free trade zone in the region. These claims are still unpersuasive.

The broadening of Mercosul to create the SAFTA was originally pro-posed by Brazil in 1993. The task would be accomplished by substituting Mercosul agreements for the old ALADI arrangements. Before Mercosul turned into a customs union, its members were signatories to bilateral pref-erential agreements with several Latin American countries under the aegis of ALADI. To prevent a perforation of the common external tariff adopted in 1995, pre-existing bilateral arrangements would be replaced by new pref-erential agreements signed by Mercosul.[30] In 1996, Mercosul signed free trade agreements with Chile and Bolivia, who were granted an associate membership status. The negotiation of a preferential agreement with the Andean Community (Bolivia, Colombia, Ecuador and Venezuela) proved to be more difficult than was originally anticipated. In any event, the

SAFTA should be the end result of Mercosul's own network of free trade agreements throughout the region.

There are good arguments in favour of this initiative. The South American region might benefit from the potential synergy between diplomacy and economic geography. Assessing the Southern Cone experience, Araújo Jr observed that 'the extraordinary growth of regional transactions in the Mercosul region after 1985 can be seen as an economic geography phenomenon. As soon as barriers were lifted, Mercosul firms began to carry out a volume of transactions that was compatible with the region's level of affluence.'[31] South American countries already constitute the principal market for Brazilian industrial goods, accounting for over 40 per cent of exports in 1998. Broadening Mercosul to include the rest of South America is also consistent with geo-economic trends that are shaping contemporary Brazil, with the gradual shift of people and capital towards the interior of the country and the new agricultural frontiers in the west and the north. Industrial deconcentration is also changing the economic landscape as firms leave the southeast in search of low-wage labour and locational advantages in the less developed regions.[32]

Physical integration through the implementation of cross-border infrastructure projects also looms large in the prospects for regional integration. As Lafer pointed out, the role of geography can be magnified 'if three vectors – logistics/transportation, telecommunications, and energy – are simultaneously developed to add value and reduce costs, thus expanding comparative advantages in a process of competitive insertion into the world economy'.[33] In 1999, Brazil designed the National Integration and Development Axes programme, an ambitious developmental blueprint that identified bottlenecks and missing links in infrastructure (energy, transport and telecommunications), social needs (education, health and housing), scientific and technological information, and environmental management. The programme developed a portfolio of 385 investment projects, which are expected to cost some US$181 billion over the next eight years. Given Brazil's increasing dependence on regional supply of oil and natural gas, economic integration with neighbouring countries via investment in joint infrastructure projects has been assigned top priority.[34]

To paraphrase Paul Krugman, the goal is 'to eliminate international economy and replace it with economic geography'.[35] What is lacking are the means to translate lofty objectives into reality. Broadening Mercosul preferences to South American countries might yield economies of scale and augment the economic efficiency of domestic producers, and hence attenuate the adjustment costs of entering a hemispheric free trade agreement at a later date. However, this possibility hinges crucially on the economic dynamism of the Mercosul partners, notably Brazil.

The Free Trade Area of the Americas (FTAA)

Taking full advantage of economies of scale to grow, however, is a viable possibility for Brazil in the context of a hemispheric free trade agreement. Differently from most countries in the Americas, Araújo Jr observed that

> Brazil and the United States have a variety of trade partners world-wide. Therefore, access to the European market, the dialogue with strategic partners such as Japan, and the strengthening of the WTO as a multilateral forum of negotiation are important priorities for both countries. On the other hand, the competitiveness of their respective export industries is particularly sensitive to economies of scale to be generated by hemispheric integration.[36]

Existing complementarities can be gleaned from trade statistics. Between 1997 and 1999, about 20 per cent of Brazil's exports went to the US. In 1999, 70 per cent of Brazilian exports to that country were manufactured goods, notably aeroplanes and motor vehicles. In contrast to the past, Brazil has been able to export more dynamic products for which demand is on the rise in the North American market. This change notwithstanding, Brazil's relative share of US imports has dwindled in recent years. In 1991, Brazil accounted for 1.4 per cent of total US imports and ranked as its 13th largest trade partner. Since 1997, Brazil's share was reduced to 1.1 per cent, precisely when the American economy was booming. Two other factors appear to be equally important. The first is the establishment of a preferential trade treatment with Mexico (through NAFTA) and China. From 1991 to 1999, Mexican exports jumped from 6.3 per cent to 10.5 per cent and China increased its volume of trade, going from 3.6 per cent to 7.9 per cent over the same period. The second factor is the intensification of antidumping suits and the imposition of tariff and non-tariff barriers against Brazilian exports, especially steel, sugar and orange juice. From Brazil's point of view, the FTAA is attractive only to the extent that it can assure the same preferential trade treatment that is already granted to its main competitors in the US market, and avoid the imposition of barriers to Brazil's exports.

Another source of concern for Brazil and Mercosul is that the FTAA goes beyond a traditional free trade arrangement seeking only tariff and other border barrier reductions to include 'agreement on domestic rules of the game – intellectual property rights, product standards, internal competition policy, government procurement and, to a lesser degree, labour and environmental standards'.[37] (Birdsall and Lawrence 1999: 128). However, the FTAA model provides no space for trade partners to share in decisions regarding the management of trade relations other than through traditional conflict resolution mechanisms. The US is pushing for a hemispheric integration model that would essentially extend to the countries south of Mexico the rights and obligations already conferred by NAFTA.[38] Actually, differences between NAFTA and Mercosul are large enough to be considered as distinct models for integration. As described by Bernier and Roy 'NAFTA represents a mostly contractual approach based on legal dynamics, and Mercosul represents a participatory approach based on political dynamics. The contractual approach focuses primarily on rules that place rigid controls on the behaviour of members, restricting government powers.'[39] How to preserve Mercosul as a preferential system within FTAA is a matter of concern. However, it only compounds the more general preoccupation that the FTAA framework might provide the US and the other NAFTA partners, with the possibility to manipulate domestic standards in order to gain a competitive advantage.

The reluctance of the US Congress to grant fast-track authority to the president has slowed progress on the FTAA negotiation. While the goal of reaching a hemisphere-wide free trade agreement by 2005 remains in force, a speedy conclusion of negotiations seems unlikely. Resistance to the FTAA has surfaced in the US as labour and environmental lobbies intensified efforts to include social and environmental clauses in the free trade agreement. Likewise, business and congressional leaders expressed strong opposition to Mercosul's demand that the US antidumping legislation be revised in the course of FTAA negotiations. In Brazil, the FTAA has also met with growing scepticism given the persistence of trade barriers to Brazil's most competitive export products.

However, it would be misleading to conclude that the FTAA is seen solely as a threat on both sides of the border. As in any complex two-level game of international negotiation, a significant part of the American and Brazilian business communities expect to benefit from wider access to each nation's respective market. Work on the FTAA negotiation clauses has proceeded rapidly since the second summit of the Americas held in Santiago in 1998.[40] However, the uncertainty surrounding the FTAA's timetable in the absence of fast-track authorisation provides an important window of opportunity for Mercosul to regroup, seek to consolidate ties to the EU, and move toward the deepening of Mercosul as leverage in the hemispheric negotiation. If these tasks are successfully accomplished, Mercosul will be in a stronger bargaining position when the FTAA negotiations reopen in 2002.

The European Union

Having been partly inspired by the Europeans' ground-breaking experience of regional integration and unification, the Mercosul partners have been more agreeably inclined to advance trade negotiations with the EU, than with the US. What matters here is that the two sides share a basic orientation towards multilateralism, they are driven by a similar vision of a multipolar international system, and that they have a keen interest in emerging borderless issues such as global warming and human rights. They are also bound by more tangible entanglements. Since 1996, the EU has been the principal source of foreign direct investments in Mercosul.

Yet, the actual conduct of trade negotiations with the EU is bound to be disappointing for Mercosul. For one thing, the EU has erected a formidable wall of protectionism, which is at least as effective as North America's. Within the EU, Mercosul exports are subject to numerous non-tariff barriers such as sanitary and phytosanitary restrictions, quotas, subsidies, anti-dumping and countervailing duties, and technical barriers in addition to relatively high tariffs. This is particularly true with respect to agricultural trade in which Mercosul has a special interest. Average tariffs on manufactured goods are around 4 per cent, whereas agricultural tariffs are in the range of 40 per cent to 50 per cent. In a free trade environment, the Mercosul industry is also likely to face competition from the EU as stiff as North America's. Since 1990, Mercosul has been the fastest growing export market for the EU. From 1990 to 1997, exports to Mercosul grew annually by 19.7 per cent, almost three times as fast as European exports to the rest of the world. However, imports from Mercosul grew a meagre 3.7 per cent annually over the same period, compared with 17.4 per cent from China. Moreover, Mercosul exports mostly farm products and raw materials to the EU while it imports mostly high value-added products such as machinery, chemicals and equipment.

The consequence of overly ambitious diplomacy, the Mercosul's interest in a trade deal with the EU serves, to a large extent, as a counterpoise to the push by the US toward the FTAA. The novelty is that it is a negotiation between regions, a new form of international relations that Grabendorff dubbed an interregional association.[41] This new type of alliance goes beyond a free trade area, involving co-operation over a wide range of policy issues such as the environment, international crime, and the development of new technologies. It is also more difficult to negotiate because 'each bloc has a distinct external agenda and both blocs face the issue of widening and deepening, an issue that is not easily reconciled either in the European Union or in Mercosul'.[42] The obvious advantage is that such an association is bound to increase both regions' bargaining power in the international system as well as in multilateral forum.

Progress to date has been slow. Formal negotiations were finally initiated in mid-1999, but there are wide areas of disagreement regarding the removal of non-tariff barriers and domestic farm subsidies that bar access of Mercosul agricultural products to the EU market. Another issue is the opening up of Mercosul to European services and industrial goods. It is unclear how these claims will be balanced in the negotiation process. It is equally unclear whether Mercosul will be able to pursue parallel negotiations with the EU and FTAA, giving similar preferences and market access to both.

CONCLUSION

The core question is whether Brazil and other South American nations can effectively manage their economies in a globalised world. Brazil's entanglement in multilateral trade disputes has greatly increased, as the country seeks to expand market access for its products. The bitter trade conflicts with Canada illustrate the difficulties that Brazil faces to overcome barriers that block its exports to world markets, ranging from commodities (beef) to high-tech products (regional jet planes). From this viewpoint, Brazil's best chances lie in a new WTO trade round. No hemispheric or transatlantic free trade agreement could offer greater potential gains for the country's negotiating efforts than a new round to liberalise world trade. However, reaching an agreement at WTO to launch a new round, hinges on factors beyond Brazil's reach.

Regionalism has been the response, but Mercosul's slow progress casts doubts as to the trade partners' ability to sustain a unified front to negotiate more favourable terms in a hemispheric integration process under the FTAA, or in a free trade area with the EU. By binding themselves to one another, Brazil and Argentina, and to a lesser extent Uruguay and Paraguay, expected that they would be better off integrating their economies and forging common stances on a range of issues than trying to fend for themselves in an adverse international environment. Despite its success as a trade bloc since its founding in 1991, Mercosul has been floundering under economic frustration and bitter trade disputes between Brazil and

Argentina. Little progress has been made in liberalising intra-bloc trade or consolidating the customs union and still less in making Mercosul a competitive platform in world trade.

'The FTAA is a choice, but Mercosul is destiny', proclaimed president Cardoso at the April 2001 FTAA summit in Quebec. That is why the initiative to 'relaunch' Mercosul represents a crucial effort, not only to overcome the trade bloc's institutional fragility and avoid a loss of power at the bargaining table, but also to unlock the trade partners' economic potential by widening and deepening their union. A rejuvenated Mercosul is a prerequisite for increasing power in international negotiations, as well as to foster the development of competitive economies in the Southern Cone. It is conceivable that the dynamics of hemispheric trade liberalisation might accelerate the speed of sub-regional integration. Motta Veiga suggested that 'the pressure to negotiate the FTAA could lead Brazil to adopt a position less resistant to issues that so far have been considered to have low priority. In fact, Brazil's proposal to make sub-regional integration schemes the building blocks of the FTAA requires that Mercosul take up the issues and subjects pertaining to the agenda for deepening the customs union.'[43] However, as important as endowing Mercosul with the institutional backbone that will allow the trade bloc to effectively co-ordinate macro-economic policies and settle trade disputes, is also the need to increase competitiveness by simultaneously increasing the exposure of the sub-regional economy to international competition and the export coefficient of domestic industry. Keeping a high common external tariff will hardly pay off as a tactic for achieving a stronger negotiating position *vis-à-vis* FTAA or the EU if it keeps Mercosul from augmenting its competitiveness. What matters in the upcoming trade negotiations is to assure that Mercosul will compete on a level playing field with other preferential trade partners of the US and the EU, and that decisive action to remove non-tariff barriers to its products be taken.

As the Southern Cone's largest nation, Brazil holds the key to the future of Mercosul. Brazil's poor export performance and its vulnerability to outside events threaten to retard growth and unravel sub-regional integration. A chronic trade imbalance and mounting current account deficits, however, are only part of the problem. A significant growth boost is unlikely to follow from a more aggressive involvement in the international political economy alone. What is needed, as Rodrik (1999) argues,[44] is a strategy that uses trade liberalisation to allow the forces of comparative advantage to push the economy toward sustained growth. After decades of high trade barriers and import substitution policies, economic and institutional reform is required to increase domestic savings and investment, create conglomerates with economies of scale, and breed an outward-looking corporate attitude. It should be stressed that Proex, the export-financing mechanism that triggered the trade row with Canada over Embraer, was set up to compensate for Brazil's high capital costs that reduce the competitiveness of otherwise efficient companies, rather than to prolong. The key, therefore, is to combine the aggressive pursuit of world trade opportunities with an equally aggressive economic and institutional reform strategy at home.

NOTES

1. Rodrick, Dani, 'Trade Policy Reform as Institutional Reform', paper prepared for a handbook on *Developing Countries and the New WTO Negotiations*, edited by B. Hoekman, 2000.
2. Huntington, Samuel, P. 'The Lonely Superpower', *Foreign Affairs* 78, 2, 1999, pp. 35–49.
3. Lafer, Celso, 'Brazilian International Identity and Foreign Policy: Past, Present and Future', *Daedalus*, 129, 2, pp. 207–38, 2000.
4. Wolf, Martin, 'Will the Nation-State Survive Globalisation?', *Foreign Affairs*, 80, 1, pp. 178–90, 2001.
5. Roett, Riordan, 'US Policy Toward Mercosul: From Miami to Santiago', in *Mercosul: Regional Integration, World Markets*, Boulder, CO, Lynne Rienner Publishers, pp. 111–24, 1999.
6. Bouzas, Roberto, 'Mercosul's External Trade Negotiations: Dealing with a Congested Agenda', in Riordan Roett, editor, *Mercosul: Regional Integration, World Markets*, Boulder, CO, Lynne Rienner Publishers, pp. 81–93, 1999.
7. Daalder, Ivo. H. 'Are the United States and Europe Heading for Divorce?', *International Affairs*, 2.
8. Castro, Antonio Barros, 'O Crescimento: Revendo o Passando e Pensando o Futuro', in Joao Paulo dos Reis Velloso, editor, *Brasil: 500 anos. Futuro, Presente, Passado*, Rio de Janeiro, Jose Olympio Editora, pp. 303–51, 2000.
9. Motta Veiga, Pedro da, 'Brazil in Mercosul: Reciprocal Influence', in Riordan Roett, editor, *Mercosul: Regional Integration, World Markets*, Boulder, CO, Lynne Rienner Publishers, pp. 25–33, 1999.
10. Sobeet, Carta, 'O Ciclo Recente de Investimentos Diretos Estrangerious no Brasil', *Carta da SOBEET*, 3, 14, 2000.
11. Souza, Amaury de, 'Cardoso and the Struggle for Reform in Brazil', *Journal of Democracy*, 10, 3, pp. 49–63, 1999.
12. Mendonça de Barros and José Roberto, 'Tres Difeceis Questoes do Comercio Externo', *Gazeta Mercantil*, November, 21, 2, 2000.
13. Bielschowsky, Ricardo, Marcos Thadeu Abicalil, José Clemente de Oliveira, Sebastião Soares and Marcio Wohlers, 'Formação de Capital no Ambiente das Reformas Econômicas Brasileiras dos Anos 90: Uma Abordagem Setorial', in Renato Baumann, editor, *Brasil: Uma Década em Transição*, Rio de Janeiro, Editora Campus, pp. 143–81, 2000.
14. McKinsey Global Institute, *Productivity: The Key to an Accelerated Development Path for Brazil*, São Paulo, McKinsey Brazil Office, 1998.
15. Motta Veiga, Pedro da, 'Brazil in Mercosul: Reciprocal Influence', in Riordan Roett, editor, *Mercosul: Regional Integration, World Markets*, Boulder, CO, Lynne Rienner Publishers, pp. 25–33, 1999.

16. Mendonça de Barros and José Roberto, 'Tres Difeceis Questoes . . .', 2000.

17. Albuquerque, José Augusto Guilhon, 'A Integração Regional e a Agenda Multilateral Pós-Seattle', in Pedro da Motta Veiga, editor, *O Brasil e os Desafios da Globalização*, Rio de Janeiro, SOBEET/Relume-Dumará, pp. 229–36, 2000.

18. De la Balze, Felipe, 'El Destino del Mercosul: Entre la Unión Aduanera y la Integración Imperfecta', in Felipe De la Balze, editor, *El Futuro del Mercosul: Entre la Retórica y el Realismo*, Buenos Aires, ABA/CARI, pp. 13–76, 2000.

19. Soares de Lima and Maria Regina, 'Brazil's Alternative Vision', in Gordon Mace and Luir Bélanger, editors, *The Americas in Transition: The Contours of Regionalism*, Boulder, CO, Lynne Rienner Publishers, pp. 133–51, 1999.

20. Rios, Sandra Polónia, 'A Influência da ALCA na Agenda Brasileira de Negociações Comerciais', in Pedro da Motta Veiga, editor, *O Brasil e os Desafios da Globalização*, Rio de Janeiro, SOBEET/Relume-Dumará, pp. 237–52, 2000.

21. Rodrick. Dan, 'How Far Will International Economic Integration Go?', *Journal of Economic Perspectives*, 14, 1, pp. 177–86, 2000.

22. Ibid. p. 180.

23. Ibid. pp. 182–3.

24. Soares de Lima and Maria Regina, 'Brazil's Alternative Vision', p. 149, 1999.

25. Araújo Jr, José Tavares de, 'ALCA: Riscos e Oportunidades para o Brasil', in Samuel Pinheiro Guimarães, editor, *ALCA e Mercosul: Riscos e Oportunidades para o Brasil*, Brasília, IPRI, FUNAG, pp. 41–106, 1999.

26. De la Balze, Felipe, 'El Destino de Mercosul . . .', pp. 31ff. 2000.

27. Ibid. p. 39.

28. Roett. R., 'A Full Plate', *Worldlink*, p. 3, 1999.

29. Rios, Sandra Polóniam 'A Influência . . .', p. 237, 2000.

30. Bouzas, Roberto, 'Mercosul's External Trade . . .', p. 82, 1999.

31. Araújo Jr, José Tavares de, 'ALCA: Riscos . . .', p. 75, 1999.

32. Campolina, Clélio Diniz, 'A Nova Geografia Econômica do Brasil', in João Paulo dos Reis Velloso, editor, *Brasil 500 Anos: Futuro, Presente, Passado*, Rio de Janeiro, José Olympio Editora, pp. 303–51, 2000.

33. Lafer, Celso, 'Multilateralismo e Regionalismo na Ordem Econômica Mundial', in *A OMC e a Regulamentação do Comércio Internacional: Uma Visão Brasileira*, Porto Alegre, Livraria do Advogado, p. 87, 1998.

34. Silveira, José Paulo, 'Os Eixos Nacionais de Integração e Desenvolvimento', in João Paulo dos Reis Velloso, editor, *Brasil 500 Anos: Futuro, Presente, Passado*, Rio de Janeiro, José Olympio Editora, pp. 295–302, 2000.

35. Krugman, Paul, *Geography and Trade*, Cambridge, MA, MIT Press, p. 69, 1991.

36. Araújo Jr., José Tavares de, 'ALCA: Riscos . . .', 1999.

37. Birdsall and Lawrence, 1999.

38. Bélanger, Louis, 'U.S. Foreign Policy and the Regionalist Option in the Americas', in Gordon Mace and Louis Bélanger, editors, *The Americas in Transition: The Contours of Regionalism*, Boulder, CO, Lynne Rienner Publishers, pp. 95–109, 1999.

39. Bernier, Ivan and Martin Roy, 'NAFTA and Mercosul: Two Competing Models?', in Gordon Mace and Luir Bélanger, editors, *The Americas in Transition: The Contours of Regionalism*, Boulder, CO, Lynne Rienner Publishers, 69–91, 1999.

40. CNI, 'ALCA: Os Avanços do Projeto de Integração Continental', Confederação Nacional da Indústria, *Comércio Exterior em Perspectiva*, 9, 12, 2000.

41. Grabendorff, Wolf, 'Mercosul and the European Union: From Cooperation to Alliance?', in

Riordan Roett, editor, *Mercosul: Regional Integration, World Markets*, Boulder, CO, Lynne Rienner Publishers, pp. 95–109, 1999.

42. Ibid. p. 106.
43. Motta Veiga, Pedro da, 'Brazil in Mercosul: Reciprocal Influence', in Riordan Roett, editor, *Mercosul: Regional Integration, World Markets*, Boulder, CO, Lynne Rienner Publishers, pp. 25–33, 1999.
44. Rodrick, Dani, *The New Global Economy and Developing Countries: Making Openess Work*, Washington, DC, Overseas Development Council, 1999.

TEN

———◄◦►———

Brazilian Foreign Policy at the Beginning of the Twenty-First Century

CLODOALDO HUGUENEY

Thinking about Brazilian foreign policy in a medium-term perspective is not an easy task. Foreign policy projects Brazil's reality and interests into the world. Consequently, a prospective vision of foreign policy depends not only on a view of Brazil's reality and how its changes will affect the definition of its interests, but also on international scenarios, which allow Brazil to set some guidelines for its diplomatic action. Such a discussion is more difficult today because we are living in transition periods at the internal and international levels. At present, new and old forms coexist and the final shape of the new forms is still unclear. The Brazilian scene is even more complex for a number of reasons:

1. At the domestic level, the challenges of modernisation in an environment of growing international integration are coupled in a medium-term perspective with the need to overcome the legacy of backwardness, particularly in the social area, while increasing democratic liberties.

2. At the external level, the challenges of globalisation offer the opportunity of a more positive and dynamic integration of Brazil into the world economy, with the external dimension functioning as an important factor of internal transformation or, on the opposite, as a threat of an unequal integration linked to the renunciation to the dream of a more autonomous international projection for Brazil and the increase of internal dichotomies between modern and non-modern sectors, with growingly unequal development.

3. As to intersections between the external and internal levels, the challenges are important too, both because the ability to influence the international situation is limited and because the specific weight restricts our degree of autonomy at the international level.

4. Finally, it is important to realise that an expansion of the international sphere is taking place, reflected in the multiplicity of the so-called global issues, and of the new actors on the international scene in growing competition with the state, as indicated by the increasing importance of public diplomacy and by the claims for transparency and legitimacy.

In a short chapter, these unavoidable issues will have to be summarily treated. The exposition will begin by identifying some simplifying views (scenarios) relating to Brazil's future and the main trends on the international scene. These scenarios and trends are only possibilities, and in some instances the text will try to warn against less desirable alternatives. Starting from those draft scenarios, I will point out and examine six central issues for Brazilian diplomacy in the coming years.

For the purposes of this discussion of the future trends in Brazilian foreign policy, we will assume that Brazil will be able to overcome the challenges of modernisation and build a more democratic and socially fair society. Such an assumption is justified, from the point of view of a proposal for foreign policy, because the alternatives of muddling through, anti-democratic nightmares, or a worsening of exclusions, would reduce the degree of autonomy of foreign policy. This would become an expiatory foreign policy with a strongly marked defensive character. An alternative would be a subordinated and excluding modernisation, which would allow an associative-type international integration in the style of peripheral realism with the absorption of some advantages of the global integration, but with an increase of internal heterogeneity and the renunciation to a larger degree of autonomy.

At the international level, the main scenario will be the deepening of globalisation combined with an open regional integration and tendencies in peripheral areas. There is nothing inescapable or immutable in this scenario. Globalisation has already been greater in other historical times, and then receded. Parallel scenarios may turn into alternative scenarios. There is nothing to justify the belief that the crises of capitalism have been overcome, and that democratic political liberties are secure. This is not new and has already proved inaccurate in the past. At the same time, it seems obvious that the present reality of globalisation is determined by economic and technological forces that shape a reality different from the reality of past times. In the past, a very high degree of universalisation, viewed as a growing integration of national areas into the international reality, was achieved.

The other assumption that can be made in relation to world configuration for the years to come is that the world will remain unipolar. The challenge of building an international order lies in the ability to manage situations of crisis in any area, in a balanced way. Furthermore, it is the ability to strengthen multipolarity factors through a more shared management of power. A positive answer would strengthen multilateralism and distribute world wealth more equitably. A negative answer would increase the temptations of unilateralism and the indiscriminate use of power with the growing disparity between rich and poor nations. Based on these assumptions, it is possible to say that:

1. The positive internal developments will project a Brazil with growing interests and the capacity to act on the international scene. This implies a more assertive foreign policy in accordance with national interests. Brazil will become a more important international partner and, as such, will have to take positions on issues of the international agenda, which will very often have little to do with its immediate interests. At the same time, Brazil's capacity to act at the international level will remain limited, due to her specific weight and to the limited resources available for foreign policy operations. This is because internal challenges will remain more important than external challenges, and the ability to face them will remain a precondition for an assertive foreign policy. The predominance of internal challenges over the international and the limitation of resources will require a clear definition of priorities for Brazil's foreign policy. This assessment would change if the international situation could set important obstacles in the way of Brazil's internal objectives. At first sight, such a possibility could arise in the context of a process of integration in the world economy. This would reduce Brazil's internal levels of autonomy or, due to changes in the immediate neighbourhood, could pose a threat to Brazil's national objectives.

2. A basic globalisation scenario in combination with open processes of regional integration and fragmentation movements would require, on the part of Brazil, an assertive foreign policy rather than a policy exacerbating differences. Such a policy involves an objective of growing integration in a global world. However, considering that

such a reality reflects a power structure which has not been defined to meet the interests of emerging countries such as Brazil, its foreign policy cannot be a mere exercise of adaptation to international reality. Nor can it be based in the naive belief that this reality can be a simple mechanism to solve our internal problems. Rather, the international reality must be considered, if not as an obstacle, then as a challenge constantly demanding a clear vision of Brazil's national interests and of the best way to defend them at the international level. At the same time, the realism dictated by the limited ability to influence the international scene, as well as a certain degree of coincidence between national objectives and the reality of globalisation, recommend that the element of criticism and opposition in Brazil's foreign policy be less important than the element of similarities.

3. The coexistence of globalisation, with the formation of economically, politically and culturally integrated areas, open to countries such as Brazil, is an important opportunity to assert their specificity, and to set up a basis for their integration into the international economy. The South American area in which Brazil is integrated is fortunately an area in which the assertion of similarities is much more natural than the building of an identity through the exacerbation of differences. The construction of a political, economic and cultural integrated area in South America through a policy of co-operation and affirmation of common values, must be the top priority for Brazilian foreign policy.

4. Such a construction will require constant attention to the challenges of fragmentation in Brazil's region, through the exacerbation of differences and social inequalities, or through the infiltration of organised crime. Considering Brazil's weight in the region, the building of an integrated area in South America needs a Brazilian leadership supported by an open, stable and expanding economy. Such leadership will not be inspired by a yearning for hegemony, but by co-operation schemes that provide space for neighbouring countries, and recognise the need to share responsibilities and the gains of the integration process.

Brazilian foreign policy is rightly proud of its continuity, of a constancy deriving from a diplomatic tradition set up since independence. Furthermore, it was derived from a predictable action due to a combination of respect for certain principles of international coexistence and, in the post-war period, of its professionalism. Projecting a foreign policy for the first decades of the century must start from a reflection on that diplomatic tradition, its principles, its basic trends and its implementation. A reflection of this kind seems extremely important in relation to the recent trends expressed in certain global issues, such as human rights, drug trafficking and the environment, in order to qualify some central principles of Brazil's diplomatic tradition. These are principles such as non-intervention and equality between states and the United Nations supremacy in the decision to use force. The mere repetition of Brazil's diplomatic tradition in a context of important changes could put it on the fringe of the international debate. On the other hand, adopting a policy determined only by pragmatism, and varying according to developments, as well as the decisions of the main actors on the international scene, would be a denial of all the diplomatic traditions, with a consequent loss of credibility. Moreover, it would act against Brazil's interests, since she would become a hostage of external pressures. Such a policy would also serve as a guarantee of the intentions in Brazil's relations with other countries.

As Brazil's international importance grows, and as she is led to take a larger part in the solution of global issues (as well as in the maintenance of peace and security), the demands will increase for the redefinition of certain principles of the diplomatic action. These principles, while keeping their essence, will have to be updated in light of the evolution of international relations. Those demands are already present in the preventive action proposals, in the temptation to use military force with low risks due to the evolution in technology, in the assertion of certain universal values which should be respected world-wide, and in the pressure from public diplomacy and the media to take decisive action. These issues will be treated below, but always from the standpoint of Brazil's diplomatic tradition: the defence of multilateralism and the rejection of unilateral solutions; the legitimacy principle in the definition of any action, both in terms of freely accepted international obligations and in terms of the need for a universal and equitable enforcement of obligations; and the strengthening of multipolarity and regional integration as protections against unilateralism.

Continuity also finds another expression: through the upholding of the main orientation of Brazilian foreign policy in the years to come. Indeed, Brazilian foreign policy has always tried to avoid sudden shifts and dramatic gestures. This trend is part of the diplomatic tradition and there is no reason to believe that, in the absence of unpredictable events, at both the international and the national levels, a completely different foreign policy should be adopted. Imagining the unpredictable does not seem possible. On the other hand, foreign policy achievements always go through a lengthy maturation process. Therefore, it seems right to presume that the present will, to a large extent, mark the future with the necessary changes being determined by the evolution of the internal and external scenarios.

THE MAJOR QUESTIONS

In recent decades, we have witnessed the emergence of a number of issues that will remain important for the definition of Brazilian foreign policy in the years to come. The objective here is simply to pinpoint those issues treated in the following sections.

The first of these questions relates to the new integration of Brazil into the global economy. The recent integration of markets and production structures supported by the fast development of information technologies will intensify three different aspects of the global economy. First, the integration and homogenising features of economic areas in globalised sectors; second, the unequal nature of globalisation; and finally, in the process, the possibility of crises and setbacks.

Next to the challenges of globalisation, the construction of a politically, economically and culturally integrated area in South America will probably remain the main priority for Brazilian diplomacy. The success of this regional integration effort will be achieved by strengthening and enlarging Mercosul. If successful, it will facilitate the integration of Brazil and the region in the global economy.

As to the political field, unipolarity will make the relation with the superpower even more complex, at both the bilateral and the regional levels. The conclusion of the ALCA negotiations will mark hemispheric relations.

Global questions will represent a new challenge for Brazilian diplomacy. Their increased presence on the international scene will require an even greater involvement in the search for solutions to them. The treatment of these issues is linked to two other important questions: the redefinition of the notion of national sovereignty, and the creation of a new international institutionality.

The fifth important challenge that Brazilian diplomacy will face in the next decades will be its attitude towards security questions, globally and in the region. Globally, a new consensus on disarmament seems a priority, as well as developing new responses to local conflicts. Regionally, a common approach to internal problems, based on dialogue and co-operation, must be developed.

Finally, in the context of globalisation and the reduction of the role of the state, new actors are gaining influence in international relations. It seems that the creation of new forms of dialogue and co-operation with these actors will be increasingly important in the years to come.

This short identification of questions, which is schematic and oversimplified, can nevertheless constitute a guideline for the discussion of Brazilian diplomacy in the first decades of the twenty-first century.

In the next sections, I will endeavour to single out priorities for Brazilian diplomacy in relation to the six major questions mentioned above: globalisation; regionalisation; unipolarity; global issues; new challenges to security; and the arrival of new actors on the world scene.

Considering the length of this chapter and its nature, the discussion will remain at a high level of generalisation and will simply try, with a few exceptions, to single out the main lines of action for Brazilian diplomacy. To make up for this limitation, a section listing some concrete initiatives in the six examined areas will be included at the end of this work.

GLOBALISATION AND THE BRAZILIAN ECONOMIC DIPLOMACY

In the recent decades, Brazilian diplomacy has been mainly an economic diplomacy. Due to the absence of serious security problems in its close neighbourhood, Brazil has primarily turned its diplomatic activity towards the opening of spaces abroad, to aid its internal development efforts. Brazilian diplomacy, without disregarding the high importance of its political dimension, or the fact that a separation between politics and economy is somewhat superficial, has concentrated on the economic field. A few examples of this range from the defence of the prices of its raw materials through international agreements between producers and consumers, to the participation as a founding member of the GATT, to the fights for textile and steel markets in the US and in Europe, and to the pioneering relations with the European Community and innovating efforts to promote exports. This tendency remains present today, despite the change in the agenda and direction due to Brazil's internal transformations, and the changes in the international economy.

Brazil is one of the first ten world economies, and therefore its weight in the region and in the world leads it to extend its international economic links. At a time where integration of productive structures and markets at the global level is growing and in which technological developments are changing growth models, an economy as important as Brazil's cannot imagine a development on the fringe of globalisation. On the contrary, it must work towards an ever-stronger integration into the international economy. The answer to Brazil's development challenges lies not in isolation, but in a positive integration.

The Brazilian economic diplomacy must continue to change from a resistance diplomacy to a participation diplomacy. For instance, in the trade area the concern is no longer restrictions to imports, but the promotion of exports. In the investment sector, the concern is the removal of barriers to access and the expansion of flows. It will be increasingly in Brazil's interest to take part in the groups deciding the destinies of the international economy rather than adopting an antagonistic stance towards these groups.

A participating economic diplomacy requires, in the context of a growing globalisation, an internal economic performance compatible with international patterns. Broadly speaking, such a performance implies significant and sustainable growth rates and the reduction of vulnerabilities, both internal (social inequality, disequilibrium of the public sector, insufficient internal savings, technological backwardness and institutional fragility) and external (deficit in current transactions, low dynamism and diversification of exports). It is apparent from the global consensus on theories of growth in an open economy, and from the reliance in this context on volatile capital, that there is a need for adequate performance as well as consistent and sustainable policies. The dimensions of the Brazilian economy and its development level give Brazil important assets but do not exempt it, as the recent crises showed, from the necessity to have an adequate and strong performance.

In the context of a daily judgement by the markets on the internal economic performance of each country, the reduction of external vulnerabilities is important. In an economy of global markets, but with international institutions endowed with a limited management and response capability, volatility and crisis will remain a part of life. This is in spite of the optimism for the 'new economy' which, ultimately, is not new and will only repeat perceptions of irreversibility common at other moments of rapid growth. A growing integration into the international economy will therefore require, in addition to a strong internal performance, a constant vigilance as to the country's external vulnerability. If not, Brazil might transform its integration in the global economy into an element of instability and crisis, rather than a factor of growth and stability.

The reduction of the external vulnerability, inherent in the process of globalisation, and the growing integration of the Brazilian economy into the international economy, seems the main task of Brazilian economic diplomacy in the coming decades. Here, three sets of actions appear to be relevant:

1. To carry on working at the global level through the reform of the international financial institutions, and gain a better coherence

between trade and finance. The objective would be to increase the manageability of the system, measured by its capacity to avoid and overcome crises, and to promote a balanced growth and development, with an increasing integration of emerging economies. Brazil should also gain a greater participation in decision-making processes that relate to these questions, at both the formal and the informal levels.

2. Contributing to the task of opening markets to Brazilian exports by promoting its swift growth and its diversification. In this case, in regards to markets and products, towards the more dynamic segments of world trade. This result will demand the internationalisation of Brazilian firms, not only through trade but also through investments.

3. Since external vulnerability results not only from realities, but also from perceptions of these realities and market interests, the economic diplomacy will have to work more at improving perceptions and identifying interests. In these tasks, a constant effort of explanation and information, as well as at the building of alliances and the identification of opposing interests, will be essential.

The tasks of economic diplomacy in the next decades should be somewhat different from those in the previous decades, especially in the context of implementing a participation strategy. However, it would be naive to presume that in an unequal world, in which the rules of the system reflect this inequality, Brazil should abandon defensive concerns in its search for a greater integration into the global economy. However, the defensive strategy will have to switch from protection at the border to the regulation of the economic activity by the state, in line with what is taking place in developed countries and at the international level. Either through changes occurring in the global economy, or through negotiating processes in line with these changes, barriers at the borders to goods, services and capital flows will disappear. Even as far as work is concerned, it is possible to foresee some loosening of immigration restrictions due to demographic transformations (ageing of the populations in the most developed countries), or to the effect of wealth on the acceptance of certain tasks. This is to say nothing of the illegal immigration caused by the sharp income disparity between the developed and the underdeveloped world.

The transition to a defensive strategy focused on regulation will require, from a country such as Brazil, a significant effort in developing the adequate regulatory agencies. This effort is already in progress. The transition can even be observed in the protectionist stronghold of agriculture, with the reduction of border barriers and the proliferation of internal barriers, as well as in the change from subsidy policies to the so-called consumer protection policies. Incidentally, this will also be important in the context of Brazil's access to world markets.

If Brazil accepts that in the next decades border barriers to goods, services and capital will disappear, it should be prepared, on the one hand, for a final negotiating effort, at the multilateral and regional levels, of its remaining barriers (in the context of integration into the global economy). On the other hand, this will entail the state setting up a sophisticated legal and institutional system, to avoid market abuses and disloyal competition. The Brazilian economic diplomacy will have to defend international rules on these matters (trade protection, consumer protection, competition, services trade, electronic trade, intellectual property and investment, among others). This will answer the needs of Brazilian development and make room for its own institutional strengthening, based on its national development needs.

Much has been written on globalisation and regionalism, but here it is appropriate to call attention to the fact that a successful integration in the global economy requires the strengthening of regionalism. On this matter, Europe's lessons are unquestionable. In a unipolar world, separation leads to unimportance, whereas unity is the only way to preserve autonomy. Acknowledging this reality will permit acceptance of the sacrifices which will be increasingly needed in order to build an integrated area in South America. The next section will develop this point.

There are two final questions regarding the need for a critical approach in the context of a participating strategy and the negative aspects of globalisation. A participating diplomacy does not mean an adaptive diplomacy. Criticism of the unequal and concentrating nature of globalisation must remain present in Brazil's diplomacy. It is a developing and unequal country and its identity, which combines globalised and backward sectors, requires a diplomacy that reflects this dual reality. In this sense, it is worth noting that the most important challenges to globalisation have not recently come from developing countries but from civil society organisations in developed countries. These organisations contributed to the failure of the MAI and the launching of a new round of multilateral trade negotiations. As to the action of NGOs, I will make some observations in the final section of this essay. Here it is worth underlining that this critical element in Brazil's diplomacy should be based on:

1. a careful examination of the definition of new rules and the creation of institutions to foster globalisation in areas where there is too wide

a gap in development among the participants. It is also necessary to examine where Brazilian development requires the preservation of the possibility to adopt internal protection policies, without which it would be difficult for Brazil to catch up to the more advanced countries;

2. a re-evaluation of the international dispute settlement system in the trade area, with its mandatory provisions and with a capacity to create case law based on paper decisions as established after the Uruguay Round with the creation of the WTO. This system, against which non-governmental organisations and some countries are concerned, involves a risk of promoting growing trade conflicts and of exacerbating the imbalances between developed and developing countries. Its recent evolution, with increasingly mandatory provisions and the capacity to establish rights and obligations through the interpretation of texts, which as the product of diplomatic negotiations are inevitably unclear, is worrying for two reasons. First, unlike the former GATT which covered only trade in goods and in which the recourse to the dispute settlement system was limited, the dispute settlement mechanism today rules over disputes involving internal policy decisions and laws in a great number of areas. This new scope of the system, together with its probable expansion to cover new areas, exacerbates the problem of the system legitimacy in confrontation with national legislation. On the other hand, this evolution has taken place in a context of great disparity in the capacity of countries to defend their cases and to retaliate. This disparity renders the system even more questionable and raises doubts on whether it would be advisable to contemplate its extension, through new rounds of negotiations, to other areas of economic activity. Facing this problem will also require a growing effort internally to explain present and possible future limitations of certain internal policies;

3. the promotion of a development agenda and a reformation of international economic institutions. The development issue will remain central in the international agenda. Unfortunately, a defence of the enlightened interest does not seem to emerge in the developed countries, in which there is a predominance of what could be termed 'a theory of containment in the handling of development issues'. The Brazilian economic diplomacy should continue to defend an alternative vision of international economic relations.

A final word about globalisation: it is neither irreversible, nor can the possibility of recurrent crisis be overruled. In this context, the reduction of external vulnerability, the diversification of economic relations and regional integration are particularly important. The first issue has already been treated, but a few words on the other two are offered. In regards to diversification, it is important to preserve it, both by maintaining a balance between the two big areas (North America and Europe) and by strengthening the relations with the Pacific area, as well as developing strategic partnerships with key-countries. In this situation, it is particularly important to keep the negotiations of the ALCA parallel with the EU and Mercosul negotiations, and to take new initiatives to promote relations with Japan and China. Regional integration, which will remain the main task of Brazilian economic diplomacy in the near future, might lead to the adoption of common strategies at the regional level, to face crisis originating in the global economy.

REGIONAL INTEGRATION AND THE BUILDING OF A SOUTH AMERICAN BLOC

The building of a politically, economically and culturally integrated area in South America, with projections in Latin America, the Caribbean and Africa, is certainly a top priority for Brazilian diplomacy in the coming decades. I would even say that it is a priority for Brazilian society since the objectives of peace and prosperity will best be achieved through an intensification of relations with neighbouring countries. Therefore, it is a real national project and, as such, it goes beyond the diplomatic field. I will not go as far as to say that without South American integration and its ramifications, a renewed and more positive integration of Brazil in the world economy would be impossible, but it would surely be more difficult.

If we look at the main trends in international relations, we can see that regional integration is a fundamental platform for countries such as Brazil and its neighbours, which are not great powers and who are facing the challenges of catching up with the more developed countries, as well as redefining their integration in the world of globalisation. In this context, the lessons of post-war Europe are enlightening: division would have led to marginalisation, and the dream of an important part for Europe in the world had to be a collective dream. It is much more realistic to think of globalisation from the standpoint of large groups, or integrated areas, in which the relations of geographical proximity and the historical and cultural affinities are enhanced. Liberalisation between more equal partners, the ability to develop an independent harmonisation of policies, and the physical and infrastructure integration possible in the regional integration processes, will set up a much stronger basis for the integration of the group. Furthermore, it will be a solid basis of integration for each one of its members into the globalised economy, and it may be a stabilising factor in crises.

On the other hand, from the point of view of a regional group, the relationship with the superpower certainly represents the potential for a larger degree of autonomy. In the same way, joint action at the international level, particularly in regards to sensitive subjects for the region (such as drug trafficking), represents a possibility to treat such issues from a more appropriate angle. Furthermore, it could enhance the international ability of each partner in the area, to act.

The same is true for security issues, in which the predominance of a regional point of view may be, in extreme cases, the only way to avoid unjustified interventions. Considering security from the perspective of the construction of a democratic area, in which there is a mutual confidence between neighbours in search of their own co-operative solutions to critical problems, is a way of individualising a region as a peaceful area, while projecting it positively into the world.

Why a South American area and not Latin American integration? There is a simple answer to that. South American integration can become an economic reality for three reasons: its members do not have exclusive relations with any area, their economies have important links with one another by reason of their sub-regional integration processes (Mercosul and the Andean Pact), and there is a vast untapped potential for expansion of the inter-regional relations. Therefore, it is possible to imagine a South American economic integration based on physical integration as well as on historical and cultural affinities. On the contrary, imagining a Latin American and Caribbean integration is a remoter reality, given the predominant links of Central American and Caribbean countries, and Mexico, with North American and European economies. Indeed, Latin America and the Caribbean are historical and cultural, rather than economic realities, and this is to a large extent the reason why integration plans for the whole region have failed. This does not mean that there is no Latin American and Caribbean identity or specificity, or that they should not be developed. The capacity of the region to survive as a group, though little articulated, in the face of all disintegration challenges, proves the existence of a strong identity that must play an important part in the foreign policy of each one of its members. In the future, this identity might even find expression in stronger economic links thanks to sub-regional integration processes. The creation of an integrated economic area in South America will contribute in a decisive way to that ultimate objective.

However, for that purpose, this area must not be considered as a closed bloc, but rather, as a preferential open area. In this area, the relations at the regional and hemispheric levels will develop in concentric circles and strategic partnerships will be built (for example, with South Africa, within the framework of a strategic notion of the South Atlantic region).

As far as South American integration is concerned, it seems important to draw some lessons from Europe. The first lesson is that the integration process has manifold aspects: political, commercial, economic, scientific, technological, social and cultural. The priorities among these aspects, and the speed of the integration process in each one, may vary in the course of time, but the process is integral. The integration project is indivisible and, in fact, its strength comes from the ability to visualise a group of countries for which the community aspect is increasingly important, in comparison with the national aspect.

The second lesson to extract is that integration is an ongoing process. Integration has no deadline and the process is constantly overcoming its limits and establishing new goals. Moreover, the crises are overcome by further integration, or by a different integration, always keeping in mind the objective of enhancing the community aspect. In addition, construction of the community space relies on the observance of the subsidiarity principle, i.e. it should proceed only when an objective can be better achieved through the expansion of the common approach.

The third main lesson is that there is a constant tension between strengthening and enlargement. There is no exclusive option: both coexist as central aspects of the process and their intensity may vary according to the circumstances. The dilemma between strengthening and enlargement is therefore a false one: both must take place simultaneously.

The other positive tension occurs between the supranational and national levels. This is illustrated by the central element of the institutional structure (Council and Commission) and by the constant evolution of the founding treaties through successive intergovernmental conferences. The central part played by the institutional and legal elements appears clearly here. Moreover, there is a constructive tension between the proposing (Commission), decision (Council) and representative (Parliament) bodies. The treaties provide for a gradual transfer of power among these institutions.

Two other aspects are worth mentioning; first, the existence of axes leading the integration process and the European identity. European construction is to a large extent the result of a Paris–Bonn axis. However, beyond this observation, there is a more complex reality, since the difficulty for the most powerful member to assert itself at the international level has opened the door to the expression of French glory. It was, however, the basic agreement among the traditional enemies, and the awareness that their enmities could only be overcome within the framework of a European construction. Within this construction, national power could find expression in the definition of common objectives, which gave momentum and direction to the integration process.

At the same time, the great architects of this process, Monnet and Schuman, have always started from a vision of Europe distinct from their national identities. This notion of a superior identity, resulting from a common historical and cultural evolution in a definite geographical area, is at the root of European integration. It is worth mentioning that the notion of Europe is not self-evident. As Jean Monnet said in his famous sentence: 'Europe has never existed. It is not the sum of national sovereignties that make an identity. It is necessary to create a real Europe.' The European identity issue was therefore present from the beginning of the process.

It is clear that the European identity notion has never been a dominant concept, except in the minds of the great dreamers of European integration. Furthermore, it has always coexisted with national idiosyncrasies. This duality is even more important today, in particular after the accession of the United Kingdom. It is important to note that this tension between the national and the supranational levels has always existed. However, with time there has been an expansion of the community space and institutions promoted by the existence of community bodies, such as the Commission and by the succession of intergovernmental conferences to reform the treaties.

The question is whether the integration process of Mercosul and South America, which was born in a different manner, should follow the same path to deepening and widening as the European. My answer to this question is a qualified yes.

The recent Mercosul crisis showed two things: the first one is that the process has a vitality, allowing it to survive difficulties. This indicates that today, Mercosul is a reality, which is considered by its members as worth preserving beyond their national interests. The second one, more questionable, is that the integration process must be transformed to survive, and that its exclusively intergovernmental aspect, with the predominance of trade liberalisation, must evolve towards a more complex process with the establishment of community institutions and the strengthening of integration in other areas such as co-operation in industrial and macro-economic policies. In short, as Mercosul's heads of states have indicated, the difficulties will be overcome by more, not less integration. The difficulty is to define whether the type of integration will remain the same, or if there will be an agreement for a qualitative leap in the process and, in that case, which turn the changes will take.

These are complex issues, but it would be appropriate here to make some preliminary and tentative proposals in regards to Brazilian foreign policy and Mercosul. First, considering Brazil's weight in the region, the process must have Brazilian leadership, in regards both to Mercosul and to its expansion in concentric circles, starting with the creation of an integrated area in South America. However, this leadership will only be possible if, at the same time, it is accepted that the weight and size of Brazil and its economy within the regional framework, require sacrifices. In that sense, regional integration must be considered a national project.

This task requires, from Brazilian diplomacy, a great external and internal effort. At the external level, a new agenda must be established, combining Mercosul's strengthening and enlargement. Strengthening should follow different lines:

1. Diversification of the economic agenda to include, in addition to trade, the aspects of macro-economic co-ordination, industrial policy with an identification of schemes for market division, the setting up of firms at the community level and the harmonisation of policies in sectors such as competition and capital markets. The aim would be to build a unified market in five to ten years.

2. Institutional development with the establishment of community institutions. These institutions would be subsidiary to the inter-governmental process, but could make proposals to contribute to the development of the agenda. Moreover, the dispute settlement procedure should be improved.

3. More importance should be given to other aspects of integration, such as internal security and social, scientific, technological and cultural co-operation.

4. Consultative and co-ordinating institutions with the participation of civil society organisations should evolve and contribute with proposals to the integration process.

5. To consolidate the process, intergovernmental conferences should be convened to define new common obligations through new international agreements.

This process should go hand in hand with Mercosul's enlargement, with the joining of Chile and Bolivia, the negotiation with the Andean Community, and the accession of Surinam and Guyana.

The successful conclusion of this process would require from Brazil, a generous attitude in terms of an asymmetric liberalisation of its markets to the neighbouring countries. This would be in addition to an acceptance of the creation of community authorities, particularly in regards to the dispute settlement process, in order to guarantee the observance of obligations and respect to agreed market access conditions. During this process, physical integration and the formation of sector-based strategic partnerships would be strengthened in order to create bi-national or multinational firms, with the capacity to compete at the global level.

THE UNIPOLAR WORLD AND THE RELATIONS WITH THE SUPERPOWER: PRESERVING AUTONOMY

Minister Luiz Felipe Lampreia quotes in his book *Brazilian Diplomacy*, Ambassador Domicio da Gama's sentence as a 'perfect guideline' for our relations with the US:

> I think each time we have resisted US claims that seemed exaggerated to us, we have done them the service to point out the limit beyond which it would be unbecoming for them to go. Brazil should not give to the US more proofs of consideration than it receives from them. On the contrary, we should place ourselves in a position to respond rather than to make approaches, since haste would only damage our reputation.

Preserving this fundamental guideline in a world characterised by unipolarity, will certainly represent a challenge for Brazilian diplomacy. Not because they have serious conflicts with the US, or because there are insuperable disputes between the two countries in regards to vital issues for both of them in the international agenda. Instead, because the US has always considered Latin America as a natural area of influence, and because unipolarity involves some risks of unilateralism.

The construction of a Latin American identity as a priority for Brazilian diplomacy has in the past been tempered by the desire to maintain special relations with Washington. On the other hand, the US has always seen, with some reluctance, the growth of Brazilian national power and the progress made in Latin American integration.

In recent years, however, this tension has been decreasing, due to internal transformations in Brazil (return to democracy, economic opening) and the constant search for a more positive and better-balanced agenda with the US. In Washington, since the Miami Summit, the relations with the region have acquired a new meaning, and in this context, as well as in others, the

Clodoaldo Hugueney

relations with Brazil and Mercosul have gained importance. Today, the extent to which the US accepts not only the irreversibility of Mercosul, but also the importance of South American integration as a means to overcome regional difficulties, remains to be seen.

This is the central question for the definition of inter-American relations: to what extent does the US consider the construction of South American integration and the assertion of Latin American and Caribbean identity at the international level as an objective, which competes with their interests in the region. This question becomes increasingly important, insofar as the integration efforts offer a real opportunity to build an integrated area. As Brazilian diplomacy works towards this aim, it will have the ability to assert itself on the international scene.

The discussion of the hemisphere integration process brings that question to light: should this process be considered as an extension of NAFTA and as a vertical integration of Latin America and the Caribbean in the North American economy? Or, is such a process compatible, as Brazil maintains, with the construction of sub-regional integration processes?

For Brazilian diplomacy, the integration of the hemisphere represents a threefold challenge: for Brazil's own economy, for Mercosul and the South American area, and for its relations with other areas, particularly Europe. At the internal level, challenges are twofold: in terms of competitiveness and in terms of a more autonomous regulation, mainly in the more modern sectors. The opening of the Brazilian economy revealed the low competitiveness of the Brazilian exporting sector, which does not seem to be due only to problems of macro-economic policies with an anti-export bias. Considering the competition inequalities, and the difference in the degrees of openness of both economies, the result of a preferential scheme with the US would lead not only to a significant increase in the share of North American exports in Brazilian total imports, but also to a growing negative trade balance for Brazil. Moreover, in regards to services, investment, intellectual property and new technology sectors such as electronic commerce, a free trade area would reduce Brazilian autonomy significantly, as far as regulation is concerned.

On the positive side, the ALCA will provide better conditions for Brazil's products into the main world economy and will favour foreign US investment in the Brazilian economy, which has lost ground in recent years. From a more general point of view, the ALCA and the set of commitments and agreements to be concluded at the hemispheric level will permit the establishment of relations between Latin American and Caribbean regions and the US on more positive and dynamic bases.

At this point it looks likely that, whatever the final details of ALCA negotiations may be, the preferential area will become a reality unless the US, due to internal reasons, lose interest in the initiative. This is unlikely because in the coming years, the imbalances of growing trade deficits and external indebtedness of the North American economy will give rise to pressures to accumulate trade surpluses. This will strengthen the objective of integration within the only area that the US has traditionally enjoyed surpluses. In such circumstances, the ALCA should become a reality and generate a renewed process of the elimination of trade barriers and define new competitive sectors in the region. Within this framework, Brazilian diplomacy will have to carry on working in three main directions:

1. In the ALCA negotiation process, by avoiding an acceleration of the process in order to allow the Brazilian economy to recover competitiveness and consolidate Mercosul and the South American integration, while gradually introducing additional liberalisation and preserving areas of autonomous regulation in the more modern sectors.

2. Consolidating, deepening and enlarging Mercosul, whose level of integration, measured by its degree of openness as well as by the harmonisation of its policies, should always be superior to ALCA's in order to turn it into a permanent integrated area in constant evolution.

3. In the negotiation of a free trade area between Mercosul and the EU, preserving the diversification of the group's economic relations and creating factors of strengthened multipolarity, so as to keep a competitive balance in Mercosul in relation to North American exports.

In the next two decades, we will probably witness almost complete liberalisation of trade barriers at the border, while protection will shift to internal regulations. What is proposed here is a deeper trade liberalisation towards neighbouring countries than the one achieved through negotiations of free trade areas with the NAFTA and the EU. The liberalisation with Brazil's neighbours should precede and be deeper than the liberalisation with developed partners, involving other sets of policies, in order to secure the identity and the future of the sub-regional integration processes.

The relations with the US go well beyond the trade aspect, although trade disputes have sometimes dominated the relation, giving it a conflicting nature. As Brazil's political and economic dimensions grow, the relations with the US should gain even more density at the bilateral, regional and international levels. The absence of serious conflicts between both countries put no limit a priori to those relations, apart from those deriving from the priority given by both sides to their development. Given the existing disparities, this priority will always be lower in the US, though this will not, as is currently the case, prevent those relations from developing and diversifying.

Another central point in the evolution of Brazil's relations relates to the possible evolution of unipolarity. There are two very distinct alternatives in the exercise of unipolar power: one recognises supremacy while accepting the need to share power; in the other, the exercise of power is more direct and unilateral. In the first case, the growing international involvement of the superpower would lead towards the establishment of partnerships and a more balanced international order. In the second case, the increasing international presence would be associated with a less qualified exercise of power, a growing unilateralism and an asserted supremacy. Both trends have always existed in US foreign policy: internationalism and isolationism. In a unipolar world, isolationism would find expression not by turning one's back to the outside world, but in an international presence determined by a limited and short-term vision of national interest.

Most probably, both trends will continue to coexist and the construction of a new international order will be marked by progresses and failures. To a large extent, these will be determined by the predominance of one trend or the other, in Washington.

Brazil's interest is that US foreign policy veers towards a participating internationalism. Although Brazil's influence in this matter is limited, US decisions will be influenced by the international climate and the attitudes of their partners. Brazil must contribute to the establishment of a new international order as far as its limited possibilities allow it to.

There are three appropriate remarks on this level. First, the multipolarity factors at the international level should be strengthened. The principles of equidistance from power centres and diversified relations should go on guiding Brazilian diplomacy, as well as the defence of a multilateralism based on fair and stable rules. In this context, Brazil should pay a growing attention to disarmament. Secondly, alliances will be important for Brazil to influence the building of a more multipolar world and the construction of a renewed multilateral system. In this matter, Europe can play an important part and the strengthening of the links between Brazil and Europe at the bilateral and regional levels should remain a priority. At the same time, Brazil should exploit its multiple forms of insertion in international life, as a developing country, as a continental country, as a Portuguese-speaking country, as an Atlantic country. These multiple dimensions will allow the conclusion of alliances, which will strengthen multipolarity. Finally, the building of an integrated area in South America and the strengthening of Latin American and Caribbean identity will be fundamental in order to ensure room to move on the international scene, as well as to preserve the region from an excessive dependence on the US.

All these movements will require an active foreign policy with growing responsibilities for Brazil at the international level. The maintenance of a critical view of unilateralism will only be consistent if Brazil is ready to share the costs of building a more positive international order.

GLOBAL ISSUES AND LIMITS TO SOVEREIGNTY

The increased interdependence and interrelations between countries caused by globalisation, combined with homogenisation of models and the mobilisation of civil society, strengthened the international character of certain issues such as environment, human rights and drug trafficking. In the coming decades, these issues will continue to mark the international agenda and Brazil will have an important part to play in the working out of solutions to many of those questions. On the other hand, the agenda of common themes will continue to expand due to the progress of globalisation and the mobilisation of civil society in those matters. Five issues relating to the so-called global issues are of interest to us here:

1. The limitations to sovereignty deriving from the internationalisation of issues, which before were considered to be within the internal jurisdiction of countries, as for instance human rights.

2. The working out of a global agenda truly reflecting the main concerns to build a fairer and more stable global order, and therefore tackling the issues of development and peace.

3. The question of international governance and its institutionality to permit a balanced multilateral treatment of those issues.

4. The role of civil society in the construction of a conscience about those issues and in the promotion of solutions.

Global issues are increasingly bringing to light the question of the limits to sovereignty. This is due to the nature of the issue, which may include transborder threats that are real or perceived as real, as in the case of environmental issues or organised crime. Furthermore, the exposure of these issues to public opinion translates them into a threat for increasingly accepted behaviour models, as in the case of human rights. Therefore, there is a tendency to consider those questions as possible global threats in the presence of which the limits of national sovereignty must be ignored in the interest of the international community.

The purpose of this text is not to discuss the issue of limits to sovereignty, but simply to mention the fact that it is increasingly present, and to draw a few conclusions for the Brazilian foreign policy. First, since Brazil is a country with Western traditions, it is not inhibited by historical or cultural considerations in the treatment of issues such as democracy and human rights. Second, such values are important in regional life where, for instance, the democratic clause in Mercosul is an incentive to the search for negotiated and constitutional solutions to the political crises, which are likely to occur. For a country such as Brazil, the regional level is, in fact, a more appropriate sphere to promote these values. Within the region Brazil has developed appropriate co-operation instruments, such as integration schemes, the Treaty of Amazonian Co-operation to promote sustainable development, among others, which can be used to face global challenges.

A word on the application of universal rights and on the use of intervention to curb violations of these rights is offered. For reasons of principle, and given the inefficiency of the mechanism, Brazilian diplomacy should keep a critical stance towards the use of force, unless it is approved by the UN. Moreover, the Latin American diplomatic tradition has always been opposed to intervention and the use of force for efficiency reasons. This is because the situations that are at the root of such violations have generally complex causes that cannot be corrected by the use of force. On the other hand, Brazilian diplomacy should continue using the criteria of respect to democratic principles and human rights as an important factor in the definition of the level of its bilateral relations.

To go back to a traditional set of themes of Brazilian diplomacy, such as the three Ds policy, it is important to place due emphasis on the issues of development and disarmament in the global agenda. (Disarmament is discussed in the next section.) As to development, it seems only natural that the development issue should be one of the main components of the diplomacy of a country with social inequalities, such as Brazil. Moreover, there is no doubt that backwardness and poverty cannot be dissociated from other global issues such as environmental degradation and some situations of human rights violation.

The difficulty of dealing with the development issue derives from the fact that the negotiating agenda on development has not produced significant results in trade or in finance, and, moreover, the mobilisation mechanisms (G-77, G-15, non-aligned countries) are not efficient anymore, either in the exercise of pressure or as a means for dialogue and negotiation. There is no doubt, however, that the development issue remains central for the building of a new international order.

It appears there is no room, either to re-formulate trade questions in terms of special and differential treatment, or to mobilise significant sums of money for development aid. Perhaps an alternative might be to discuss more general questions of development conception and strategy, with an emphasis on social inequalities as a basis for a new international consensus on the issue. This might lay the foundation for the drafting of a new agenda for North–South relations. Another possibility, particularly significant for Brazil and other developing countries of a similar weight in international economic relations, would be to participate more fully in the discussion of the so-called global governance issues. These issues concern the international community as a whole.

Previously, I mentioned the fact that the global issues agenda is constantly changing. Those changes will occur both through the addition of new topics (for example, security of information sent by electronic channels or water resources in certain regions), and through the change of focus or emphasis in more traditional questions, such as environment. In that field, for instance, if there is confirmation of the estimates of global warming, the issue of climactic change will increasingly draw attention. Brazil will have to continue to show concern for the balance in the agenda, and for the balance in the proposed solution and adjustment costs. Here, the central issue is to preserve the capacity to adopt policies consistent with the development objectives. Despite the important effort required and the need to mobilise scarce resources, Brazil will have to devote more attention to global issues, by creating alliances and contributing to the consensus building.

Finally, it will be necessary to set up new fora for the co-ordination of developing countries, in addition to the present plenary ones. Maybe the co-ordination at regional levels could be strengthened, in the case of Latin America through the ECLAC, and we should also take advantage of the restructuring of UNCTAD to invest again in the organisation. Moreover, NGOs could contribute to mobilisation of public opinion in developed countries, as they are already doing, for instance, with proposals for the rescheduling of external debt of highly indebted countries.

A brief mention of two other issues: international governance and the role of civil society. As globalisation progresses, the deficiencies of the international system become increasingly apparent in dealing with what could be called the negative externalities of market liberalisation, such as financial crises. In time, development considerations could inspire a review of the so-called architecture of the monetary and financial system, as well as the coherence between the financial and the trade aspects of international economic relations. Here, two questions will be important: the inclusion of a larger number of countries in the decision-making process, and the search for new forms of market discipline. The present debate in favour of reforms of the Fund, the World Bank and the WTO could, in the medium term, lead to a deeper understanding of the need for a new institutionality for the international economic system.

The civil society organisations, which have mobilised around those issues, could move from an obstructionist role to a more constructive stance in favour of the reforms of these institutions. Brazil should take part in this debate by defending a major transparency and contributing, with its own vision, to this reform process.

THE SECURITY CHALLENGES

Brazil's continental dimensions, her specific weight in South America, and the fact that the region has been a peaceful area (away from the centres of international tension and, to a large extent, spared the consequences of the ideological dispute of the Cold War), have combined to make the security issues less prominent in Brazilian foreign policy. The consolidation and the definition of Brazil's borders through negotiation contributed decisively to this situation, allowing for the construction of friendly and co-operative relations with all its neighbours.

Although this situation will not change in the foreseeable future, the growing international presence of Brazil (which could mean a permanent seat in the Security Council), combined with the new configurations that the security problems can take in the post-Cold War world (including in its close neighbourhood), might require major attention in regional and international security from Brazilian diplomacy.

In a unipolar world, superpower leadership in international security issues is decisive. At the same time, it is not advisable, as Europe acknowledged after the crisis in the Balkans, to rely solely on that leadership and not to develop a national approach to international security problems, particularly in neighbouring regions. This would, of course, involve assuming greater responsibilities in crisis prevention and management.

With the end of the Cold War and in a world dominated by democratic regimes and interdependent open and integrated economies, it seems possible to rethink peace and security issues. This rethinking is more positive than it was in a world defined by ideological expansionist competition and strategic balance of power.

However, unipolarity entails the danger of the search for international supremacy, with risks of unilateralism. There is always a tendency to identify new enemies, whether emerging powers or rival civilisations, or even global challenges, such as the threat of nuclear proliferation or drug trafficking. Therefore, it seems important to re-examine those issues, from both a global and a regional point of view.

At the global level, four issues seem relevant. The first relates to the answers to local crises, resulting from tensions which, during the Cold War, were held in check by the bipolar game. The second issue concerns the new security challenges, such as organised crime and the ecological risk. The third relates to strategic supremacy and the threats of a new arms race. Finally, the last matter concerns international institutionality, and the reform of the Charter of the United Nations.

In regards to the first aspect, the recent evolution in Latin America towards democratic regimes and the absence of serious cultural or ethnical tensions in the region protect, to some extent, the region from those tensions. In the whole area, social inequalities and income concentration are the main causes of tension. The regional democracies will have to solve these problems to consolidate definitively their position. Progress in regional integration may contribute to this result. Moreover, it would also be important to solve the existing border disputes, sources of occasional tensions, and to improve the political dialogue in the region. In regards to tensions in other areas, given the limited resources of the Brazilian state and the fact that such tensions do not present a threat to Brazilian security, it does not seem relevant to imagine a Brazilian involvement. That is unless it is justified by historical or other reasons, as could be the case in some areas of Africa. Such an involvement would only take place within the framework of United Nations decisions, as is currently the case.

In regards to global issues perceived as threats to security, a distinction has to be made between reality and fantasy, be it intentional or not. For instance, as far as environmental issues are concerned, this distinction is unclear. Moreover, there is often a temptation to use those 'threats', especially in relation to problems in developing countries, such as deforestation in tropical forests, as a way to achieve other objectives. This does not mean that the problems are not real and that they cannot sometimes be serious, but there is a big difference between saying this and claiming that they represent a threat to security.

Brazilian diplomacy will have to tackle these issues on three fronts: first, on the perception front, by discerning the real nature of the problem and the means to solve it, which in most cases, requires combined efforts from multiple actors; second, in regards to drug trafficking, such as a strategy attacking both supply and demand. The co-operation in the search for multilaterally accepted global solutions to those questions is important. Third, at the regional level, through internal actions and co-operation with neighbours to avoid, by all means, problems in the region becoming threats to security and therefore open to a military solution. The most important of these questions is clearly the concern of drug trafficking.

In regards to the risks inherent in unipolarity in terms of the search for an undisputed supremacy, there are two significant questions, which can only be briefly examined in this essay. The first concerns the power divisibility and the possibility to combine economic and military supremacy. Here it is important to note the possibility that an economic multipolarity might give rise to fierce competition for markets. On the other hand, the second concerns the appropriateness of military solutions to post-Cold War questions. The quest for supremacy can lead to economic difficulties. In this context, a decision on the installation of an anti-missile system seems to pose important challenges since it involves the possibility of a renewed arms race and an increase in international tension. Besides, localised crises and peripheral tensions, given their complex nature, do not seem susceptible to military solutions.

In both cases, more permanent solutions could be found, not by a repetition of past models of behaviour, but in an approach that would restore to the negotiating table the two central issues of disarmament and development. Brazil, as a developing and non-nuclear country with an important relative weight, is in a position to help build consensus in both fields.

In trying to build a new consensus on disarmament and development, it is important to bear in mind the need for a new international institutionality. The reform of the United Nations and the Security Council should lay the foundation for a greater participation in the solution of these issues, and in the management of international crises. Brazil, given its characteristics, is entitled to aspire to a permanent seat in the Council. However, this is only one part of the question, since the aim of an institutional reform must be to develop a new approach to post-Cold War crises. This must be in the context of revisiting the central issues of disarmament and development.

A final word on regional security. Within the framework of the construction of Mercosul and an integrated area in South America, the dialogue on military and security issues should be intensified. There are already some important initiatives, both at the Mercosul level and between Brazil and its neighbours. It seems appropriate to improve this dialogue to increase mutual confidence and develop mechanisms for the solution of regional crises. Through this, neighbouring countries could co-operate to eliminate centres of tension. Such initiatives should always respect the non-intervention principle, and their aim would be to develop the solution of conflict situations at the regional level through political dialogue and co-operation schemes. The solution of the Peru and Equador border dispute, as well as the solution of the institutional crisis in Paraguay through the co-operation among Mercosul members, are examples that come to mind in this context.

THE NEW ACTORS

The influence of new actors in international relations, in competition with states and the consequent development of a public diplomacy, is a question which will continue to gain importance. This is both because of the growing incapacity of the state to answer problems, and because for various reasons some of these actors will play an increased role both internally and externally in the context of the so-called global issues. Mergers fostered by markets integration are creating new corporations whose revenues exceed the GDP of most countries. Global issues are mobilising civil society. Traditional actors on the international scene, such as the Church, are developing a new diplomacy. As globalisation weakens the limits between the internal and the external, issues that were previously considered to be within the competence of countries are gaining an international dimension. Furthermore, internal organisations specialised on these issues, such as human rights or the indigenous populations, are gaining a growing influence at the international level.

As patterns of behaviour are becoming more homogeneous and as countries are being 'judged' along the same parameters (in regards to both public deficit and the defence of democratic liberties), transparency and information are gaining importance too. Image and reality are merged in the often hasty and ill-founded judgement of investors and NGOs.

Diplomacy, while competing for limited resources, must also justify itself to internal public opinion. Congresses have an increasing part to play in that field, not only as supervisory and controlling bodies, but also in the definition and defence of national positions. A diplomacy supported by Congress and the internal public opinion is a strong diplomacy. Therefore, there is a growing challenge to Brazilian diplomacy in regards to the building of a strong internal basis through transparency and dialogue and with reference to the presentation abroad of its reality and positions. These developments are positive, and the Brazilian Foreign Office has always been an institution devoted to consensus building. Two important examples of this are the establishment of Mercosul and the definition of Brazil's position in relation to ALCA.

The diplomacy of the twenty-first century will increasingly tend to be a dialogue diplomacy with a multiplicity of actors, both internally and externally. In this dialogue, arrogance should be avoided as much as innocence, for, neither foreign services have the monopoly of truth, nor are all motivations devoid of vested interests. Interests will always be present, determined by financing sources or by myopic views and single-minded opinions.

There is, in all this issue of new actors and their competition with the state, a question of harmonisation of interests and legitimacy. Civil society organisations have specific causes to defend and, here, their visions are partial. To a large extent, they do not have to worry about the harmonisation of conflicting interests.

Both because democratically elected authorities are responsible for the harmonisation of conflicting interests and because the states keep their capacity for management and international negotiation, they will have to remain the central actors on the international scene. However, this supremacy will take place within the framework of an increasingly open and participating society.

At the beginning, which is only natural, NGOs tended to assume an obstructionist and protesting stance. Their success lay them open to the need to build a constructive agenda. At this stage, the dialogue with NGOs is becoming more creative. In the case of Brazilian diplomacy there is a recognition that developing a working relationship with civil society organisations is important. Fortunately, this dialogue has produced areas of convergent views.

As those organisations incorporate more and more development issues into their agenda, such a convergence of views will tend to increase, for instance, in matters such as negotiations in the WTO or intellectual property rights. Brazilian diplomacy should be able to work increasingly with NGOs in the promotion of a development approach to global issues and the fight against poverty, as exemplified by the concept of sustainable development. Disarmament should also be a part of this common agenda. In many cases, it will be possible not only to preserve the independence of each actor, governmental and non-governmental, but also to institutionalise the dialogue.

In regards to the other aspect of Brazilian public diplomacy – image building – it will be important to count on a mobilisation of resources in order to allow a change of the country's image abroad. Here, two areas should have priority: the economy and the culture. The presentation of Brazil's economic performance data transparency should go hand in hand with the identification of partnerships and the development of a web of shared interests, such as in the financial and investment areas. In the cultural area, the promotion of Brazilian culture abroad will help consolidate links with other cultures, especially with its neighbours, preserving diversity in globalisation.

ELEVEN

————◄○►————

Conclusion

HÉLIO JAGUARIBE AND ÁLVARO DE VASCONCELOS

THE INTERNATIONAL SYSTEM

This book has offered an in-depth analysis of the position of some countries of the European Union and of Mercosul *vis-à-vis* the present international system. An attempt to extract conclusions from different papers and authors, although all geared to the same general purpose, can be approached in two distinct ways. First, one could try to find the common and reciprocally compatible elements in all chapters, eventually indicating their more important discrepancies. Second, one could offer personal reflections on what can be gathered about the subject matter, in light of these chapters.

These brief concluding remarks follow the second approach and attempt to convey what we, the editors, were led to believe after considering the different chapters on the subject. The General Introduction to this research was written as a way of providing the other contributors with the editors' views, without the benefit of knowing their own views. These final remarks are therefore written with the advantage of having evaluated our initial views against the opinions of the writers.

After evaluating the concerns of the international system and the trends for the formation of a new world order, it appears that our original views were predominantly confirmed by the other writers. We are living under the global predominance of the United States (US). In such conditions, the US is increasingly inclined to proceed unilaterally in the international scenario and to avoid its engagement in multilateral arrangements. That same behaviour, however, is increasing international resistance to US unilateralism and stimulating growing pressures in the direction of a multilateral world order. There is growing awareness in the European Union (EU) that it must discharge its responsibilities, primarily in the European continent. There is also dissatisfaction with American unilateralism among its members, particularly in France and Germany but also in Great Britain, despite its Atlanticism. This has led the EU to adopt, since the beginning of the 1990s, a number of measures to give purpose, coherence and visibility to a common foreign and security policy. As part of this initiative, an independent European defence policy with the corresponding military assets is being constructed, although – at least for the time being – there is no intention to duplicate or bypass NATO.

As Christoph Bertram has stressed, neither world hegemonies have ever been historically permanent, nor can the international system be regulated in a stable and rational way under a regime of unilateralism, even if exercised by an apparently benign power as during the Clinton mandate. Multilateralism is necessary, desirable, and, sooner or later, will inevitably come to prevail. It is preferable for the US to engage in it for its own self-interest, while being the predominant power, rather than being compelled to do so when a future multipolarity will impose – in conditions much less advantageous to the US – a new international order that could be more unstable than one based essentially on norms and rules.

Jean-Marie Guéhenno has argued that the European Union has a clear interest in a system close to its own model, based neither on US supremacy nor on the pursuit of independence and sovereignty, a third model that aims to be an institutional and political response to interdependence.

Charles Grant analyses the likelihood of the EU becoming a political and security actor, given the fact that in the present international circumstances and the shift in US policies towards more unilateralist power, even the British see that their national interests are better served by a more coherent and effective common European foreign policy with a defence component. This conclusion is encouraged by the fact that most of the security challenges in Europe can be dealt with by the Europeans. The conditions exist for France, Germany and Britain to head up a European Union process to be more then just a civilian power.

Multilateralism, as observed by most of the authors, will depend on the ability of the European Union to assert itself as a global political actor. Is this likely to happen in the near future? In the first decade of the twenty-first century, the European Union will concentrate on the enlargement process and in making the necessary reforms for a union of 27 states to be manageable. At the same time, it will be consolidating the achievement of Economic and Monetary Union, as exemplified by the euro. As a political power, the Union will be primarily concerned with its regional environment and in gradually developing the military instruments for the

European Defence Policy. In short, the Union will become a formidable economic power, speaking with a single voice in trade negotiations and financial institutions but it will take time to transform this weight into equivalent global political influence. Furthermore, the speed of this process could be challenged by external events, such as a more isolationist or even a more unilateralist America – as seems to be the case under the Bush administration.

MERCOSUL

What about Mercosul? The preceding studies, for one thing, have emphasised, even stronger than the General Introduction, the relevance of Mercosul for South America in general, and for Argentina and Brazil in particular. Pinheiro Guimarães presents a very hard picture of the US strategy – practically unopposed by other world powers – to bring the southern half of Latin America, under the guise of a Free Trade Area of the Americas, under the same influence already achieved over its northern part. Only Mercosul, or even Brazil individually, are capable of resisting the satellisation of South America. However, for this, Mercosul must be significantly strengthened, and Brazil and Argentina, among other requirements, have to consolidate, in reciprocally advantageous terms, their operational alliance.

Strengthening Mercosul is not merely a question of intention. Aldo Ferrer shows that the troubles currently affecting Mercosul are neither accidental, nor do they result from bad will from some (supposedly Argentine) interlocutors. Rather, they result from structural reasons, derived from the 'four capital sins' incurred by Argentina and Brazil. Overcoming some of those sins requires a lot of time. Two of them are particularly serious, if less time demanding. One, of an attitudinal nature, concerns the extent to which, particularly but not exclusively in Argentina, the neoliberal ideology has contaminated the ruling strata, converting them into accomplices of South America's subordination to the US. The other, of a structural character, is derived from the excessive financial dependence of both countries (but particularly Argentina), due to systemic deficits of their balance of payments, on the international finance system, controlled by the US.

Mercosul weaknesses are also stressed by Markwald. He underlines the extent to which the lack of a minimally satisfactory degree of institutionalisation prevents the isolation of merely commercial controversies – inevitably, to occur often – from political contamination. Everything becomes political in Mercosul, constantly menacing its inner coherence. However, that lack of institutionalisation is not accidental, but rather due to structural and strategic reasons. Structurally, Brazil is so many times larger than the other participants that any voting system becomes unacceptable, and only a continuous political consensus can regulate Mercosul's affairs. Strategically, Brazil wishes to keep open its condition and possibilities as a global trader, Mercosul absorbing a minor part of its exports. Moreover, Brazil's expectation of exercising a consensual regional leadership requires the minimisation of institutional ties in Mercosul.

The problem, as illustrated by Clodoaldo Hugueney, is that in the short and medium terms, the US holds the conditions to impose the adoption of the FTAA on South America. This is provided that Mercosul (keeping its unity), or even Brazil alone, in a sustained way, do not frontally oppose it. It is Mercosul's internal unity, however, which is now seriously threatened. In addition, it is Brazil's independent disposition, to say and sustain a 'no' to the FTAA project, which is also at stake.

THE ALTERNATIVES

The EU is gradually increasing its internal consistency and enlarging its membership, moving to become a system that covers most of Europe with the exception of states of the former Soviet Union. That system is not likely to become, in the foreseeable future, a federal state. Rather, it will have a growing influence in contributing to the prevalence of a multilateral world regime. The EU favours the consolidation of Mercosul. It sees it as an attempt to adopt its own institutions and a significant contribution for the multilateralisation of the world. It is not prepared, however, to drop its agricultural policy in exchange for closer ties and a free trade agreement with Mercosul. An important agreement, however, could be adopted with Mercosul if, as suggested by Pinheiro Guimarães, the agricultural question is postponed for future discussion. Such agreements would significantly enhance Mercosul's international strength.

However, an important question is emerging as the result of radical shifts in Argentina's foreign policy. As emphasised by Pérez Llana, the Argentinean foreign policy, commanded in the 1980s by political considerations, shifted under Menem, to economic priorities in the 1990s. The Brazilian alliance, formerly crucial, could now be replaced with advantage by the US. This view was shared by the former Economics Minister. Although the de la Rua government did not follow the policies of its predecessor and he is personally more favourable to Mercosul, close relations with the US continue to be a priority in Argentina, particularly taking into account the delicate financial position of the country. The Argentinean position, if maintained by de la Rua, transfers most of the burden of dealing with US pressures and the FTAA challenge to Brazil. What is Brazil likely to do?

Amaury de Souza's paper discusses the many limitations currently afflicting the Brazilian state, its financial debility and narrow margins of manoeuvre. On the other hand, however, Brazil is confident of its great future and will do everything possible not to jeopardise it, preserving its maximum international autonomy. Hence, Brazil's willingness to achieve a durable and reciprocally convenient understanding with Argentina, adjusting Mercosul to such a purpose, as well as the willingness to promote an independent South American system of political and economic co-operation before, and preferably in place of, any agreement on the FTAA. The Presidential Summit of August 2000 in Brasilia was an important first step in that direction.

What is the more likely outcome? The appointment in February 2001 of Celso Lafer, enjoying a most favourable reputation in Argentina as Brazil's Foreign Minister, indicated the beginning of a serious effort to restore on solid ground the Argentinean–Brazilian relationship, a policy which is also pursued by the present government. President Cardoso's firm declarations that Brazil would not join the FTAA if the US did not remove all non-tariff barriers – something strongly opposed by politically very influential American lobbies – created a serious obstacle that President Bush may not be able to surmount. US alternative strategy, as is already apparent, will consist of obtaining support for the FTAA from other South American countries, so placing Brazil in the position of either joining FTAA or becoming isolated in South America.

Brazilian reluctance to join FTAA is based on a well-founded estimate that, particularly with American non-tariff barriers, a regime of free trade will systematically favour the US. This has been reinforced by Canada's arbitrary embargo of Brazilian meat, under the pretext that Brazilian cattle could, theoretically, have been contaminated by a few animals imported from Europe. Although the ban was enforced for a very short time, it was seen in Brazil as an ugly stratagem to harm the country in the international competition between two medium-range jet builders, Canada's Bombardier and Brazil's Embraer. Brazil's Agriculture Minister, Pratini de Moraes, declared that this abusive Canadian measure had buried forever the prospect of Brazilian adoption of the FTAA. Rhetoric discounted, serious damage has been inflicted by Canada on its relationship with Brazil and, consequently, on the possible attractiveness of the FTAA project to Brazil.

At the time of writing, the outcome of the whole question concerning the FTAA, a possible independent South American system and the future of Mercosul is not yet clear. It will mainly depend on what Brazil does. Brazil's interests are envisaged differently, domestically, by a powerful minority sector, integrated by multinational corporations, representatives of foreign interests and members of the traditional elite. They are strongly pro-America and, consequently, pro-FTAA, and a much larger sector, although insufficiently articulated, stressing an independent position for Brazil. The latter sector favours the strengthening of Mercosul, the organisation of an independent South American system, closer relations with Europe, and well-balanced relations with the US.

In the short term the issue was to be decided by the Brazilian government,[1] whose preferences are strongly oriented in the second direction, but whose sharp sense of realism and clear perception of the current limitations of the Brazilian state impose on it a very cautious behaviour. As a matter of fact, in the short term the issue will be strongly influenced by the extent to which President Bush is both willing and capable of removing the non-tariff barriers that block Brazilian exports in exchange obtaining Brazilian adherence to FTAA.

The relevance of that question for Brazil is of such a nature that an eventual acceptance of FTAA, even with the suppression of American non-tariff barriers, was to be the object of passionate discussions in the electoral campaign for his succession.

What is at stake, for Brazil, is its willingness and capability for assuming, in the last resort, an isolated opposition to FTAA in Latin America. As observed by Markwald, Brazil, by its large population, immense natural resources and as the ninth largest economy in the world, enjoys the conditions to be a 'lonely runner'. Moreover, such a position would attract important support from the EU and other independent powers and, after a critical period, would consolidate a Brazilian consensual leadership in South America. However, it would have to face, at least initially, the most serious financial challenges. It is ultimately a choice between a bravely sustained national independence, and a dollar prone to inflation.

The terrorist attack of 11 September 2001 on New York and Washington occurred after the conclusion of this study. There is no doubt that the attack aroused universal and intense indignation, while America's presumed invulnerability – to be enhanced by the proposed anti-missile – proved vulnerable to airliners on domestic flights hijacked by a group of terrorists. The incident was to reveal the existence of a large-scale terrorist network, generally known as al-Qu'aida, an extremist Islamic group operating from Afghanistan with the support of the Taliban.

It is not the purpose of this brief final comment to analyse the innumerable aspects and consequences of that monstrous crime. Suffice it to recall that it aroused the widest possible international condemnation, and that the UN Security Council authorised military intervention in Afghanistan. Additionally – and more importantly – it led President George W. Bush to acknowledge the need for, and American public opinion to support, the construction of a very large international coalition to contain and, ultimately suppress, international terrorism. Initially, this was seen as an indication of America's favourable predisposition towards multilateralism. However, it did not take long for the innate unilateralist tendencies of the new American administration to surface again, as exemplified by its opposition to the International Criminal Court and a vast number of multilateral conventions. The manner in which the Bush administration has responded to the question of Iraq has been a further example of the dominant role played by unilateralists within the administration itself. However, the response of the United Nations Security Council to this American project has demonstrated the continued prevalence of multilateral norms within the international community. Yet the divisions within the European Union over the way in which to respond to the unilateralism of the Bush administration have demonstrated two important aspects of the Union's role in international affairs. On the one hand, it has demonstrated the Union's difficulty in articulating a coherent common position over its vision of international order. On the other hand, it has revealed the vital role that Europe must play in engaging the United States in a multilateral approach to international affairs. Indeed its position as the world's only superpower does not confer – contrary to the assumptions made before 11 September 2001 – invulnerability on the United States. In fact, the extent to which the management of global interests and national protection depend on wide-ranging, multilateral co-operation has become evident from the crisis. This is the case, not only in the fight against terrorism but also in confronting an enormous variety of crises and problems in order to promote international security and justice.

NOTE

1. This was written before the 2002 presidential elections in Brazil which brought Luiz Inacio Lula da Silva to power.

Index

References to footnotes are denoted by page number, followed by 'n' and note number

Index

For Product Safety Concerns and Information please contact our EU
representative GPSR@taylorandfrancis.com Taylor & Francis Verlag GmbH,
Kaufingerstraße 24, 80331 München, Germany

Printed and bound by CPI Group (UK) Ltd, Croydon, CR0 4YY

11/04/2025

01844008-0016